D0850664

AQIVA'S CONTRIBUTION TO THE LAW OF *ZERA'IM*

STUDIES IN JUDAISM IN LATE ANTIQUITY

EDITED BY

JACOB NEUSNER

VOLUME TWENTY-TWO

CHARLES PRIMUS

AQIVA'S CONTRIBUTION TO THE LAW OF *ZERA'IM*

LEIDEN
E. J. BRILL
1977

AQIVA'S CONTRIBUTION TO THE LAW OF *ZERAᶜIM*

BY

CHARLES PRIMUS

Assistant Professor
Department of Theology
University of Notre Dame

LEIDEN
E. J. BRILL
1977

ISBN 90 04 04881 2

PRINTED IN THE NETHERLANDS

FOR ROMANA

CONTENTS

PREFACE

This study surveys traditions on agricultural laws ascribed to Aqiva ben Joseph (d. ca. A.D. 132) in the earliest strata of rabbinic literature. Tradition assigns to Aqiva, one of the foremost authorities at Yavneh, a prominent role in shaping the literature of earliest rabbinic Judaism. Scholars during the past century have in the main reproduced the traditional view. Thus it is alleged, notably by the distinguished literary critic, Y. N. Epstein (see "The Mishnah of R. Aqiva," in *Tannaim*), that Aqiva organized a collection of traditions which served as the prototype for Mishnah. This view presumably depends upon two sorts of evidence, the first formal and focused on literary traits of traditions, the second substantive and focused on the legal content of larger units of traditions. The former sort of evidence would have to show that Aqivan traditions in M.-T. reflect literary forms and patterns which stand prior to those of M.-T. The latter would have to show that Aqivan interests shape the legal issues which are developed in the individual tractates in M.-T. Neither sort of evidence can be discerned, however, in the traditions surveyed in this study. The forms in which Aqivan traditions circulated prior to redaction in Mishnah (at least sixty years after Aqiva's death) cannot be determined; obviously no conclusions can be drawn concerning the literary format of pre-mishnaic Aqivan collections of materials, if any existed. Furthermore, in no case do Aqivan legal interests determine the agenda of specific tractates. Aqiva contributes formative legal principles in only a few instances; the discussions in the different tractates range far beyond the issues of Aqiva's traditions. My work suggests that Aqiva's role in earliest rabbinic Judaism should be judged by reference to the unfolding of the logic of Tannaitic legal concerns and not by reference to the development of particular sorts of literature.

I focus on Aqiva's traditions in the first Order of Mishnah-Tosefta, *Seder Zera*ᶜ*im* (The Order of Seeds). (The first tractate in the Order, *Berakot*, is excluded, for unlike the other ten tractates in *Seder Zera*ᶜ*im* it does not deal with laws related to agriculture.) *Seder Zera*ᶜ*im* contains approximately one-sixth of the total number of Aqivan traditions in M.-T. The primary sources are formal and highly stylized. They do not claim to derive in present form directly from the mouth or pen of Aqiva. Furthermore, they deal with a narrow range of legal problems, many of which had become theoretical following the destruction of the Temple in Jerusalem in A.D. 70. In other words, mishnaic literature does not provide the raw materials for biography. Pericopae in M.-T. do not provide facts concerning events in the life of Aqiva or explicit statements concerning the master's religious, philosophical or political opinions. The procedures used in this study therefore focus on, first, the literary characteristics of, and second, the legal positions expressed in, discrete traditions. These procedures follow from those first applied to early rabbinic literature by Jacob Neusner in *Development of a Legend. Studies on the Traditions concerning Yoḥanan ben Zakkai, (Leiden, 1970)* and subsequently refined in *The Rabbinic Traditions about the Pharisees before 70*, (Leiden, 1971), *Eliezer ben Hyrcanus. The Tradition and the Man*, (Leiden, 1973), and *A History of the Mishnaic Law of Purities*, (Leiden, 1974-1977). Neusner has shown that legal traditions in M.-T. provide the best sources for the study of earliest rabbinic Judaism. This investigation of Aqiva's legal traditions is a contribution to that study.

This volume has been revised from a dissertation written at Brown University under the direction of Professor Jacob Neusner. At each stage in my work Professor Neusner has provided direct and indirect counsel. I take his scholarship as a model toward which to strive. His many professional and personal courtesies are deeply appreciated.

Professors Ernest S. Frerichs and Horst R. Moehring have read the entire manuscript and made valuable suggestions. Professors David R. Blumenthal and B. Barry Levy have read and commented on portions of Part One. In less tangible ways my work benefits from the opportunity to study at Brown with Professors Wendell S. Dietrich, David Goodblatt (now of Haifa University), Stephen Gero, and Sumner B. Twiss, Jr. and with Rabbi Joel H. Zaiman. In addition, I have benefited in two ways from my graduate-student colleagues. First, they have paid close attention to my work throughout the different stages of its development. And second, I have profited from reading their work on topics closely related to my own. I gladly acknowledge my debt to Professor Gary G. Porton, University of Illinois; Professor William S. Green, University of Rochester; Professor Baruch M. Bokser, University of California at Berkeley; Rabbi Shammai Kanter; Mr. Joel Gereboff; Professor Jack Lightstone, Concordia University; Professor Tzvee Zahavy, University of Minnesota; Rabbi David Eisenman; Mr. Irving J. Mandelbaum; and Professor Richard S. Sarason, Brown University. I am grateful to each of these individuals for the consideration they have shown me and my work. I alone, of course, am responsible for the shortcomings of this study.

Mrs. Marion Craven has typed the manuscript. I thank her for her patience and good humor. Mr. Bruce Fingerhut prepared the indices.

The Memorial Foundation for Jewish Culture provided a generous fellowship for the preparation of the dissertation upon which this book is based. I thank the Foundation for its support. The National Foundation for Jewish Culture granted an honorary fellowship as well.

In previous years I have been privileged to study with many exceptional teachers. In particular I would like to express my appreciation to Miss Esta Johnson and Miss Rhoda Robinson of the public schools of Oak Park, Illinois; to Mr. Ruric Jordan and Mr. Irving Williams of the public schools of Mount Kisco, New York; to Professors William G. McLoughlin, Jr., Salo W. Baron, and the late Klaus Epstein, Brown University; and to Professors Ismar Schorsch, Joel Roth, and Gerson D. Cohen, Jewish Theological Seminary.

The University of Notre Dame has provided valuable assistance in the publication of this book. I gratefully acknowledge my debt to the University, particularly to the staff of Ms. Carmela M. Rulli.

The publication of this book has been made possible through the aid of the following, to whom I express my deep appreciation: Mr. and Mrs. Bert Liss; Mr. M. Mendel Piser; Mr. and Mrs. Harry Rosenstein; Mr. Bernard H. Natkow; The Jesselson Foundation.

My family, parents, grandparents, sisters and brothers, have encouraged me in all of my endeavors. My children, Richard, Ida, Michal, and Aryeh, have contributed to my work in ways they cannot imagine. In particular I have relied upon the tolerance, good sense, and encouragement of my wife, to whom this book is dedicated.

South Bend, Indiana
24 Tammuz 5735
3 July 1975

CHARLES PRIMUS

ABBREVIATIONS

A.Z.	= ᶜ*Avodah Zarah*
b.	= Bavli, Babylonian Talmud
B.B.	= *Bava*ᵓ *Batra*ᵓ
B.M.	= *Bava*ᵓ *Meṣi*ᶜ*a*ᵓ
B.Q.	= *Bava*ᵓ *Qamma*ᵓ
Ber.	= *Berakhot*
Bert.	= *Bertinoro.* Obadiah b. Abraham of Bertinoro, d.c. 1500. From reprint of Mishnah, ed. Romm.
Bes.	= *Beṣah*
Bik.	= *Bikkurim*
C	= Cambridge. W. H. Loewe, ed., *The Mishnah on which the Palestinian Talmud Rests,* (Cambridge, 1883; repr., Jerusalem, 1967).
Danby	= Herbert Danby, *The Mishnah,* (London, 1933).
Dem.	= *Dema*ᵓ*i*
E	= Erfurt ms., Tosefta. Cited in Lieberman.
Ed.	= ᶜ*Eduyyot*
Eliezer	= J. Neusner, *Eliezer ben Hyrcanus. The Tradition and the Man,* (Leiden, 1973).
Epstein, *Tannaim*	= Y. N. Epstein, *Introduction to the Literature of the Tannaim* (Heb.), edited by E. Z. Melamed, (Jerusalem and Tel Aviv, 1957).
Epstein, *Mishnah*	= Y. N. Epstein, *Introduction to the Text of the Mishnah* (Heb.), (Jerusalem and Tel Aviv, 1954[2]).
Erub.	= ᶜ*Eruvin*
Ex.	= Exodus
Gen.	= Genesis
Git.	= *Giṭṭin*
GRA	= Elijah ben Solomon Zalman ("Elijah Gaon" or "Vilna Gaon"), 1720-1797. From Mishnah, ed. Romm (Vilna, 1887).
Hal.	= *Ḥallah*
HMLP	= J. Neusner, *A History of the Mishnaic Law of Purities,* (Leiden, 1974-1977).
Hul.	= *Ḥullin*
Is.	= Isaiah
Jastrow	= M. Jastrow, *A Dictionary of the Targumim, the Talmud Babli and Yerushalmi, and the Midrashic Literature,* (reprint N.Y., 1967).
Jer.	= Jeremiah
K	= Georg Beer, *Faksimile-Ausgabe des Mischnacodex Kaufmann A 50,* (reprint, Jerusalem, 1968).
Kel.	= *Kelim*
Kil.	= *Kila*ᵓ*yim*
Lev.	= Leviticus
Lieberman, TK	= Saul Lieberman, *Tosefta Kifshutah. A comprehensive commentary on the Tosefta,* (N.Y., 1955-).
M	= Babylonian Talmud Codex Munich (95), (reprint, Jerusalem, 1971).

M.	= Mishnah
M.-T.	= Mishnah-Tosefta
Ma.	= *Ma^caserot*
Maim.	= Maimonides, *Mishnah ^cim Perush Rabbenu Moshe ben Maimon.* Trans. Joseph David Qappaḥ, (Jerusalem, 1967).
Maim., *Code*	= Maimonides, *Mishneh Torah,* (reprint, Tel Aviv, 1959).
M.Q.	= *Mo^ced Qaṭan*
MR	= *Mishnah Rishonah*; Ephraim Isaac of Premysla. Published in 1882. From reprint of Mishnah, ed. Romm.
M.S.	= *Ma^caser Sheni*
MS	= *Melekhet Shelomo.* Shelomo bar Joshua Adeni, 1567-1625. From reprint of Mishnah, ed. Romm.
N	= *Mishnah ^cim Perush Ha Ramban. Defus Rishon Napoli [5] 252 (1492),* (Jerusalem, 1970).
Num.	= Numbers
Oh.	= *Ohalot*
P	= *Shishah Sidré Mishnah. Ketav Yad Parma DeRossi 138,* (Jerusalem, 1970).
Par.	= *Parah*
Pe.	= *Pe^ɔah*
Pes.	= *Pesaḥim*
Phar.	= J. Neusner, *The Rabbinic Traditions about the Pharisees,* (Leiden, 1971).
Ps.	= Psalm
Qid.	= *Qiddushin*
Rabad	= R. Abraham ben David. Supercommentary to Maimonides, *Code.*
Rabad, Sifra	= Commentary to Sifra. From Sifra, ed. Weiss.
R.H.	= *Rosh Hashanah*
Romm ed.	= Edition of Mishnah (Vilna, 1887).
Sanh.	= *Sanhedrin*
Sens	= Samson ben Abraham of Sens, ca. 1150-1230. From reprint of *Mishnah Seder Zera^cim* in Babylonian Talmud, Romm ed.
Shab.	= *Shabbat*
Shev.	= *Shevi^cit*
Sifra, Weiss	= *Sifra,* ed. I. H. Weiss, (reprint, N.Y., 1947).
Sifré Num., ed. Horovitz	= H. S. Horovitz, ed., *Sifré d'be Rab,* (Jerusalem, 1966).
Sifré Deut., ed. Finkelstein	= L. Finkelstein, ed., *Sifré on Deuteronomy,* (N.Y., 1956).
Suk.	= *Sukkah*
T.	= Tosefta
T., Lieb.	= Saul Lieberman, ed., *The Tosefta according to Codex Vienna with variants from Codex Erfurt, Genizah mss. and Editio princeps (Venice, 1521),* (N.Y., 1955-)
T., Zuck.	= M. S. Zuckermandel, ed., *Tosephta. Based on the Erfurt and Vienna Codices, with parallels and variants,* (reprint, Jerusalem, 1963).
Ta.	= *Ta^canit*
Tem.	= *Temurah*
Ter.	= *Ṭerumot*
TY	= *Tiferet Ya^caqov.* Jacob Ṣevi Shapira. From reprint of Mishnah, ed. Romm.

TYT = *Tosafot Yom Ṭov.* Yom Ṭov Lipman Heller, 1579-1654. From reprint of Mishnah, ed. Romm.
TYY = *Tiferet Yisrael, Yakhin.* Israel ben Gedaliah Lipschütz, 1782-1860. (With supercommentary of Baruch Isaac Lipschütz.) From reprint of Mishnah, ed. Romm.
V = Vienna ms., Tosefta. Cited in Lieberman.
y. = Yerushalmi. Palestinian Talmud.
Y.T. = *Yom Ṭov*
Yev. = *Yevamot*

TRANSLITERATIONS

א	= ʾ	מ ם	= *m*
ב	= *b*	נ ן	= *n*
ג	= *g*	ס	= *s*
ד	= *d*	ע	= ʿ
ה	= *h*	פ ף	= *p*
ו	= *w*	צ ץ	= *ṣ*
ז	= *z*	ק	= *q*
ח	= *ḥ*	ר	= *r*
ט	= *ṭ*	שׁ	= *š*
י	= *y*	שׂ	= *ś*
כ ך	= *k*	ת	= *t*
ל	= *l*		

INTRODUCTION

i

Every legal system has its own logic. My purpose is to identify the logic internal to the legal sayings ascribed to Aqiva b. Joseph in *Seder Zeraᶜim* of Mishnah-Tosefta. [1] M.-T. consist predominantly of legal, that is, prescriptive sayings. Through such statements rabbinic Judaism expresses positions on the meaning of existence, the nature of being, and the relation between the sacred and the profane. The study of law in early rabbinic literature thus is a subject of interest for the history of religions.

Several considerations require attention in this Introduction. First, the roles generally assigned to Aqiva the man are specified. Second, the nature of literary materials in M.-T. is discussed. Third, the procedures which delimit this study are explained. In this connection I also briefly specify certain frequently encountered views concerning Aqiva and concerning mishnaic literature which do not enter into this study.

Aqiva plays a central role in the activities at Yavneh in the years between the two wars against Rome. Later tradition reports Aqiva's activities as exegete of Scripture, mystic and martyr. [2] M.-T. know

---

[1] Minus M.-T. Ber. Traditions relevant to pericopae in M.-T. in related literature are also considered.

[2] Convenient summaries are provided in articles by L. Ginzburg, *Jewish Encyclopedia*, (New York, 1912), I:304-10 and H. Freedman, *Encyclopedia Judaica*, (Jerusalem, 1972), I:487-91. Abraham Joshua Heschel, in an effort to create a typology by which to understand rabbinic Judaism, makes extensive use of traditions in which Aqiva functions as an exegete of Scripture and as a mystic, *The Theology of Ancient Judaism* (Heb.), (New York, 1962-65). Aqivan traditions are arranged thematically in I. Konovitz, *Rabbi Akiba Collected Sayings, in Halakah and Aggadah in the Talmudic and Midrashic Literature* (Heb.), (Jerusalem, 1965). G. Scholem briefly describes the "*Hekhaloth* Books," early examples of literature in which Aqiva figures prominently as a mystic, in *Major Trends in Jewish Mysticism,* (New York, 1961³), pp. 45-48, 63-67. Scholem also discusses statements ascribed to Aqiva in the "Lesser *Hekhaloth*" in "The *Halakhic* Character of *Hekhaloth* Mysticism," "The Four Who Entered Paradise and Paul's Ascension to Paradise," and "The Theurgic Elements of the Lesser *Hekhaloth* and the Magical Papyri," in *Jewish Gnosticism, Merkabah Mysticism and Talmudic Tradition*, (New York, 1965²), pp. 9-13, 14-19, and 75-83. E. E. Urbach discusses the exegetical and mystical activities of Aqiva and Aqiva's disciples in "The Traditions about *Merkabah* Mysticism in the Tannaitic Period" (Heb.), in *Studies in Mysticism and Religion Presented to Gershom G. Scholem,*

Aqiva, however, only as the authority to whom numerous legal sayings are attributed. His is in fact by far the largest corpus of traditions in M.-T. ascribed to a Yavnean. Two inferences follow: first, the Aqiva of M.-T. must be sharply distinguished from the Aqiva of later biography; and second, the Aqiva of M.-T. will be of interest as a legal philosopher and metaphysician.

The nature of the literary composition of M.-T. suggests the advantage of focusing on the corpus of traditions of a single master. Individual sayings occur in small units of tradition which in turn are organized in larger units up through chapters and tractates on related legal topics. The sayings obviously are the building-blocks of the literature, and the study of individual masters' traditions provides a felicitous approach for sorting out different strands in the documents. Studies of major Yavnean figures, Eliezer b. Hyrcanus, [3] Ishmael, [4] Joshua, [5] Gamaliel, [6] show that the corpora of individuals reflect consistent patterns of thought; taking the traditions of a single master as a point of departure, it becomes possible to identify larger issues which are addressed through discrete legal statements in Tannaitic literature. My work shows that this holds true for the Aqivan corpus, because recurring interests and viewpoints find expression in Aqivan discussions on different agricultural issues.

Insofar as we investigate the history of the law, however, we encounter significant limitations by focusing on the traditions of a single master. First, to understand the work of one individual, the work of his contemporaries and of his predecessors must be known. Contributions of one Yavnean must be measured by reference to the activities of other Yavneans and of pre-70 figures. The second problem here is that the bulk of traditions in M.-T. is not ascribed to any specific master. Studies of all assigned traditions would account for only part of the total corpus. This consideration has recently led Professor Jacob Neusner to begin the investigation of the "final product" of M.-T., the legal topics formally redacted in individual tractates. [7] Working with relatively large quantities of materials related to a

(Jerusalem, 1967), pp. 1-28 (Hebrew section), esp. pp. 10-17. For a critical survey of views on Aqiva as patriot and martyr, see G. S. Aleksandrov, "The Role of ᶜAqiba in the Bar Kochba Rebellion," in J. Neusner, *Eliezer,* Vol. II, pp. 422-36.

[3] J. Neusner, *Eliezer.*

[4] G. Porton, *The Traditions of R. Ishmael. Part One. The non-exegetical Materials,* (Leiden, 1976).

[5] W. Green, *Joshua,* (Unpublished Ph.D. dissertation, Providence, 1974).

[6] S. Kanter, *Gamaliel,* (Unpublished Ph.D. dissertation, Providence, 1974).

[7] J. Neusner, HMLP, Vol. I, p. xiii.

limited number of legal topics, one may distinguish with some confidence developments in the law, refinements in legal theory, and the contributions of many different individuals. By contrast, in focusing on the corpus assigned to an individual master, one necessarily deals with a large number of legal topics none of which is treated in any depth.

How then can focusing on the tradition of a particular master be justified? There are two considerations here. One attends, albeit tentatively, to the details of the history of the development of law, and the other one relates not to those details but rather to the rationale for the enterprise itself.

First, it is possible systematically to raise the question of Aqiva's contribution to the individual tractates in *Seder Zera^{c}im.* I do this in Chapter Five. Obviously my results are tentative; we await future studies of the individual tractates. For the present, however, I distinguish among different sorts of tractates. Certain tractates include issues and refinements of principles important to Aqiva (Kil., Ter.). Others include principles which Aqiva assumes along with other masters (Pe., Shev., Ma.). In others Aqiva contributes principles of interest which are not central to the agenda of the tractates (M.S., Hal.). And in some tractates Aqivan sayings play little or no role at all (Dem., Or., Bik.).

Beyond tentative conclusions about the development of details of law, however, it is possible to raise the question of the rationale for the enterprise itself. Here we move beyond the recognition that Aqiva's corpus on agricultural laws of itself yields almost no firm information concerning the development of principles within the strata of literature redacted in M.-T. Instead we note that the issues to which Aqivan sayings time and again return in different legal contexts yield information about the philosophical and religious principles embedded in the discussions of law. In *Seder Zera^{c}im* we identify two main areas of Aqivan concern: first, the fixing of boundaries, the definition of domains, in time and in space; and second, the efficacy of human intention. Frequently Aqiva tries to relate the two by fixing boundaries by reference to human intention as signaled by some sort of action. [8] Aqiva's interest in the issue of intention is familiar from traditions in M.-T. Kel.; Neusner shows that Aqiva focuses on the role of intention in the determination of the status of a utensil. [9] The issue of the

[8] E.g., M. Pe. 3:2.
[9] HMLP, p. 333.

nature of the human will is also familiar, of course, from other sorts of Jewish literature of the period. The prophet of the Ezra Apocalypse, for instance, sees in the destruction of Jerusalem punishment for the sins to which the corruption of the will had led man; the prophet declares that, in view of their fate, men would be better off without consciousness.[10] Similarly, Paul alleges that men cannot perform the good even when they intend to do it.[11] Aqiva's view is quite different, as the following examples make clear.

At T. M.S. 2:16 Aqiva discusses the nature of the sanctity attached to the city of Jerusalem. The legal issue concerns the status of Second-tithe produce which is brought to Jerusalem and which is subsequently discovered to have contracted uncleanness. Aqiva asserts that the disposition of the produce, that is, whether it may remain in the city or whether it must be taken outside and redeemed for cash and eaten there, depends upon the location at which the uncleanness was contracted. On Aqiva's view the sanctity attached to Jerusalem pertains to an area circumscribed by an invisible boundary which runs parallel to, but is separate from, the city's wall. Aqiva assumes that the holiness of the city is not "active," for it can be contained by a fiction of law, an invisible boundary-line. What is of particular interest for us is that the discussion to which Aqiva contributes takes place after the destruction of the Temple. The issue is wholly theoretical as regards bringing Second-tithe produce to Jerusalem. The discrete legal issue provides the occasion for a discussion of the nature of holiness.

A second tradition, at M. M.S. 5:8, suggests what is at stake in Aqiva's program. Judah, an Ushan master, states that "formerly" produce from which tithes had not been separated was, at the time for "removal" shortly before Passover during the fourth and seventh years of a seven-year cycle, destroyed without regard to whether the particular crop had in fact become liable for tithes. Presumably the "tithe-element" was regarded as holy, and at the time of "removal" an Israelite was charged to declare that he had removed all that was holy (*qwdš*) from his house (Deut. 26:13). Judah reports that Aqiva exempted from the law of removal produce which had not yet become liable for tithing. On Aqiva's view the holiness attached to produce is not

[10] IV Ezra 7:62-64; 8:35.

[11] Romans 7:15. Professor Horst Moehring has called my attention to a major difference between the explicit frame of reference of Paul's discussions and that of Aqiva's traditions in M.-T. *Zeraᶜim.* Paul frequently focuses on matters of everyday life, e.g., gossip, envy, pride, deceit. By contrast, in the materials I survey Aqiva focuses on prescriptions relating to the defunct Temple-cult.

inherent in the crop itself; it is a function of the legal status of the crop. Since the exercise of the intellect is at the center of a legal system, it is evident that Aqiva accords a substantial role to the human mind in the task of mapping out spheres of holiness. This is all the more evident in view of the theoretical nature of the discrete legal issues which Aqiva addresses. The question of the relation between Aqiva's assumptions and the apparent explosion of legal materials, ultimately redacted in M.-T., in the century and a half following the destruction of the Temple lies outside the boundaries of this study. We may speculate, however, that for Aqiva the patterns of coherence which previously converged on the Temple shift their focus to the law formulated by Tannaitic masters.

ii

The sources are given in translation in Part One, along with brief exegetical comments. Part Two deals with literary, form-critical, redactional and legal problems.

In Part One the sources are surveyed in the order that they occur in M.-T. I treat Tosefta as its name implies, as a "supplement" to Mishnah.

Fresh translations have been provided for each pericope. Danby provides an admirable translation; it is problematic, however, for purposes of literary criticism. I try to render the translation as close as possible to the Hebrew text. On occasion Danby's paraphrase of a particularly intractable phrase is cited.

A brief statement of the legal problem at issue is given for each pericope. In this regard I do not claim to advance the exegetical enterprise, and I gladly acknowledge my debt to the genius and erudition of previous commentators, especially Maimonides, Samson of Sens, the authorities on the page of the Romm Mishnah, the Gaon, Elijah of Vilna, and, in the twentieth century, Professor Saul Lieberman.

The literary structure of each pericope is examined. The number of units within a particular source is specified. If more than one unit occurs, I ask whether the different elements relate closely, or whether they address disparate topics.

The formal characteristics, that is, the forms and formulary patterns in which particular sayings occur, are also noted for each pericope.

The context in which each tradition occurs is also considered. In this regard I take up questions concerning the redaction of larger units of materials.

Historical or biographical issues are also discussed in the context of discussions of particular pericopae.

In Part One my contribution goes little beyond presenting the sources in systematic fashion. Part Two represents the greater part of my own contribution to the study of Aqiva's traditions. I proceed as follows:

First, the tradition is surveyed as a whole (Chapter Two). In this regard the remarkably well-balanced distribution pattern of Aqiva's traditions is noted.

Second, the forms and formulary patterns in which Aqivan sayings occur are discussed (Chapter Three). The results here are mostly negative: forms are an aid of considerable value for the exegesis of law but not for the study of its development. This conclusion in turn points to the substantial work done by the redactors of materials in M.-T. They have set the parameters of my study; the formal shape of Aqiva's traditions prior to redaction in M.-T. cannot be recovered, at least not by the methods used in this study.

Third, attestations are considered (Chapter Four). An attestation provides a *terminus ante quem* for a particular saying, the earliest time that we can say that the form or substance of an opinion was known. With one, or possibly two, exceptions, no firm attestations for Aqivan traditions prior to occurrence in M.-T. can be identified.

Finally, Aqiva's legal interests are compared with the agenda of the individual tractates in *Seder Zera^cim* (Chapter Five). In conclusion I describe the principles which recur in Aqivan traditions on disparate legal topics.

iii

Three areas of interest relating to Aqiva's role in the history of early rabbinic Judaism find no echo in the evidence which I survey in Part One. I therefore omit extended discussions of these three issues. I think it would be well, however, to state these issues clearly.

First, there is the question of Aqiva's exact words. Sources in M.-T. are formulaic and stylized. On the face of it, it is highly improbable that they record *verbatim* transcripts of Tannaitic discussions. In Part One I translate statements introduced by "said" or "says" inside quotation marks; I do so, however, only in accordance with normal English usage. I take "said" and "says" in Aqiva's traditions to be the equivalent of "is of the opinion that."

Second, there is the question of the enforcement of Aqiva's legal decisions. Aqiva's traditions in *Seder Zera^cim* suggest little or no interest in the enforcement of the master's legal decisions. His opinions obviously are of interest to his disciples. [12] In only one instance, however, is it alleged that a community followed Aqiva's legal decision. [13] Indeed, Aqiva's traditions in M.-T. *Zera^cim* provide no evidence concerning the contribution which the legal discussions of Yavnean and Ushan masters made to the actual life of the majority of Jews in Palestine during the second century.

And third, there is the question of the shape of Tannaitic collections of legal materials prior to the redaction of Mishnah (ca. A. D. 200). It has been suggested that Tannaim collected legal traditions and arranged them by topic as early as the Houses of Hillel and Shammai. [14] It is frequently alleged that Aqiva shaped a specific collection which, although further augmented and refined by subsequent tradents, served as the basis of the Mishnah authorized by Judah the patriarch around A.D. 200. Y. N. Epstein, who subscribes to this theory, calls Aqiva "the father of ... Our Mishnah." [15] In Aqiva's traditions on agriculture I see no evidence to suggest the existence of an Aqivan proto-mishnah. Aqiva is not responsible for the literary structure or legal agenda of any of the tractates in *Seder Zera^cim.* Nor are the forms and formulary patterns in which Aqivan traditions circulated prior to redaction in M.-T. available, at least not by means of the methods used in this study. At this time I can propose no answer to the question as to whether Aqivan traditions, prior to redaction in M.-T., circulated individually or in collections organized by legal topic, by theme, or by formal literary traits.

For convenience I omit diacritical marking in spelling Aqiva. The name is transliterated according to the spelling given in the Kaufmann Mishnah-Codex.

Translations of Scriptures are taken from the RSV, of passages in the Pseudepigrapha from Charles' edition.

Hoffmann's abbreviations and numbering system are followed for references to passages in the *halakhic* midrashim. [16]

In Part One a reference-number precedes each pericope. Each number consists of three parts: (1) an upper case Roman numeral; (2) a

[12] M. Shev. 8:9-10.

[13] T. Dem. 4:13.

[14] E.g., D. Hoffmann, *Die erste Mischna und die Controversen der Tannaim* (Berlin, 1882).

[15] Y. N. Epstein, Tannaim, p. 71.

[16] D. Hoffmann, *Zur Einleitung in die halachischen Midraschim*, (Berlin, 1886-7).

lower case Roman numeral; and (3) an Arabic numeral. The first two numerals indicate the stratum and document in which the source occurs. I.i, for instance, designates sources from the primary stratum (I. = M.-T.), and specifically from Mishnah (i). The sources from particular documents are numbered consecutively, and it is to this that the Arabic numerals refer. Thus I.i.1 refers to the first pericope cited from Mishnah, I.i.2 to the second, I.i.3 to the third, and so on. The strata and documents surveyed are as follows:

I.i	Mishnah
I.ii	Tosefta
II.i	Sifra
II.ii	Sifré Numbers
II.iii	Sifré Deuteronomy
III.i	Pericopae in y. introduced by *tny* or by *tny*ᵓ
III.ii	Pericopae in b. introduced by *tny* or by *tny*ᵓ
IV.i	Pericopae in y. not introduced by *tny* or by *tny*ᵓ
IV.ii	Pericopae in b. not introduced by *tny* or by *tny*ᵓ

PART ONE

CHAPTER ONE

THE SOURCES

i. *Pe*ᵓ*ah*

I.i.1

A. "At any time [the landowner] may give [part of his harvested crop] for *pe*ᵓ*ah* (*nwtn mšwm p*ᵓ*h*), and is exempt from tithes [due for the part of the crop given as *pe*ᵓ*ah*], until he finishes the process of stacking [the harvest].

B. "And [the landowner] may renounce ownership (*nwtn mšwm hpkr*) [of part of his harvested crop] and is exempt from tithes [due for the part of the crop declared ownerless], until he finishes the process of stacking [the harvest].

C. "And [the landowner] may feed [part of his harvested crop] to cattle, to a wild animal or to birds and is exempt from tithes [due for the part of the crop used to feed the animals], until he finishes the process of stacking [the harvest].

D. "And [the landowner] may take [part of his harvested crop] from the threshing floor and sow [what he takes] and is exempt from tithes [due for the part of the crop used for sowing], until he finishes the process of stacking [the harvest]," words of R. Aqiva.

M. Pe. 1:6a (y. Ma. 5:1, 51c)

The pericope is a collection of traditions which repeat the principle that the obligation of tithing is incurred when the process of harvesting a crop in finished. A, B, C and D apply this principle to uses of harvested crop which usually exempt a landowner from paying tithes. For example, *pe*ᵓ*ah*, the gleanings which Lev. 19:9-10 mandate be left for the poor to gather in the corners of harvested fields, normally is given from standing crop and is exempt from tithes. A specifies that *pe*ᵓ*ah* may be given "at any time," but if a landowner gives *pe*ᵓ*ah* after the harvesting process is finished, he must pay tithes for the harvested crop given as *pe*ᵓ*ah*. Similarly, tithes apply to harvested crop that is used as ownerless property (B), as fodder (C) or as seed-grain (D) after the harvesting process is finished.

The pericope would be appropriate in a section of traditions about tithing. It probably occurs in M. *Pe*ᵓ*ah* because of the substance of A, which answers the question, When may *pe*ᵓ*ah* be given?

I take *words of R. Aqiva* to refer to all A-D. The sayings share the same implicit subject (the landowner) and follow the same formulation (participle + object + "exempt from tithes until he finishes..."). In addition, the four sayings apply the same legal principle to related issues of law. We can therefore consider A-D to be a composite, that is, a complex unit of traditions which applies a single principle to several closely related issues of law. [1] Traditions about the Houses circulated in composites, [2] and the attribution to Aqiva, the only master named in the pericope, suggests that Aqiva's traditions circulated in at least one highly developed literary form comparable to the forms of the Houses' traditions.

I.i.2

A. [Concerning] one who harvests his field selectively (literally, "makes his field spotty," *hmnr śdhw*) and left [unreaped] unripe stems—

B. R. Aqiva says, "He gives *peʾah* [omitted in P and K] from every one."

C. But (*w*) sages say, "From one [section] for all."

D. But (*w*) sages agree with R. Aqiva with regard to sowing dill or mustard seed in three [separate] places [in a single field], that one gives *peʾah* from every one."

M. Pe. 3:2 (A-C, b. Men. 71b)

A-C are in dispute-form. Aqiva's and the sages' opinions, in B-C, neatly balance in a 1-2-2-1 order:

Aqiva: *mkl ʾḥd wʾḥd*
Sages: *mʾḥd ʿl hkl*

The agreement-saying in D takes over Aqiva's phrase, "from every one." MR notes that D focuses on "sowing"; by contrast, the superscription in A refers to harvesting.

The pericope addresses a fundamental issue, the definition of a field. The case concerns *peʾah* given from produce which grows in a single field but which is not harvested all at the same time. Aqiva assumes that units of produce harvested at different times, although from the same field, are each individually liable for *peʾah*. That is, Aqiva considers the element of time to be relevant to the definition of a field for the purposes of giving *peʾah*; on Aqiva's view, different units of produce, each harvested at different times, constitute separate fields. By contrast, the unnamed sages allege that all the *peʾah* due for the contents of the field can be taken from any one of the units of harvested produce. On the sages' view, the field is defined by its physical boundaries. The sages presumably agree with Aqiva with regard to

[1] Cf. J. Neusner, *Eliezer,* Vol. II, pp. 61ff.
[2] Cf. J. Neusner, *Phar.*, Vol. II, pp. 333-44.

dill and mustard seed (D) because those plants regularly grow in separate beds within a single field. [3]

The apodosis of our dispute-form ("*pe᾿ah* from every one" vs. "from one for all") recurs in two other pericopae of M. Pe. chapter three:

A. [Concerning] plots of grain [sown] among olives:
B. House of Shammai say, "*Pe᾿ah* from each one."
C. House of Hillel say, "From one for all."
D. But they agree that if the ends of the rows were confused, that he gives *pe᾿ah* from one for all."

M. Pe. 3:1

A. [Concerning] plots of onions [sown] among green vegetables —
B. R. Yosé says, "*Pe᾿ah* from each one."
C. But sages say, "From one for all."

M. Pe. 3:4b

Following is a synopsis of all three traditions:

M. Pe. 3:2	*M. Pe. 3:1*	*M. Pe. 3:4b*
1. One who harvests his field selectively and left unripe stems —	1. Plots of grain among olives —	1. Plots of onions among green vegetables —
2. R. Aqiva says,	2. House of Shammi say,	2. R. Yosé says,
3. "He gives *pe᾿ah* from	3. "*Pe᾿ah* from each one."	3. " " "
4. But sages say,	4. House of Hillel say,	4. But sages say,
5. "From one for all."	5. " " "	5. " " "
6. But the sages agree with R. Aqiva	6. But they agree	6. — — —
7. With regard to sowing dill or mustard in three places,	7. That if the ends of the rows were confused,	7. — — —
8. That he gives *pe᾿ah*	8. " " "	8. — — —
9. From each one.	9. From one for all.	9. — — —

The traditions give different superscriptions (no. 1). Our pericope, however, stands apart from the other two, which, although they specify different items (grain/olives, 3:1, vs. onions/green vegetables, 3:4b), at least follow the same pattern of phrasing. 3:1 adds an agreement-saying (nos. 6-9) to the dispute, but it is not comparable to the agreement-saying in our pericope. Strikingly, 3:1 attributes its dispute to the Houses, 3:2 attributes its dispute to Aqiva, a Yavnean, and 3:4b attributes its dispute to Yosé, an Ushan. Each of the traditions is first attested by its occurrence in M. Do we have three versions of the same dispute?

[3] So MR. See Felicks, *Agriculture in Palestine*, p. 78.

T. Pe. 1:9 gives the following, which recalls the pericope in M.:

A. [If] one harvested half [of his crop] and sold what he had harvested,
B. [Or if] one harvested half [of his crop] and dedicated what he had harvested,
C. He gives *pe*ʾ*ah* from the one for all...
D. And if the ends of the rows were confused,
E. He gives *pe*ʾ*ah* from one for all.
F. One who harvests selectively (*hm*ʾ*rg*)
G. Is obligated at its beginning and is obligated at its end.

T. Pe. 1:9 (Lieberman ed., p. 44 lines 38-42)

"*Pe*ʾ*ah* from one for all" (C, E) is familiar from the pericopae in M. (no. 5 in the synoptic table, above). D+E, in fact, give the case about which the Houses, in M. Pe. 3:1, agree. And F+G in T. refer, albeit in different language, to the same case as our pericope, M. Pe. 3:2. [4] *hm*ʾ*rg* (F of T.) is no less novel a term than *hmnmr* (A of M. 3:2); in my translation I follow Lieberman, who equates the terms. [5] G of T., "obligated at its beginning and obligated at its end," can be equated with "from every one" attributed to Aqiva in M. 3:2B; the result of both opinions is the same—a landowner must give *pe*ʾ*ah* both from the first unit that he harvests and also from the last. Since the language of F-G of T. differs completely from that of our pericope, it seems most likely that T. records an independent version of the same, basic dispute. A-C of T. give still other variations on the same problem.

What is that problem? Clearly it relates to determining boundaries, both in time and in space. Our pericope deals with determining the status of units of the same crop harvested at different *times.* Aqiva holds that differences in the times of harvesting matter; the sages hold that such differences are not normally considered relevant. The Houses' and Yosé's disputes in M. deal with determining boundaries in *space* between mixed crops in a single field. In each instance the biblical requirement of giving *pe*ʾ*ah*, surely not something newly discovered in the second century, provides the point of departure for raising the issue. y. Pe. 3:1, to which we now turn, understands Aqiva's position in the light of this issue.

IV.i.1

A. R. Ba [b.] R. Ḥiyya [said] in the name of R. Yoḥanan, "It came about that R. Meir [followed] the system of R. Aqiva, his master:

---

4 Lieberman, *TK, Seder Zera*ʾ*im*, pp. 137-38.
5 Lieberman to T. Pe. 1:9, p. 44.

B. "Just as R. Aqiva said [that] unripe and ripe [things] are two separate [categories], so R. Meir says [that] unripe and ripe [things] are two [separate] categories."

y. Pe. 3:2, 17c

Ba b. Ḥiyya, a fourth-century Palestinian master, presumably refers to Aqiva's opinion at M. Pe. 3:2. Meir's opinion occurs at M. Pe. 2:1b:

A. [Concerning] one who cuts [a crop] to use for fodder —
B. "[The harvested crop] serves as a boundary (literally, "cuts off")," words of R. Meir.
C. But sages say, "It serves as a boundary only if [the area is] ploughed up."

M. Pe. 2:1b

Meir considers harvested crop as sufficiently different from unharvested crop so as to be able to constitute a physical boundary between patches of the latter. Aqiva, at M. Pe. 3:2, distinguishes between ripe and unripe crop for the purposes of giving *pe᾿ah*: each unit of crop becomes obligated for *pe᾿ah* only as it ripens and is harvested; ripening, and subsequent harvesting, marks the point at which the obligation of *pe᾿ah* is incurred. According to Ba b. Hiyya, Meir turns Aqiva's chronological boundary into a physical one.

Ba b. Ḥiyya, a fourth-century Amora, claims that Aqiva is Meir's master. The traditions surveyed in this study provide no evidence to support that assertion. To the contrary, in pericopae in *Seder Zeraᶜim*, not once does Meir refer to an Aqivan tradition.

I.i.3
A. R. Eliezer says, "Land of the size of a quarter [*qab*] is liable for *pe᾿ah*."
B. R. Joshua says, "That which produces two *se᾿ahs*."
C. R. Tarfon says, "Six by six handbreaths."
D. R. Judah b. Bathyra says, "[Sufficient] so as to harvest and to repeat [the process]."
E. And the *halakhah* is according to his words.
F. R. Aqiva says,
G. "Land of any size (*qrqᶜ kl šh᾿*)
H. "Is liable
I. "For *pe᾿ah*
J. "And for first fruits
K. "And to write a *prosbul* on its basis
L. "And to be acquired along with movable property by money, or (*w*) by document, or (*w*) by presumption."

M. Pe. 3:6 (y. Pe. 3:6,7; b. Qid. 26a;
b. B.B. 27a-b, 150a)

Aqiva's sentence, F-L, stands independent of the preceding dispute. P splits off F-L from A-E as a separate pericope. For the dispute, see Neusner, *Eliezer*, Vol. I, p. 34. G+H read well with either I or J, or with both. The infinitive phrases in K and L break, however, the pattern of the foregoing.

Aqiva focuses on obligations (H, I) and privileges (K, L) which "land of any size" incurs. By contrast, the preceding dispute focuses solely on the first of the four issues to which Aqiva refers, namely, the minimum area of land obligated for *pe᾿ah*. Aqiva's "land of any size" is far smaller than any of the measures proposed by the other masters. Indeed, Aqiva's view may assume a definition of *pe᾿ah* different from that assumed in the other masters' opinions, for Aqiva all but divorces the obligation for giving *pe᾿ah* from considerations of owning land. As at M. Pe. 3:2 Aqiva introduces into the calculus of the laws of *pe᾿ah* an element beyond that of the physical dimensions of the field, namely, the element of time, so here in our pericope Aqiva transforms the land-owning requirement, expressed by the other masters in concrete, physical terms, into an abstract conception of obligation. The difference between Aqiva and the other masters could be readily expressed in a dispute-form composed of A+F+G:

> Eliezer: Land of the size of a quarter *qab* is liable for *pe᾿ah*.
> Aqiva: Land of any size.

Cp. Aqiva's view on giving Heave-offering at M. Ter. 4:5.

The discussion of M. Shev. 10:6 about the *prosbul*, a court-document which entitles a creditor to collect a debt otherwise cancelled by the Sabbatical year, assumes Aqiva's principle:

> They write a *prosbul* only on the basis of land. If [the debtor] has no [land], [the creditor] gives him title to part of his own [i.e., the creditor's] field, however small (*kl šh᾿*).
>
> M. Shev. 10:6a

That is, a court can issue a *prosbul* only if the debtor owns real property; in extreme circumstances that requirement can be satisfied by the creditor ceding to the debtor even land "of any size"—Aqiva's measure. The final item, L, assumes the distinction between, on the one hand, acquiring land and, on the other hand, acquiring "movable property," that is, anything other than real property. M. Qid. 1:5 notes that in the former case, acquisition is effected by transferring money, by drawing a document, or by establishing a presumption of ownership;

with movable property, however, acquisition is effected only by taking physical possession of the articles. M. Qid. 1:5 further notes that if both land and movable property are to be acquired in a single transaction, the rules applying to land pertain. L of our pericope means that, regardless of the size of the land included in a transaction of the last type, the rules about acquiring real property pertain. The discussion at M. Qid. 1:5 does not necessarily assume Aqiva's principle. Is each of the items integral to Aqiva's list? At most the evidence, literary and legal, suggests that K and L be distinguished from G+H+I/J. In any case, a single sentence, formulated as a list of diverse items, is unique among Aqiva's traditions in M.-T. *Zeraᶜim.*

Aqiva's saying obviously occurs at M. Pe. 3:6 because it repeats "land — is liable for *peᵓah*" from the superscription (A) of the Eliezer-Joshua-Tarfon-Judah dispute. Interestingly, the following pericopae, 3:7-8, do not relate to *peᵓah* at all; instead they deal with deathbed gifts (3:7a), bequests (3:7b), and manumission (3:8). Each tradition, however, uses the phrase, "land of any size." Aqiva's saying, along with M. Pe. 3:7-8, may have comprised a discrete unit of materials prior to its redaction at the end of M. Pe. chapter three. But this is no more certain than the possibility that F-G was attached to the preceding dispute-form, with H-L (and M. Pe. 3:7-8) added subsequently.

I.i.4

A. Three searches (*ᵓbᶜywt*) [are made] during the day: in the morning, and at midday, and at [the time of] the afternoon offering (*mnḥh*).

B. Rabban Gamaliel says, "They said this only lest they decrease [the number of searches]."

C. R. Aqiva says, "They said this only lest they add [to the number of searches]."

D. [The men] of Bet Namer used to give the poorman's share according to the rope-measurement and *peᵓah* from each and every row.

M. Pe. 4:5 (y. Pe. 4:3, 18b)

The pericope discusses the number of times during the day that the poor may enter a field to gather *peᵓah*. Gamaliel and Aqiva dispute as to whether *three* is a maximum or a minimum specification.

A-C are in dispute-form. The balanced opinions in B and C respond, however, only to the first part of A, *three searches.* A is an independent saying which specifies three searches, no more, no fewer, and their times.

According to Gamaliel, a landowner must allow at least three searches. Aqiva says that there may be no more than three searches. It is not clear whom either opinion favors, whether the poor or the landowner. To increase the number of searches, for instance, might give the poor greater access to *pe'ah*; on the other hand, it might also allow the landowner to tax the poor by parcelling out *pe'ah* in many small quantities. Conversely, to decrease the number of searches might decrease the quantity of *pe'ah* that the poor could gather; or, on the other hand, it might make it more convenient for the poor to gather *pe'ah*.

S. Kanter suggests [6] that D supports Gamaliel's formulation, for giving *pe'ah* "from each and every row" may imply that the poor were occupied in gathering many small quantities of *pe'ah*.

I.i.5

A. What is gleanings (*lqṭ*)?

B. Whatever drops down at the moment of the reaping.

C. He cut a handful, he plucked a fistful, a thorn pricked him, [what he had cut or plucked] fell from his hand to the ground—this belongs to the landowner.

D. [What falls from] within the hand or within the sickle—to the poor.

E. Back of the hand or back of the sickle—to the landowner.

F. Top of the hand or top of the sickle—
1. R. Ishmael says, "To the poor."
2. R. Aqiva says, "To the landowner."

M. Pe. 4:10

Lev. 19:9-10 mandate that "gleanings" be left in a field at harvest-time for the poor to gather in addition to *pe'ah*. A-B define gleanings by reference to produce which drops to the ground during the harvesting-process. C-F do not mention gleanings but do take up issues related to produce which falls to the ground at the time of reaping a crop. C notes that produce which falls because of an accident unconnected with the harvesting process belongs to the landowner. D-F address the problem of produce which falls to the ground during the harvesting procedure. By contrast to C, D-F distinguish between different places from which the produce falls; the concern is to define the moment at which "harvesting" is accomplished. Thus what has been taken within the hand or sickle clearly has been harvested and consequently, if it falls, belongs to the poor (C). Produce not taken within the hand or

[6] *Gamaliel*, p. 30.

sickle, "back of the hand or back of the sickle," just as clearly has not been harvested and consequently, if it falls, does not belong to the poor (D). But what of produce which falls from the "top of the hand or top of the sickle" (F), that is, off the fingertips of the reaper or off the edge of his sickle (Bert.)? Ishmael holds that such produce is considered as harvested and consequently belongs to the poor. Aqiva's view favors the landowner and assumes that the harvesting process is not in fact accomplished so long as the produce is not taken within the hand of the reaper or within his sickle.

F is in dispute-form. The masters' sayings in the apodosis balance ("To the poor" vs. "To the landowner"). The protasis, "Top of the hand or top of the sickle," as with the statements in D and in E, is unintelligible without the notion of "falling," which is introduced in the preceding statements in the pericope. We note, however, that B and C use different verbs for falling (B: *nšr*; C: *npl*). A-B and C could in fact stand separate from each other. G. Porton suggests that A-B, C, and D-F are independent units of tradition which have been brought together in the redaction-process of our pericope. [7]

I.i.6

A. [Concerning] a vineyard which comprises only defective clusters (*šklw ᶜwllwt*),

B. R. Eliezer says, "[The produce of the vineyard belongs] to the landowner."

C. R. Aqiva says, "To the poor."

D. Said R. Eliezer, " 'When you gather the grapes of your vineyard, you shall not take the defective clusters' [Deut. 24:21]. If there is no grape-gathering, how can there be defective clusters?"

E. Said R. Aqiva, " 'And from your vineyard you shall not take the defective clusters' (Lev. 19:10)—even if the whole consists of defective clusters. If so, why is it said, 'When you gather... you shall not take the defective clusters'? The poor have a right to the defective clusters before the vintage."

M. Pe. 7:7

"Defective" grapeclusters lack both shoulder and pendant (M. Pe. 7:4). At harvest-time they are supposed to be given to the poor. In this pericope Eliezer and Aqiva dispute regarding the ownership of the product of a vineyard which comprises only defective grapeclusters.

A-C is in dispute-form. A is the topic-phrase. Eliezer's opinion depends upon and completes the phrase in A. Aqiva's saying in C,

---

7 *Ishmael*, pp. 27-28.

like B, depends upon and completes A. D-E add a debate, reported in the past tense (*Said*...), between the two masters.

The debate in D-E supplies reasons for the positions of the two masters. Eliezer fixes on the first clause of Deut. 24:21, "When you gather the grapes." If a vineyard contains only defective clusters, there will be no grape-gathering. Eliezer consequently holds that the second clause of Deut. 24:21, "you shall not take the defective clusters," becomes moot: it applies only at a time of harvesting.

Aqiva interprets Lev. 19:10 as a straightforward injunction to leave defective clusters for the poor. Aqiva, unlike Eliezer, uses Deut. 24:21 to limit the ruling, rather than to decide the main issue, that is, whether the contents of the vineyard belong to the poor or to the landowner.

The debate in D-E gives Aqiva the last word. It is not stated what use Eliezer makes of Lev. 19:10.

I.i.7

A. They do not give the poor at the storehouse less than (*m*)
B. Half a *qab* of wheat
C. Or (*w*) a *qab* of barley.
D. R. Meir says, "Half a *qab*."
E. A *qab* and a half of spelt
F. Or (*w*) a *qab* of dried figs
G. Or (ʾ*w*) a *maneh* of fig-cake.
H. R. Aqiva says, "*Prs* [i.e., half a *maneh*]."
I. Half a *log* of wine.
J. R. Aqiva says, "A quarter [*log*]."
K. A quarter [*log*] of oil.
L. R. Aqiva says, "An eighth [of a log]."
M. And [regarding] all other produce:
N. Said Abba Saul, "[Sufficient quantities] so that by their sale (literally, "Should he sell them") provisions for two meals can be purchased."

M. Pe. 8:5 (b. Erub. 29a)

The pericope focuses on Poorman's tithe. By contrast to *pe*ʾ*ah* and gleanings, which the poor gather for themselves, Poorman's tithe must be measured out by the landowner. The question in our pericope is, In what quantities should a landowner apportion Poorman's tithe?

B+C+E+F+G+I+K comprise an anonymous list which responds to A. Meir (D) and Aqiva (H, J, L) challenge four of the measures specified in the list. Dispute-forms for the masters' opinions could be constructed as follows:

1. They do not decrease ... less than a *qab* of barley.
   Meir: Half a *qab*.
2. They do not decrease ... less than a *maneh* of fig-cake.
   Aqiva: *Prs*.
3. They do not decrease ... less than half a *log* of wine.
   Aqiva: A quarter.
4. They do not decrease ... less than a quarter *log* of oil.
   Aqiva: An eighth.

Each of these disputes could be further reduced to,

> They do not decrease ... less than X [quantity] of ...
> Meir/Aqiva: Half [of that quantity].

Meir's and Aqiva's phrases stand within the formulaic framework of the anonymous list, by contrast to M-N, which give a new superscription (M), a different attributive formula ("Said X," N, vs. "X says," D, H, J, L), and a new legal principle formulated in a sentence-fragment.

How does Meir's opinion relate to Aqiva's? As noted above, within the framework of A-L the two masters share the same working principle, 'half of the quantity specified anonymously.' But obviously neither opinion depends upon the other. M. Or. 3:7, discussed below, p. 117, gives a slightly more complicated case in which opinions attributed to Aqiva and to Meir have been redacted together, obviously relate to one another, but nonetheless remain formally quite separate. As in our pericope, Meir's opinion at M. Or. 3:7 precedes Aqiva's.

How does Aqiva's view (as well as the other views reflected in B-L) differ from that of Abba Saul? Whereas Aqiva provides fixed quantities to set the limits beyond which *peʾah* cannot be diminished, Abba Saul provides a somewhat more subjective criterion, geared to the amount of food in a poorman's meal. The two views can be related to differing interpretations of the biblical injunction "to eat and be filled" (Deut. 14:29, 26:12).[8]

Do the specific items mentioned in the pericope necessarily relate to *peʾah*? In fact each of the items occurs elsewhere in contexts dealing with *ᶜerubim*, that is, the demarcation of limits for travel on the Sabbath (MS, TYY).[9] Abba Saul's general principle, "sufficient — for

---

[8] y. Pe. 8:5, 20d; Sifré Deut. 110, Finkelstein ed., p. 171; Sifré Deut. 303, Finkelstein ed., p. 321. See MR.

[9] E.g., T. Erub. 6:1. See Lieberman, *TK, Seder Moᶜed*, p. 411; Maim., *Code*, H. Ned. 9:9.

two meals," also occurs with reference to ᶜ*erubim*; at T. Erub. 6:3 (Lieberman ed., p. 119) the phrase defines the quantity of food required to constitute an ᶜ*erub*. Indeed, T. there applies the principle specifically to wine (the subject of I-J of our pericope) and to oil (K-L of our pericope).[10]

Contrast Epstein, *Tannaim*, pp. 162-63.

I.ii.1

A. [Concerning] the ears that are in the straw and in the *fields* [E reads, rows]—

B. Lo, these belong to the landowners.

C. Said R. Aqiva, "In this landowners behaved generously (*nhgw* ... ᶜ*yn yph*).

T. Pe. 2:21 (Lieberman ed., p. 49 lines 45-46)

Ears of corn that fall to the ground during the harvesting process belong to the poor. This pericope relates, however, to ears of corn that fall to the ground other than during the harvesting, for instance, when the sheaves are bound following the harvest (Lieberman).

A supplies the topic sentence. B depends on A. C, introduced by *said*, glosses A-B. Aqiva does not dispute the anonymous statement in B. Instead he adds information: landowners "behaved generously," presumably by allowing the poor to take the ears. The effect of C, of course, is to reverse the ruling in B.

Aqiva's comment attests to the ruling in A-B.

IV.i.2

A. Said R. Yosé, "A man is not obligated [by the law of] Forgetting for olive trees."

B. But (ʾ/ʾ) R. Aqiva,

C. Who expounded "afterwards" (Deut. 24:20)/"afterwards" (Deut. 24:21),

D. [Holds that] at present (*m*ᶜ*th*) [the law of] Forgetting does not apply to olive trees.

E. As [does] R. Yosé, who does not expound "afterwards."

y. Pe. 7:1, 20a

y. focuses on an issue which M.-T. does not associate with Aqiva. It also attributes to Aqiva a type of exegesis which does not occur in the master's traditions in M.-T. *Zera*ᶜ*im*.

By contrast to A, a complete sentence with a standard attributive formula, B-E give a run-on sentence and do not attribute any specific saying to Aqiva. "But," in B, suggests that Aqiva's opinion conflicts

[10] Our pericope, M. Pe. 8:5, provides the occasion for y. Pe. 8:5, 20d (bottom). The discussion there, however, explicitly focuses on the issue of T. Erub. 6:3, the specification of which materials, and in what quantities, may constitute ᶜ*erubim*.

with Yosé's; as E notes, however, D in fact agrees with A. The relative clause in C obviously assumes a scriptural exegesis—but what is it?

The pericope connects Aqiva with both (1) the question as to whether or not olive trees are subject to the law of Forgetting, namely, the scriptural mandate to leave sheaves "forgotten" in a field for the poor (Deut. 24:19) and also (2) the exegetical tradition on Deut. 24:20-21. The former, the question about olive trees, provides the context for the discussion at y. Pe. 7:1. Yosé's opinion (A) is consistent with that attributed to him at M. Pe. 7:1, the occasion for this discussion in y. What should Aqiva's view be? The pericope suggests that originally Aqiva held that the law of the Forgotten Sheaf *does* pertain to olive trees. "But — at present" (B+D) implies a change in Aqiva's view: previously his opinion differed from that of Yosé, but "at present" it does not. We could construct a dispute-form for the two masters' prior opinions; it would be odd, however, for the chronology is wrong. The *baraita*-editor in fact merely pursues one of the items on the agendum of *gemara*, the comparison of the theoretical views of Tannaim without regard to chronological relationships.

What can we make of the scriptural exegesis alluded to in C? Obviously an editor implies that Aqiva interpreted the repetition of the word, "afterwards," in Deut. 24:20-21 to mean that the law of Forgetting pertains to olive trees. As is apparent from the two verses, Aqiva's interpretation is external to their content:

Verse 20 — When you beat your olive trees, you shall not go over the boughs afterwards ...

Verse 21 — When you gather the grapes of your vineyard, you shall not glean it afterwards ...

Neither verse mentions the law of Forgetting. Only verse 20 mentions olive trees. Deut. 24:19, however, does focus on the law of Forgetting:

Verse 19 — When you reap your harvest in your field and have forgotten a sheaf in the field, you shall not go back to get it ...

Aqiva focuses on a purely formal similarity between 20 and 21. He infers from the repetition of "afterwards" in 20 and 21 that something external to both cases, namely, the law of Forgetting of verse 19, applies both to olive trees (20) and to grapes (21). Obviously there are at least two alternative exegeses: (1) "When ... you have forgotten ... you shall not go back to get it" (19), "You shall not glean it afterwards" (20), and "You shall not go back to get it" (21), have essentially the same meaning, and the law of Forgetting, explicitly mentioned only in 19, therefore properly pertains also to the cases in 20 and 21; or (2) Forgetting is mentioned only in the first case, and it therefore does not pertain to the second and third cases. [11] As it happens, we can identify the latter exegesis with Yosé's view; and immediately following our pericope y. reports, without attribution, the former interpretation as an alternative. Both of these exegeses, in marked contrast to Aqiva's interpretation, remain internal to the scriptural citations.

We have no example of a similar sort of exegesis attributed to Aqiva in M.-T. *Zeraᶜim.* Few of his exegeses are reported at all, and those focus conventionally on details internal to the scriptural texts. They are altogether unexceptional by reference to exegeses attributed to contemporary masters, e.g., Eliezer, [12] or Ishmael. [13] Does our pericope, y. Pe. 7:1, give us a glimpse of a category of traditions about Aqiva which circulated prior to the redaction of M. and which were not included, in recognizable forms, among the redacted materials? Sifré Zuṭṭa attests to at least one corpus of materials, allegedly Aqivan, different from that redacted in M. [14] Our pericope obviously suggests nothing about the form in which a tradition prior to it might have taken. We are left with a thematic correspondence: a concern for the application of the law of Forgetting to olive trees (and for the legal exegesis of Deut. 24:19-21) would be appropriate for a Yavnean master, [15] although it is not specifically reflected in Aqiva's traditions in M.-T. *Zeraᶜim.*

ii. *Demaʾi*

I.ii.2

A. Said R. Yosah,

B. "*mᶜśh š-* A shipment (*grn*) of beans arrived in Meron.

C. "And they came and asked R. Aqiva,

D. "And he permitted them [to buy all beans in] the market [without incurring any obligation for tithing].

E. "[Subsequently] they said to [Aqiva], 'Master, the [supplies of imported beans] have diminished.'

F. "And the market returned to its previous condition."

T. Dem. 4:13b (Lieberman ed., p. 80 lines 32-34)

---

[11] See also Sifré Deut. 244 (Finkelstein ed., p. 301) and 245 (Finkelstein ed., p. 302).

[12] Cp. J. Neusner, *Eliezer,* Vol. II, pp. 387-98, esp. 397-98.

[13] G. Porton, *The Traditions of R. Ishmael. Part Four,* (forthcoming).

[14] See Epstein, *Tannaim,* p. 742; Lieberman, *Sifré Zuṭṭ* (N.Y., 1968), pp. 11-2.

[15] Cp. M. Pe. 7:7, T. Pe. 2:21.

B-G, a story in the *mᶜśh š-* form, concern *demaʾi*-produce, that is, produce about which there is doubt as to whether or not first-tithe and second-tithe and Poorman's tithe have been separated. The discussion preceding our pericope assumes that the laws of *demaʾi* apply only to produce grown in the land and not to imported foodstuffs. The law obviously puts domestic produce at a disadvantage relative to imported foodstuffs. Yosah's story about Aqiva provides a precedent for the protection of domestic production by suspending the *demaʾi*-regulation. We are to understand that tithe-exempt beans have arrived in Meron, a city in northern Galilee, from abroad. Aqiva holds that, as long as the imported beans are readily available, domestic beans should be released from the laws of *demaʾi* (D). When imported beans are no longer readily available Aqiva reimposes the regulation concerning *demaʾi*-produce, for the domestic crop no longer faces competition from tithe-exempt, imported beans (E). The story is unusual in that it suggests that Aqiva exercises jurisdiction in economic affairs.

This pericope is the only source which connects Aqiva with Meron.

I.ii.3

A. 1. *mᶜśh š-* Our rabbis entered Samaritan villages along the road [between Judaea and the Galilee].

2. Samaritans set vegetables before them.

3. R. Aqiva jumped to tithe them [as one would tithe] wholly untithed produce (*wdʾy*).

B. Said to him Rabban Gamaliel,

1. "How does your heart prompt you (literally, "how full is your heart") to transgress the words of your colleagues?"

2. Or, "Who gave you permission to tithe?"

C. 1. He said to him, "And have I established a *halakhah* in Israel [by doing this]?"

2. He said to him, "I tithed [only] my own vegetables."

D. He said to him,

1. "Know that you established a *halakhah* in Israel,

2. "Because (*š-*) you tithed your vegetables."

E. And when Rabban Gamaliel went among them [i.e., the Samaritans] he declared (*ᶜśh*) their grain and beans *demaʾi*-produce and all the rest of their produce wholly untithed.

F. And when Rabban Simeon b. Gamaliel [Lieberman prefers the reading in the first printed edition, "Rabban Gamaliel"] returned through them, he saw that they had become negligent [about tithing]; and he declared all their produce wholly untithed.

T. Dem. 5:24 (Lieberman ed., p. 93 lines 100-106)

The pericope reflects two polemics, one against Aqiva and the other against the Samaritans. The latter provides the setting for the former.

We can identify two separate traditions: first, the story, introduced by *m*ᶜ*śh š*-, in A-D; and second, the narrative in E-F. I shall first discuss A-D. Then I shall refer to a different Aqiva-Gamaliel dialogue which will point up the patriarchal polemic in the story in our pericope. Finally I shall discuss E-F, which modify the anti-Aqivan polemic in the foregoing.

The controversy concerning the status of Samaritans' vegetables provides the setting for the attack on Aqiva in A-D. A1-2 set the scene. Aqiva's action in A3 implies that Samaritans cannot be trusted to tithe their crops to any extent; by contrast, Israelites are minimally assumed to separate Heave-offering from their produce. Other evidence shows that Yavneans disputed regarding legal issues relating to Samaritans. [16] Aqiva's position in our pericope is consistent with a view which can be inferred from M. Shev. 8:10. There he suppresses Eliezer's lenient ruling concerning the use of Samaritans' bread; here he maintains an extremely strict view on the use of Samaritans' vegetables. For Aqiva, Samaritans' produce cannot be considered like that of Israelites; Samaritans are thus considered to be like gentiles.

In B-D Gamaliel rebukes Aqiva. Gamaliel assumes that Samaritans' vegetables should not be considered like wholly untithed produce. The point of the rebuke in B1 centers, however, on the patriarch's notion of legal authority; Gamaliel alleges that Aqiva errs in acting against the opinion of (presumably the majority of) his colleagues. "Or" in B2 signals that B1 and B2 give separate statements. "Who gave you permission...?" probably is to be understood as a stock-phrase; otherwise B2 would raise an issue, namely, obtaining permission, secondary to the question of whether Samaritans' produce should be considered as wholly untithed or as *dema*ᵓ*i*. The repetition of "He said to him" in C1 and 2 suggests a secondary addition to the tradition. C1 in fact seems to have been generated by D1; this is because C1 does not specifically respond to anything said by Gamaliel in B. "Because" in D2 suggests a gloss.

The following table shows that B-D give a nicely balanced set of dialogue:

	Issue I. Authority	*Issue II. Tithing*
B.	1. Transgress words of colleagues.	2. Who gave you permission to tithe?
C.	1. Have I established a *halakhah*?	2. [Only] my own.
D.	1. You established a *halakhah*.	2. Because you tithed.

[16] See J. Neusner, *Eliezer*, Vol. I, pp. 36-7, 41-3; Vol. II, pp. 297, 348, 350.

Can we say what a primary dialogue would look like? I infer it would consist of B2+C2+D1. This is because I take C1 and D2 to be secondary additions to the tradition. The question thus becomes, to what do C2+D1 best respond? And it is evident that Aqiva's vapid answer, "I tithed my own," responds to "Who gave you permission to tithe?" more directly than it does to B1, which does not state the substance of the colleagues' rule. The attraction of this reconstruction is that it focuses Gamaliel's attention on the notion of an individual's conduct as precedent for law.[17] B1 is striking because it identifies Gamaliel with a different principle of authority, one presumably less congenial to the patriarchate, namely, the law follows the opinion of the majority of the sages.

The expansion of the primary dialogue, as I have reconstructed it, turns the patriarch into the champion of the sages. This is all the more striking because Aqiva, clearly one of the giants among the masters at Yavneh, is made the butt of the tradition. He does not know the law concerning the Samaritans' vegetables. He does not know that the actions of an individual become precedent for law. He does not, in effect, meet his responsibilities as a rabbinic master. This is strong criticism. It is also excellent patriarchal propaganda, especially with B1 added to B2; Gamaliel allegedly combines in his person both the authority of the patriarchate and also the authority of the learning of a majority of the masters.

This picture of the patriarch as the champion of the sages differs significantly from the portrait in the following tradition:

A. *m*ᶜ*śh b-* Rabban Gamaliel and the elders (*wzqnym*) were reclining in Jericho.

B. They set dates before them, and they ate.

C. R. Aqiva jumped to say one blessing [after eating the dates].

D. Said to him Rabban Gamaliel, "Aqiva, why do you poke your head into a dispute [i.e., the preceding pericope reports that Gamaliel holds that one says three blessings after eating dates; unnamed sages there require only one blessing]?"

E. He said to him, "You have taught us, 'Follow the majority' (Ex. 23:2). Even though you [hold one opinion, i.e., three blessings] and your colleagues [hold a different opinion, i.e., one blessing], the *halakhah* follows the words of the majority."

T. Ber. 4:15b (Lieberman ed., p. 21 line 53—p. 22 line 57)

---

[17] S. Kanter, *Gamaliel*, pp. 355-61.

Here Aqiva champions the view that one must follow the ruling of a majority of the sages and not that of an individual, even of the patriarch. Aqiva cites Gamaliel against himself (E); this exegesis is not identified with Gamaliel in any other context. Both T. Ber. 4:15b and our pericope assume that Gamaliel shares what we may call the rabbinic perspective of the sages. The contrast between the two traditions, however, is evident: at T. Ber. 4:15b Aqiva, the sage, vanquishes the patriarch; in A-D of our pericope, T. Dem. 5:24, Gamaliel, the patriarch-master, rebukes an irresponsible colleague. For the former, Aqiva is the paragon; for the latter, Gamaliel combines power and authority, and Aqiva is an inferior rival.

In our pericope E-F, by contrast to A-D, give a more characteristic picture of the activities of the patriarchate. The patriarch makes personal inspections and, on his own judgment, issues legal decrees. E-F do not mention Aqiva, but the connection of the narrative with A-D is clear: the patriarch is brought over to Aqiva's view concerning Samaritans' vegetables. In the end the patriarch decrees that all Samaritans' produce must be considered wholly untithed.

The addition of E-F to A-D, which surely can be considered pro-Aqivan, points to the conservatism of the ultimate authority behind the tradition. Although Aqiva's opinion triumphs and is finally accepted even by his opponent, prior, severe criticism of Aqiva has obviously not been suppressed.

iii. *Kilaʾim*

I.i.8

A. 1. The turnip and the radish,
2. and the cabbage and the cauliflower,
3. the beets and the orach;

B. Added R. Aqiva,
1. The garlic and the wild garlic,
2. [L, M, "and"] the onion and the wild onion,
3. and (omitted in K, N, M) the lupine and the wild lupine

C. Are not [considered] Mixed-kinds [when they grow] beside each other.

M. Kil. 1:3

Lev. 19:19, which specifies provisions of the law of Mixed-kinds, prohibits sowing a field with two kinds of seed. A gives a list of three pairs of vegetables and, in B, Aqiva "adds" three additional pairs. The two lists become intelligible only by reference to C, which states that none of the pairs is considered Mixed-kinds when sown together in a single field.

The two lists, in A and B, could stand independent of one another. The redactional significance of "added" in B is not clear.

I.ii.4

[...(1:1b) "The cucumbers and the gourds, and the melons and the muskmelons are not [considered] Mixed-kinds [when they grow] beside each other; and they give Heave-offering and they set aside tithes from one for the other," words of R. Meir. R. Judah and R. Simeon say, "[They are considered] Mixed-kinds [when they grow] beside each other, and they do not give Heave-offering or set aside tithes from one for the other."]

A. Added R. Aqiva, "The garlic and the wild garlic, and the onion and the wild onion, and the lupine and the wild lupine."

B. Said R. Simeon, "R. Aqiva taught only with regard to these [first] two pairs; but the lupine and the wild lupine are not [considered] Mixed-kinds [when they grow] beside each other."

T. Kil. 1:2 (Lieberman ed., p. 203 lines 6-8)

A gives the same list for Aqiva's "additions" as does M. Kil. 1:3, with slight spelling changes. T. does not specify, however, whether Aqiva lists items which are or which are not Mixed-kinds when planted together in the same field. By contrast M. Kil. 1:3C states that the items are not considered Mixed-kinds. Simeon, in B of T., however, quite clearly assumes the opposite, namely, that the three pairs listed by Aqiva are considered Mixed-kinds when planted together. Against that latter view, which contradicts the position given in M., Simeon presents a third version of Aqiva's opinion: Aqiva in fact regarded only the first two pairs as Mixed-kinds; the third pair is not considered Mixed-kinds and the homogeneous list of three pairs attributed to Aqiva is wrong.

The saying in B supplies an Ushan attestation to a list of three pairs, presumably the list which occurs both in A and in M. Kil. 1:3. B also suggests that different traditions about what Aqiva taught concerning the laws of Mixed-kinds circulated at Usha.

As in M. Kil. 1:3, the redactional significance of "Added" (A) is not clear.

III.i.3. Words in Aramaic are italicized.

A. The turnip (*hlpt*) and the raddish (*whnpws*), the cabbage (*hkrwb*) and the cauliflower (*whtrwbtwr*)—

B. [It is] *a tender cabbage* (*krwb dqyq*).

C. The beets (*htrdyn*) and the many-colored *orach* (*wh*ᶜ*l*ᶜ*wnyn hm*ᶜ*wyyn*)—

D. Added R. Aqiva, "The garlic (*hšwm*) and the wild garlic (*whšwmnyt*)"

E. [They are] *garlic plants* (*twmnyth*).

F. The onion (*hbṣl*) and the wild onion (*whbṣlṣwl*)—

G. [It is a] *dwarf-onion* (*pllgwlh*).

H. The lupine (*htwrmws*) and the wild lupine (*whplwslws*)—

I. [It is a] *lupine* (*prmwᶜh*).

J. And it is not [considered] Mixed-kinds [when they grow] beside each other.

y. Kil. 1:3, 27a

B, E, G, and I interpolate Aramaic explanations of Hebrew words in the text of M. Kil. 1:3.

I.i.9

A. [If] one's field was sown with [one type of] vegetable, and he seeks to plant in its midst a row [P omits "row"] of another [kind of] vegetable,

B. R. Ishmael says, "[He may not do so] unless there is an open furrow (*tlm mplš*) extending from one end of the field to the other."

C. R. Aqiva says,

1. "[An area in] length six handbreadths
2. and *rḥb mlwʾw*."

D. R. Judah says, "[Its] width [must be as great] as a *prsh*."

M. Kil. 3:3b

I.i.10

E. [If] one's field was sown with onions and he seeks to plant in its midst rows of gourds,

F. R. Ishmael says,

1. "He uproots two rows [of onions] and plants one row [of gourds in their place].
2. "And he leaves onions standing in [the next] two rows.
3. "And he uproots [the next] two rows [of onions] and plants one row [of gourds in their place]."

G. R. Aqiva says,

1. "He uproots two rows [of onions] and plants two rows [of gourds in their place].
2. "And he leaves onions standing in [the next] two rows.
3. "And he uproots [the next] two rows [of onions] and plants two rows [of gourds in their place]."

H. But (*w*) sages say, "If there is not between one row and the next [a space of at least] twelve *amot*, one should not allow what is planted between [the rows] to grow."

M. Kil. 3:6

M. Kil. 3:3b and 3:6 present separate versions of the same problem. Different species of plants in a single field have been separated, following the biblical requirement against Mixed-kinds. The pericopae address a fundamental question of M.-T. Kil., namely, what must be done to protect against the appearance of Mixed-kinds. How great must the separation be between different crops? The protases in A and E give similar formulations ("If one's field was sown with..., and he seeks to plant in its midst..."). E states "rows," instead of "row," which A gives. E also substitutes specific items, onions and gourds, for the general term, vegetables, of A. Gourds present an exceptional problem. Leafy and lengthy, the foliage of gourds spreads and becomes enmeshed with nearby plants, thus giving the gourds and the nearby plants the appearance of a mixture.

The apodoses of the masters differ significantly. B-C are not balanced. B attributes to Ishmael a sentence-fragment which depends upon A. A "furrow" is the plowed area in which seeds are planted. Ishmael's point is that the area in which the new kind of vegetable is sown must be clearly distinguishable as a separate field; thus the new furrow must intersect the entire field. Aqiva's saying, in C, would be unintelligible without the foregoing. By contrast to B, C introduces a linear measurement for "length." Maim. takes C to refer to the length of the furrow; against Ishmael, Aqiva thus alleges that the furrow need be only six handbreadths long. Alternatively, however, C refers to the area of separation required between rows of different kinds of plants; the standard minimum measure for that area for vegetables is six handbreadths square.[18] Aqiva presumably holds that the new row of vegetables can be planted anywhere in the field so long as the row is separated from the old crop by an area at least six handbreadths square. C thus does not respond directly to Ishmael's saying, which focuses on the length of the furrow. The point of Aqiva's saying is that no special precautions need be taken against the appearance of Mixed-kinds; the standard separation is adequate. On this view *rḥb mlwʾw* (C2) means "fully as wide."[19] Judah's saying, in D, depends upon Aqiva's. It is explained at y. Kil. 3:3 that a *prsh*, or footstep, is one handbreadth in length; Judah thus proposes a shorter measurement for the width of the required separation.

By contrast to B-C, F-G give a perfectly balanced apodosis. F1 and

---

[18] See M. Kil. 2:10.

[19] So Bert., TYT., TY. Contrast Maim., **GRA.**

3 differ in language from G1 and 3 only on one row vs. two rows; otherwise the language in F1-3 and G1-3 is identical. Maim. explains F1 and 3 to mean that the single row of gourds is planted in the middle of the space formerly occupied by two rows of onions; Ishmael requires that a special cleared area separate a row of gourds, an exceptional species, from rows of other vegetables, here represented by onions. Aqiva holds, however, that gourds may be planted in rows like other species. This assumes that only the standard separation divides the new rows from the old crop (Maim., TY, MR).

The sages in H obviously stand outside the dispute-form in F-G. H focuses on "allowing to grow." The sages assume that thick foliage of gourds extends at least six handbreadths from the plants; thus unless at least twelve *amot* separate two rows of gourds, vegetables planted in the intervening area will become emmeshed in the foliage of the gourds and will give the appearance of a violation of the laws of Mixed-kinds. Maim. notes that a row is not less than four *amot* in width and that the sages therefore agree with Ishmael's opinion in F on the space required to separate two rows of gourds. H does not speak, however, to the issue of the space necessary to separate a row of gourds from a row of, for instance, onions, which is the issue in F-G (see Sens; contrast MR). The issue of "allowing to grow" recurs in an Aqivan pericope at T. Kil. 1:15a, discussed below.

I.i.5

A. *qṣr* [y. reads, *qwṣb*; Lieberman suggests, *qṣb*] the words of both of them.

B. R. Ishmael says, "Ten *amot* [y. reads, "twelve"]."

C. R. Aqiva says, "Eight *amot* [y. reads, "eight"]."

T. Kil. 2:12 (Lieberman ed., p. 211 lines 46-48; y. Kil. 3:6, 28d)

Lieberman connects this pericope with M. Kil. 3:6. Ishmael's and Aqiva's opinions have been translated into the terms of the sages in the other pericope. Unlike Ishmael's, the opinions attributed to Aqiva in the different sources are consistent.

I.i.11

A. [If] one was passing through a vineyard and seeds [of, e.g., grain] fell from him,

B. Or [if it happened] that (*š*) [seeds of, e.g., grain] were scattered [in a vineyard] along with the manure or with the water.

C. [Concerning] one who sows [e.g., seeds of grain]

D. And the wind blows [the seeds] behind him [and into a vineyard]:

E. It is permitted [for the person to derive benefit from the crop in the vineyard].

F. [If] the wind blew (*s^{c}rtw*; K, P, C, read, *wsy^{c}tw*, "helped it") [the seeds] in front of him—

G. R. Aqiva says,

1. "If shoots (*^{c}sbym*) [begin to sprout], one should plow them under.

2. "And if [the intruding crop has reached] an early stage of ripening, one should shake it out.

3. "And if it produced [ripened] grain, it should be burned."

M. Kil. 5:7

The pericope assumes that the laws of Mixed-kinds do not pertain to seeds planted unintentionally. The literary construction of the pericope is complicated. A and B give separate instances of the same problem: unintentionally seeds of, e.g., grain, are intruded into a vineyard. Neither A nor B states what is to be done. C-D introduces another case dealing with the same basic problem. C+D+E could stand alone. E could serve A(+B) almost as well, however. The point of the editor is clear enough: in each case (A, B, C-D) the crop in the vineyard is not forfeited.

F clearly enough introduces a case in which the sower knows that seed enters the vineyard. F depends upon C and balances D. But Aqiva's saying (G) is much longer than the anonymous "It is permitted" (one word in Hebrew, *mtr*) in E. A tighter formulation would state, "It is forbidden," to balance E; in any case, the effect of Aqiva's view is to prohibit deriving benefit from the crop intruding into the vineyard. As it happens, T. reports the balanced unit—without, of course, any attribution to Aqiva:

A. R. Simeon b. Judah said in the name of R. Simeon,
B. "[Concerning] one who sows—
C. "And [if] the wind blows it behind him,
D. "It is permitted,
E. "For it is an accident.
F. "[If] the wind helps it in front of him,
G. "It is forbidden."

T. Kil. 3:12a (Lieberman ed., 216 lines 45-47)

The gloss in E of T. makes explicit what our pericope in M. assumes.

Aqiva's saying in G focuses on the product of seeds sown in a vineyard. That produce must be removed as soon as a person becomes aware of it. This is consistent with the view expressed anonymously in the preceding pericope, M. Kil. 5:6:

> If one saw vegetables growing in the vineyard and said, "When I reach them I shall pick them," they are not forbidden; [if he said,] "When I come back again I shall pick them," [the vegetables] are forbidden, even if they have grown only another two-hundreth part."

M. Kil. 5:6 assumes that, in delaying to remove vegetables from a vineyard, a person signals the intention to benefit in some way from the product of Mixed-kinds of seeds. In our pericope Aqiva similarly brooks no delay; this implies that delaying would signal the person's intention, as assumed in M. Kil. 5:6. T. Kil. 1:15a attributes this opinion to Aqiva in a different literary formulation; see below.

I.i.12

A. And how much [space] is [required for] the tillage of the vine (ᶜ*bwdt hgpn*)?

B. Six handbreaths in every direction.

C. R. Aqiva says, "Three."

M. Kil. 6:1b (y. Kil. 6:1, 30b)

A-C are in a variation on the dispute-form. A asks a question. B, an anonymous statement, responds to A. And Aqiva's saying depends upon and challenges B. As in the list at M. Pe. 8:5, discussed above, Aqiva's one-word saying gives a measure one-half that which it disputes.

Aqiva holds that a single vine needs for its tillage a circular area with a radius of at least three handbreadths (slightly more than one-quarter of a meter). Other vegetation planted within that area becomes subject to the laws of Mixed-kinds.

I.i.13

A. Said R. Yosé,

B. "*m*ᶜ*śh b-* One who (*š*) sowed his vineyard during the Seventh-year,

C. "And the case came before R. Aqiva;

D. "And he said,

E. " 'A man cannot forfeit something which does not belong to him.' "

M. Kil. 7:5 (y. Kil. 7:3, 31a)

Under normal circumstances grain or vegetables sown in a vineyard would be forfeited under the laws of Mixed-kinds. Deut. 22:9 states, however, "You shall not sow *your* vineyard with Mixed-kinds of seeds."

The story in B-E assumes that produce which grows in the Seventh-year is considered ownerless; that is, the person in B does not actually own what grows in his vineyard. E thus implies that the product of Mixed-kinds of seeds sown in a vineyard during the Seventh-year is not forfeited according to the prohibitions against Mixed-kinds.

The saying in E occurs elsewhere. In fact, in the preceding pericope, M. Kil. 7:4, it is attributed jointly to Yosé and to Simeon, another Ushan. The *mᶜśh b-* story here presumably supplies a precedent for that previous opinion.

The story suggests nothing concerning the enforcement of Aqiva's "ruling." Since it gives a case which exemplifies the confluence of two separate principles, the pericope resembles a legal conundrum.

I.ii.6

A. One who sows [Mixed-kinds of seeds]

B. And one who weeds [an area planted with Mixed-kinds of seeds, thereby aiding their growth]

C. And one who blows (*whmnpḥ*; E reads, *whmḥph*, "One who covers [Mixed-kinds of seeds with dirt, thereby aiding their growth]")

D. Transgresses a negative rule (*lʾ tᶜśh*).

E. R. Aqiva says,

F. "Also (*ʾp*) one who allows [Mixed-kinds of seeds] to grow (*hmqyym*)

G. "Transgresses a negative rule."

T. Kil. 1:15a (Lieberman ed., p. 205 lines 37-38; y. Kil. 8:1, 31b)

A-D stand as a complete unit. Aqiva adds a fourth item, namely, allowing Mixed-kinds of seeds to grow (F), to the three things listed in A-C. G repeats D.

How does 'allowing to grow' differ from sowing (A), weeding (B), and blowing (or covering with dirt) (C)? Each of the latter depends upon a positive action. And in each case the action signifies the intention of a person to transgress the biblical injunction (the "negative rule" in D), "You shall not sow your field with two kinds of seed" (Lev. 19:19). Aqiva adds that no positive action is required; delaying to uproot Mixed-kinds of seeds, once they are observed, also signals the intention of a person to violate the biblical law. This view is consistent with that expressed by Aqiva at M. Kil. 5:7, discussed above.

The issue of "allowing to grow" recurs in the sages' lemma at M. Kil. 3:6H.

IV.ii.1

A. [Concerning] one who weeds
B. Or (*w*) one who covers [with dirt]
C. Mixed-kinds of seeds—
D. *lwqh* [i.e., that person is punished with lashes].
E. R. Aqiva says,
F. "Also (*ᵓp*) one who allows [Mixed-kinds of seeds] to grow."

b. Mak. 21b (b. M.Q. 2b; b. A.Z. 64a)

The *baraita*-editor shifts the focus of the pericope away from the issue of intention. Instead he emphasizes the punishment for the violation of a biblical law, a separate issue. The following synoptic chart shows how the *baraita*-editor builds upon the pericope from T. to effect the shift:

T. Kil. 1:15a	*b. Mak. 21b*
1. One who sows	1. — — —
2. *w* + one who weeds	2. One who weeds
3. *w* + one who blows/covers	3. *w* + one who covers
4. — — —	4. Mixed-kinds of seeds
5. Transgresses a *lᵓ tᶜśh*	5. *lwqh.*
6. R. Aqiva says,	6. ,, ,, ,,
7. "Also one who allows to grow	7. ,, ,, ,,
8. "Transgresses a *lᵓ tᶜśh.*"	8. — — —

b. omits no. 1, for which a biblical text explicitly mentions a penalty; Deut. 22:9 states, "You shall not sow your vineyard with Mixed-kinds of seeds lest the whole yield be forfeited..." Instead b. narrows its concern to the actions which are one step away from the negative biblical rule (Lieberman); the *baraita* takes the Tannaitic issue of intention for granted. In no. 4 the *baraita*-editor identifies the context of the Tannaitic pericope which he is using. T. obviously assumes that the pericope relates to the laws of Mixed-kinds. By contrast, b. draws upon the discussion of Mixed-kinds for a discussion of a theory of punishment, the larger context at b. Mak. 21b. The change in terms in no. 5 makes this clear. The notion, familiar from Amoraic literature, that lashes are the punisment for the violation of a negative biblical rule (for which no other penalty is specifically stated) does not occur explicitly in materials attributed to Aqiva in M.-T. No. 8 is superfluous, and the *baraita*-editor drops it.

I.ii.7

A. And [concerning] greens (*whyrqwt*) which stretch into the midst of [E reads, "under"] the vine,

B. Abba Saul says,

C. "R. Aqiva says, 'One returns [the greens to their proper place].'
D. "Ben Azzai says, 'He trims [them].' "

T. Kil. 4:10b (Lieberman ed., p. 220 lines 36-37; y. Kil. 7:5, 31a)

This pericope follows discussions of (1) vine-shoots that stretch over and cover a nearby crop of grain (both vine and grain are forfeited) and (2) grain which, as it grows, stretches under a nearby vine (the grain is returned to its proper place without forfeit). A states the topic. The attributive formulary in B introduces C-D, which resemble an apodosis for a standard dispute-form.

The question here is in what sense C-D respond to the topic sentence, A. Aqiva holds that the offending greens should be returned to their proper place. The immediately preceding pericope in T. gives the same ruling for grain which stretches under a vine; and M. Kil. 7:7 combines the two rules in the following anonymous statement: "[Concerning] grain which stretches under the vine, and so too with vegetables (*byrq*),—one returns it [to its place] without forfeit." Does ben Azzai disagree with this view? "He trims," in D, speaks to how the greens should be disentangled from the vine. Lieberman explains that "trimming" was the usual method for disentangling vegetables and that very little of a plant was actually lost in the process. Ben Azzai, on this view, addresses a secondary issue; he states that the disentangling should proceed "as usual." There is no dispute between the masters, for Aqiva does not speak to the question of the specific method by which vegetables should be separated from a vine. And, of course, it is not clear that he would object to ben Azzai's opinion. (MS to M. Kil. 7:7 gives the alternative view: "he trims" implies that the vegetables are forfeited.)

iv. *Shevi*ᶜ*it*

I.i.14

A. Until when were they called seedlings?

B. R. Eleazar b. Azariah says, "Until [their fruit] becomes common-produce."

C. R. Joshua says, "Seven years old (C reads, "Until seven years old"; K reads, "Until ninety years.")."

D. R. Aqiva says, "A seedling is as its name [implies] (*kšmh*)."

E. "[Concerning] a fruit-tree which was razed and [subsequently] put forth shoots: [if the stump stands one] handbreadth or shorter, [it is adjudged] as a seedling; [if the stump stands one] handbreadth or taller, [it is adjudged] as a fruit-tree," words of R. Simeon.

M. Shev. 1:8

The pericope focuses on the definition of a "seedling." The legal issue concerns work which may be done in the months immediately prior to the beginning of the Seventh-year, that is, prior to the year which Lev. 25:1-7 mandate as a time during which Israelites' land must lie untilled. Fruit-trees, for instance, may not be tended from approximately six months prior to the beginning of the Seventh-year. The assumption is that it takes at least half a year to bear fruit; effort expended on fruit-trees during the six months prior to the beginning of the Seventh-year thus results in produce which will be brought forth after the beginning of the Seventh-year. An owner may derive no benefit from such produce. Seedlings are exempt from the ban on tending during the six-month period prior to the beginning of the Seventh-year (M. Shev. 1:6).

A asks, For what period of time is a plant considered a seedling? Eleazar, in B, defines seedling by reference to the laws of *ᶜorlah*, according to which fruit cannot be used during the first three years after a tree or vine has been planted; in the fourth year the fruit is dedicated in the manner of Second-tithe produce. Eleazar's statement means that fruit-trees are considered seedlings until the *ᶜorlah*-restrictions no longer apply, that is, until the fifth year or until the time when the fruit is dedicated during the fourth year (Maim.). Joshua, in C, alleges that trees are considered seedlings until their seventh year. In a different tradition, reported at T. Shev. 1:3b, however, Joshua mentions three separate periods of time (five years, six years, and seven years), and Judah the Patriarch explains that Joshua holds that different kinds of fruit-bearing plants are considered seedlings for different periods of time (thus olive trees—six years; fig trees—five years; grape vine—four years). [20]

By contrast to the first two opinions, Aqiva's saying in D does not respond directly to the question in A. D answers a slightly different question, namely, What is a seedling? Also by contrast to the sayings in B and C, Aqiva's view divorces the definition of seedling from considerations regarding the fruit of particular kinds of plants. Aqiva restricts the term seedling to newly planted trees, probably one-year old or less (Sens, TY), without regard to fruit. Maimonides suggests that Aqiva's saying means that plants are considered seedlings as long as men customarily call them seedlings. This view avoids restricting Aqiva's designation to any specific period of time, such as one year; it

---

[20] Lieberman, *TK Zeraᶜim*, p. 487.

keeps Aqiva's view independent from those of the other masters which explain "seedling" by reference to laws which explicitly refer to "fruit-trees."

E stands outside the question-answer framework of A-D. Simeon assumes a definition of seedling. E focuses on an unusual legal problem, the case of a tree-stump which puts forth shoots. To solve the problem Simeon applies a definition of seedling formulated in terms of physical measurement, namely, whether the stump stands shorter or taller than one handbreadth. The Ushan master's definition by reference to a linear measurement obviously stands at variance from the views of Eleazar and Joshua, whose opinions relate to periods of time and to the fruit-bearing process. The relationship between the definitions assumed by Simeon and by Aqiva is not so clear.

I.i.15

A. One who erects a fence separating his own [property] from public domain is permitted to dig down to the depth of the rock (*slᶜ*).

B. What should he do with the dirt [which he digs up]?

C. "He piles it up in the public domain, and he straightens it out (*wmtqnw*; K, P, N read, *wmtqynw*)," words of R. Joshua.

D. R. Aqiva says, "In the [same] way (*kdrk*) that they do not make a clutter (*mqlqlyn*) in the public domain, so (*kk*) they should not straighten it out (*lᵓ ytqnw*)."

E. What should he do with the dirt?

F. He piles it up inside his field in the [same] way (*kdrk*) those who manure [the field set up their compost heaps].

G. And so too (*wkn*) the one who digs a pit or (*w*) a trench or (*w*) a cave.

M. Shev. 3:10

Even the appearance of tilling a field during the Seventh-year is prohibited. The preceding pericopae, M. Shev. 3:5-9, discuss the movement of stones and rocks in a field during the Seventh-year for purposes unrelated to tilling the field. 3:6-7, for instance, focus on the removal of stones from a field; they specify when stones may be removed, and by what means, without giving the appearance of preparing the land for future tillage. A of our pericope, 3:10, continues the discussion of work in a field permitted during the Seventh-year. By contrast to A, B-D do not necessarily relate to the Seventh-year. The difference between Joshua's and Aqiva's opinions hinges on whether or not an individual may "straighten out" (*mtqn*) the public domain. That is, the question in B, "What should he do with the dirt?", relates not to the problem of giving the appearance of violating the laws of the Seventh-year, but rather relates to the issue of effecting a change in the public domain. (The same verb, "straighten out," *mtqn*, frequently refers in contexts related to the Seventh-year to the preparation of a field for future tillage; e.g., "They do not build steps on the sides of ravines at the end of the sixth year after the rains have ended, because [by this] one prepares them (*mtqnn*) for the Seventh-year" (3:8).) Joshua holds that an individual may pile up dirt, obstructing the public domain, so long as he subsequently removes the obstruction (C). Aqiva's opinion assumes a ban on cluttering up the public domain; by analogy with that ban, which presumably prohibits effecting a change for the worse, Aqiva argues that an individual should make no change whatsoever in the public domain. GRA suggests the following reasoning behind Aqiva's view: leveling heaps or filling in holes in the public domain will injure the interests of individuals in certain circumstances as much as heaping up obstructions or digging holes will injure the interests of other individuals in other circumstances; Aqiva therefore prohibits effecting any kind of change in the public domain.

A is a complete sentence and could stand alone. Clearly enough A generates the question, "What should he do with the dirt?" But that question occurs twice, once in B and once again in E. I suspect that E-G continue the discussion, begun in A, concerning dirt dug up in a field during the Seventh-year. The tradition about Joshua and Aqiva is inserted because it also deals with a problem of creating an obstruction in the public domain. The tradition about Joshua and Aqiva recurs in a slightly different formulation in a discussion of doing damage to the public domain at T. B.Q. 2:12, a more apposite context, and also at T. Shev. 3:5, to which we now turn.

I.ii.8

A. "They clear away stones (*msqlyn*) via (*drk*) the public domain," words of R. Joshua.

B. R. Aqiva says, "Just as (*kšm*; T. B.Q. reads, "In the same way," *kdrk*) one does not have the authority to make a clutter (*lqlql*), so (*kk*) one does not have the authority to clear away stones (T. B.Q. reads, "so one should not clear away stones.").

C. And if one cleared away stones, he should dump (*ywṣyʾ*) [them] into the sea or the river or the craggy ground.

T. Shev. 3:5 (Lieberman ed., p. 175 lines 10-12; T. B.Q. 2:12, Zuckermandel ed., p. 349 lines 13-14)

As in M., the tradition about Joshua and Aqiva does not deal with the restrictions of the Seventh-year.[21] The following is a synopsis of the two versions of the tradition about Joshua and Aqiva:

M. Shev. 3:10	*T. Shev. 3:5 (T. B.Q. 2:12)*
1. "He piles it up	1. "They clear away stones
2. "in the public domain,	2. "via the public domain,"
3. "And he straightens it out,"	3. — — —
4. words of R. Joshua.	4. " " "
5. R. Aqiva says,	5. " " "
6. "In the way	6. "Just as ("In the way")
7. "that they do not make a clutter	7. "one does not have the authority to make a clutter
8. "in the public domain,	8. — — —
9. "so they should not straighten it out."	9. "so one does not have the authority to clear away stones ("so one should not clear away stones")."

T. focuses on the removal of stones (no. 1). In M. Joshua's saying is formulated as a response to the question about piling up dirt (no. 1). The tradition in T. does not mention "straightening out" (nos. 3, 9). T. may be a subtle comment on M., for it separates the Joshua-Aqiva tradition from the context concerning the removal of dirt dug during the Seventh-year. Indeed, it is not clear at all why, except by reference to M., the tradition occurs in T.

I.i.16

A. [If] one trims vines

B. Or (*w*) [if] one cuts reeds [during the Seventh-year]—

C. R. Yosé the Galilean says, "He should do no cutting closer than a handbreadth (lit., "He should keep at least a handbreadth (away from the ground].")."

D. R. Aqiva says, "He cuts in his usual way."

E. Whether with the axe, or with the sickle, or with the saw, or with whatever he desires.

M. Shev. 4:6

The masters in C and in D respond to B, rather than to A. T. Shev. 3:19 reports the following tradition which lacks the reference to trimming vines:

[If] one cuts reeds—
He raises [the cutting tool] a handbreadth [from the ground] and cuts.

The saying of Yosé the Galilean, in C, is taken to mean the same thing as "He raises a handbreadth and cuts" in T.[22]

Reeds, in B, unlike vines (A), olive trees (4:4), or fig trees (4:7),

---

[21] *Ibid.*, p. 514.
[22] *Ibid.*, p. 522.

do not bring forth edible produce. Do the laws of the Seventh-year apply to them? Yosé the Galilean, in C, holds that at least one Seventh-year regulation does apply to cutting reeds, namely, the prohibition against doing work which, although it is not itself prohibited, nonetheless might lead to work that is prohibited (e.g., clearing land to prepare for plowing). In D Aqiva holds that no prohibition applies to cutting reeds. Lieberman suggests that, because reeds grow in marshy land, there is no concern about preparing such land for plowing or sowing.[23]

Yosé's and Aqiva's saying differ in diction. The two sayings respond independently to B, but only D explicitly repeats "cuts." E is a gloss.

I.i.17

A. [In the Seventh-year] in Syria they work with [crop which is] detached (*btlwš*)[from the land], but not with [that which remains] attached (*bmḥbr*) [to the land].

B. 1. They thresh and winnow [grain] and trample [grapes] and bind [wheat] into sheaves,

2. but they do not reap [grain] or gather [grapes] or harvest [olives].

C. R. Aqiva laid down (*ʾmr*) a general rule: Everything which is similar to what is permitted in the land of Israel is permitted in Syria (literally, "they do it in Syria").

M. Shev. 6:2

The pericope assumes the anomalous legal status of Syria, the area to the northeast of the land of Israel. Agricultural laws generally apply only to produce which grows in the land of Israel; certain laws also pertain, however, to Syrian produce. With regard to the laws of the Seventh-year, A distinguishes between crop which has been "detached" from the land and crop which is not yet detached. A alleges that in Syria the prohibitions of the Seventh-year apply to the latter but not to the former. B specifies particular activities to illustrate the distinction. "Detached" crop is threshed, winnowed, trampled and bound (B1); but the technical terms in B2 pertain specifically to unharvested types of produce. Aqiva, in C, introduces a general rule which makes produce grown in Syria comparable to produce grown in the land of Israel. The rule is formulated in terms of "what is permitted" and thus is susceptible of two interpretations. On the one hand, Aqiva may hold that Palestinian and Syrian produce are comparable, for the purposes of the laws of the Seventh-year, only with respect to activities which are permitted in the land of Israel. On this view, no conclusions may

---

[23] *Ibid.*

be drawn concerning Aqiva's views on the relationship between activities prohibited in Palestine and activities prohibited in Syria during the Seventh-year. On the other hand, the general rule in C may mean that in Aqiva's view Syrian produce is fully comparable to produce grown in the land of Israel; Aqiva thus would hold that activities prohibited in the land of Israel are also prohibited in Syria. This view would be in accord with the position attributed to Eliezer, who, with regard to liability for tithing and the laws of *ᶜorlah*, makes Syrian produce comparable to Palestinian produce, and thus includes Syria within the Israelite inheritance. [24]

In any case, the relationship between Aqiva's saying and the anonymous statement in A remains unclear. The complex of laws on the Seventh-year distinguishes between different categories of "detached" Palestinian produce, but the general rule in C obviously fails to spell out the master's presuppositions concerning what is permitted in Palestine and what is not. A(+B) and C could stand independent of one another.

I.ii.9

A. R. Aqiva agrees that [during the Seventh-year] they neither sow nor plow nor hoe in Syria, for none of [of these kinds of work] is similar to what is permitted in the land [of Israel].

B. For (*š*) everything which is similar to what is permitted in the land [of Israel] is permitted in Syria (literally, "they do it in Syria").

T. Shev. 4:12 (Lieberman ed., p. 181 lines 30-32)

The tradition in T. quite clearly assumes that Aqiva considers Syrian produce fully comparable to Palestinian produce, for in A Aqiva agrees to apply the negative corollary of the general rule. By contrast to M., T. does not specifically attribute the general rule to Aqiva. On Aqiva's presuppositions, see Lieberman, *TK Zeraᶜim*, p. 538.

I.i.18

A. [Concerning] a hide which one has anointed with oil of the Seventh-year—

B. R. Eliezer says, "It is to be burned."

C. But (*w*) sages say, "He should eat [produce of] equal value (*yʾkl kngdw*)."

D. They said before R. Aqiva, "R. Eliezer used to say, 'A hide which one has anointed with oil of the Seventh-year is to be burned.' "

E. He said to them, "Silence. I shall not tell you what R. Eliezer says concerning it."

M. Shev. 8:9

---

[24] See J. Neusner, *Eliezer*, Vol. I, pp. 80, 84; Vol. II, pp. 98, 177.

I.i.19

F. And further they said before him, "R. Eliezer used to say, 'He who eats the bread of Samaritans is like one who eats the flesh of a pig.' "

B. He said to them, "Silence. I shall not tell you what R. Eliezer says concerning it."

M. Shev. 8:10

The pericope refers to Aqivan tradents' interest in traditions about Eliezer. It is interesting that E and G state explicitly that Aqiva suppressed reports about Eliezer's true opinions.

A-E and F-G deal with separate legal problems. A-E continue from the preceding pericope, 8:8, a discussion concerning the misue of different sorts of Seventh-year produce. 8:8 states, for instance, that if oil of the Seventh-year is used to anoint vessels a quantity of common produce of value equal to the oil must be purchased and consumed, as though it were Seventh-year produce, in place of the oil. A of our pericope takes up the same problem with reference to anointing a hide. The statement of the sages, in C, corresponds to the opinion given in 8:8 concerning anointing vessels: a quantity of common produce equal in value to the misused oil should be purchased and consumed in place of the oil. Eliezer, in B, introduces a different consideration, namely, the status of the hide after being anointed. Eliezer takes an extreme position. He alleges that no benefit may be derived from the hide; it must be destroyed. The tradents in D ask Aqiva about Eliezer's position. Since (1) D gives Eliezer's position as it occurs in B and (2) Aqiva refuses, in E, to confirm the report, it follows that Eliezer in fact holds a different view, one obviously more lenient than, "[The hide] is to be burned." Conceivably Eliezer agrees with the position of the sages in C: the hide may be used, but the oil must be replaced. Neusner suggests, however, that Eliezer in fact holds a still more lenient opinion, namely, that Seventh-year oil may be used without incurring any penalty.[25] Such an opinion differs considerably from the strict views which pre-70 Pharisaism probably held regarding the laws of the Seventh-year.[26]

E-F take up a legal issue unrelated to the laws of the Seventh-year, namely, the status of Samaritans' produce. F, like B, attributes an extreme position to Eliezer; an Israelite may not eat Samaritans' bread. G repeats E *verbatim*, and once again it is possible to suggest that Aqiva

[25] *Ibid.*, Vol. I, pp. 42-43.

[25] *Ibid.*, Vol. II, p. 102.

implies that Eliezer holds a different, obviously more lenient view. We may speculate that Aqiva does not agree with Eliezer's lenient views regarding Seventh-year oil and Samaritans' bread, and thus suppresses these opinions. (T. Dem. 5:24 reports a tradition in which Aqiva assumes that Samaritans' vegetables are to be considered wholly untithed.)

The two different legal traditions (A-E: Seventh-year oil; F-G: Samaritans' bread) have been redacted according to the following formula:

> They said before R. Aqiva, "R. Eliezer used to say,..."
> He said to them, "Silence. I shall not tell you..."

Neusner suggests, first, that a list of disparate traditions in the name of Eliezer stands prior to the two rulings discussed in our pericope, [27] and second, that a progression from story to legal formulation may be discerned in the development of the traditions about Eliezer. [28] The significant point here is that Aqivan tradents are taking over and developing Eliezer-traditions .

I.i.20

A. [If] one gathers fresh (lit., "moist") vegetables [which have grown in the Seventh-year, he may use them] until the moisture [of the ground] dries up.

B. And [if] he collects dry [vegetables he may use them] until the second rainfall [after the Seventh-year] falls.

C. Leaves of reeds and leaves of vines [may be used] until [the leaves which remain in the field] fall from their stems.

D. And [if] he collects [leaves of reeds or leaves of vines when they are] dry, [he may use them] until the second rainfall [after the Seventh-year] falls.

E. R. Aqiva says, "In all [cases Seventh-year produce may be used] until the second rainfall [after the Seventh-year] falls."

M. Shev. 9:6

The pericope focuses on the problem, What time limits apply to using produce which grows in the Seventh-year? The rule is that a man must destroy his unused stocks of Seventh-year produce when, for any reason, no more of the produce is available in the fields where it grows.

A specifies that fresh vegetables which grow and are gathered during the Seventh-year may be used as long as the land contains enough

[27] Cp. Ilai's list of disparate rulings attributed to Eliezer at M. Eruv. 2:6 and see discussion at *Eliezer*, Vol. II, p. 59.

[28] The story in D-E generates A-C, and possibly also the *y*ʾ*kl kngdw* series in the preceding pericope, 8:8; F-G, which has not yielded the same development, shows that in this case the story is primary. See *Eliezer*, Vol. I, p. 42.

moisture to keep the vegetables in the field fresh. B specifies that dry vegetables which grow during the Seventh-year may be used until the second rainfall in the year following the Seventh-year. The rule is that Seventh-year produce is not to be used after the Seventh-year, but an extension, *until the second rainfall,* is granted in order to provide sufficient time for the ripening of the first, post-Seventh-year crops.

C specifies a case like that in A. "Leaves of reeds and leaves of vines" which have been properly gathered but not yet used must be destroyed from the time that leaves fall off reeds and vines that remain standing in the field. D adds that if a man collects dry leaves he will not incur the obligation to destroy what remains from what he has gathered until after the Seventh-year.

The opinion attributed to Aqiva in E takes a more lenient position than the opinions expressed in A and in C. E applies the time-limit "until the second rainfall" to all cases, regardless of the nature of the procedure involved.

The couplets in A-B and C-D occur in similar formulations:

(A) Topic + ᶜ*d š*, time-limit	(B) "*And if dry*" + *d š*, 2nd rain
(C) Topic + ᶜ*d š*, time-limit	(D) "*And if dry*" + *d š*, 2nd rain

B and D are identical. A and C differ in diction in specifying their topics and the time-limits relevant to their topics. Both A-B and C-D, however, focus on the same distinction, namely, *fresh* vs. *dry*.

"In all [cases]" in E depends upon the anonymous sayings in A-D. "Until the second..." is the same as the phrase used in B and in D.

It cannot be claimed that Aqiva glosses antecedent law here, for it would be relatively easy to formulate conventional disputes between A and E and between C and E. "In all [cases]" could be a redactor's addition.

I.ii.10

A. 1. The grain

2. and the small fruit (*whqtnywt*) which have grown one-third before New Year's day are tithed for the past [year] and are permitted in the Seventh-year.

But (*w*) if [they are] not [one-third grown] they are forbidden in the Seventh-year and are tithed for the following year.

B. R. Simeon Shizuri says,

1. "Egyptian beans

(a) which they planted from the outset for sheaves (*lᶜmyr*),

2. and also (*wkn*) large beans

3. and everything which is like them are tithed for the past

[year] and are permitted in the Seventh-year.
But (*w*) if [they are] not [one-third grown] they are forbidden in the Seventh-year and are tithed for the following year.

C. 1. Said ben Azzai before R. Aqiva
2. in the name of R. Joshua,
3. "Even after they have taken root (*ᶜp mšhšryšw*)."

D. Aqiva reversed (*ḥzr*) [his opinion] so as to teach (*lhywt šwnh*) according to the words of ben Azzai.

T. Shev. 2:13 (Lieberman ed., pp. 172-73 lines 46-51)

Joshua and Simeon Shizuri differ regarding the moment at which Egyptian beans become obligated for tithes. D implies that Aqiva initially followed Simeon Shizuri's opinion but subsequently adopted Joshua's view, as reported by ben Azzai. Curiously, D has Aqiva teaching according to the words of ben Azzai, rather than Joshua, in whose name ben Azzai cites the opinion in C. I shall first discuss the legal problem at issue in the pericope, and then I shall return to the problem of the tradents.

All the elements in the pericope assume that the moment at which a crop becomes obligated for tithing determines its status with regard to Poorman's tithe, Second-tithe, and the laws pertaining to the Seventh-year. Thus if a crop incurs the obligation during the first, second, fourth or fifth years of the seven-year cycle, it becomes obligated for Second-tithe; if during the third or sixth years, for Poorman's tithe; and if the moment of obligation occurs during the seventh, then obviously it incurs no obligations for tithing although the restriction of the Seventh-year pertain. A states that with regard to grain and small fruit (*qtnywt*; so Jastrow, p. 1358, col. I) tithes are incurred at the moment that crop becomes one-third grown. Our interest focuses on the first item which Simeon Shizuri lists in B, "Egyptian beans," that is, one particular type of small fruit. Simeon specifies Egyptian beans which are planted "for sheaves." Lieberman explains that the phrase, "planted... for sheaves," means that the crop will be eaten; by contrast, at M. Shev. 2:8, Simeon refers to Egyptian beans which are "planted for seed," that is, will be used for future seeding and will not be eaten. [29] Simeon asserts that the latter incur the obligation for tithing from the moment that they take root (Sens). Simeon's tradition in B of our pericope presumably depends upon the operative distinction in A, namely, *qtnywt* become obligated for tithes from the moment

[29] *TK*, *Zeraᶜim*, p. 508.

that they are one-third grown. Simeon thus distinguishes between Egyptian beans that are grown for seed and Egyptian beans that are grown for consumption; the former become obligated for Second-tithe, Poorman's tithe, or the laws of the Seventh-year from the moment that they take root, the latter from the moment that they become one-third grown. Joshua, according to ben Azzai in C, challenges Simeon's view concerning Egyptian beans grown for consumption; Joshua holds that they too become obligated from the moment that they take root.

The foregoing interpretation obviously assumes that T. provides a unitary pericope. Simeon's tradition, in B, does not actually specify the moment at which Egyptian beans become obligated for Second-tithe, Poorman's tithe, or the laws of the Seventh-year. Furthermore, ben Azzai's saying, in C, ignores most of A-B. We would prefer a formulation which focuses on the following:

> Concerning one who plants Egyptian beans for consumption:
> Simeon b. Shizuri says, From when they have grown one-third.
> Joshua says, From when they have taken root.

And, of course, it is only by implication (D: *Aqiva reversed* [his opinion]) and the assumption of a unitary pericope that we deduce that Aqiva initially held the opinion attributed to Simeon Shizuri.

What can we make of the tradental problem in C-D? First let us note that this pericope provides the only point of intersection of traditions about Aqiva and ben Azzai in M.-T. *Zera*ᶜ*im* (Pe.-Bik.). Throughout M.-T. slightly less than one-half of all traditions about ben Azzai intersect with traditions about Aqiva (seventeen out of a total of approximately forty).[30] Second, we note that ben Azzai cites an opinion of Joshua against Aqiva's view. In three other traditions ben Azzai also criticizes Aqiva on the basis of traditions ascribed to Joshua.[31] And finally, we note that the attributive formulas in C-D ("Said ben Azzai before R. Aqiva in the name of R. Joshua... R. Aqiva

---

30 Danby, p. 838, gives twenty items for ben Azzai, ten of which intersect with Aqiva (*ibid,* p. 812). Zuckermandel, p. xxxiii, gives twenty-five items for ben Azzai, eleven of which intersect with Aqiva (*ibid.*, p. xxxix). Only four traditions, by my count, occur in both M. and T. (M. Sheq 4:6 = T. Sheq. 2:8; M. Yoma 2:3 = T. Y.K. 1:13; M. Sot. 9:15 = T. Sot. 15:3; M. Bekh. 9:5 = T. Bekh. 7:9).

31 M. Yom. 2:3 (= T. Y.K. 1:13); M. Ta. 4:4; and M. Yeb. 4:13. This evidence is not sufficient for conclusions to be drawn concerning ben Azzai's relationships with Aqiva and with Joshua. In other traditions ben Azzai criticizes Aqiva, without reference to Joshua's traditions (e.g., M. B.B. 9:10), or studies Aqiva's teachings (e.g., T. Ber. 4:18), or simply occurs as an independent colleague of Aqiva (e.g., T. Kil. 5:10).

reversed...") recur in connection with a different legal problem at M. Ta. 4:4. A comparison with the tradition there is instructive.

A. 1. "...when an Additional Offering would be brought, no *Ma^c^amad* assembled at the Closing [of the Gates];

2. "when a Wood-offering would be brought, no *Ma^c^amad* assembled in the afternoon,"

words of R .Aqiva

B. 1. Said to him ben Azzai,

2. "Thus R. Joshua used to teach (*hyh...šwnh*)

3. " 'When an Additional Offering would be brought no *Ma^c^amad* assembled in the afternoon;

4. " 'when a Wood-offering would be brought no *Ma^c^amad* assembled at the Closing [of the Gates].' "

C. R. Aqiva reversed (*ḥzr*) [his opinion] so as to teach (*lhywt šwnh*) according to ben Azzai.

M. Ta. 4:4

The following is a synopsis of the relevant portions of the two traditions at T. Shev. 2:13 and M. Ta. 4:4; omitted are the specific legal rulings:

T. Shev. 2:13	*M. Ta. 4:4*
1. R. Simeon Shizuri says,...	1. "...," words of R. Aqiva
2. Said ben Azzai before R. Aqiva	2. Said *to him* ben Azzai,
3. in the name of R. Joshua,	3. "Thus R. Joshua used to teach
4. "..."	4. "..."
5. R. Aqiva reversed	5. " " "
6. so as to teach	6. " " "
7. according to	7. " " "
8. the words of	8. — — —
9. ben Azzai.	9. " " "

The literary formulation clearly works out at M. Ta. 4:4 better than it does at T. Shev. 2:13. Both traditions allege that Aqiva "reversed" his opinion, but only M. gives Aqiva's previous view. Thus M. begins with Aqiva's ruling (no. 1), and then has ben Azzai address Aqiva (no. 2). By contrast, T. begins with Simeon Shizuri's ruling (no. 1) and introduces Aqiva only as ben Azzai's auditor (no. 2). Similarly the tradition in M. reports what "Joshua used to teach" (no. 3) and then alleges that Aqiva reversed "so as to teach" (no. 6). By contrast, the tradition in T. notes that Aqiva reversed "so as to teach" (no. 6) but does not report Joshua's ruling as something which the master "used to teach" (no. 3). Finally, T. concludes that Aqiva followed "the words of" (no. 8) ben Azzai. This is problematic, as noted above, for ben

Azzai in fact reports the teaching of Joshua. M. notes that Aqiva taught according to ben Azzai, thus omitting "the words of" in no. 8, only slightly lessening the difficulty.

Clearly enough the tradition at T. Shev. 2:13 reflects a tradental process or circle of tradents which finds no other echo in Aqiva's traditions on agriculture.

See Epstein, *Tannaim,* p. 97.

I.ii.11

A. *mᶜśh b-*: R. Aqiva picked an *etrog* on the first [day of the month of] *Shevat*

B. And acted with it (*nhg bw*) according to the words of the House of Shammai and according to the words of the House of Hillel.

C. R. Yosah b. R. Judah [says], "According to the words of Rabban Gamaliel and according to the words of R. Liezer."

T. Shev. 4:21 (Lieberman ed., p. 185 lines 71-73)

A gives a story about Aqiva. B depends upon that story. And C, in turn, depends upon B. The opinions in B and C are balanced. A-C in fact constitute a sort of dispute-form; B and C differ as to whether the story in A relates to the issue of a Houses' dispute (B) or to the issue of a Gamaliel-Eliezer dispute (C). The pericope does not explicate the issues of either of those disputes.

"R. Aqiva picked an *etrog* on the first of *Shevat*" obviously can serve either a law dealing with the first day of *Shevat* or a law dealing with an *etrog.* B assumes the former, for it presumably refers to the following Houses' dispute.

The first of *Shevat* is the New Year for the [fruit-] trees according to the words of the House of Shammai.
But (*w*) the House of Hillel say, "On the fifteenth [day of the month]."

M. R.H. 1:1b

The House of Shammai would rule, for example, that fruit becomes liable for Poorman's tithe in the third and sixth years on the first day of *Shevat.* The House of Hillel would hold, however, that fruit continues to be liable for Second-tithe until the fifteenth day of the month. Lieberman, following the *baraita* at b. R.H. 14a, cited below, suggests that B interprets A as follows: when Aqiva picked the *etrog* on the first day of *Shevat*, he separated Second-tithe, thus satisfying the view of the House of Hillel, and he also redeemed the *etrog* for money which he gave to the poor, thus satisfying the view of the House of Shammai.[32]

Yosah, in C, assumes that the story about Aqiva refers to the second possibility, namely, a law relating to an *etrog*. M. Bik. 2:6 reports a relevant tradition about Gamaliel and Eliezer. The former holds that the *etrog*, like a vegetable, is liable for tithes in the year that it is picked; the latter alleges that the *etrog*, as a fruit, is liable for tithes in the year that it is formed. The two masters thus disagree, for example, concerning an *etrog* which is formed in the second year and which is subsequently picked in the third year. C assumes that an *etrog* picked on the first of *Shevat* provides such a case; if, as the *baraita*-editor suggests, Aqiva gave two tithes when he picked the *etrog*, he satisfied both Eliezer's and Gamaliel's rules.

Neither M. nor T. explicitly states Aqiva's opinion regarding either the date of the beginning of the New Year for trees or the nature of the *etrog*.

Yosah b. R. Judah (C) stands at the end of a chain of tradents—Ilai, Judah b. Ilai, Josah/Yosé b. Judah—who maintained their independence to some extent from Aqivan circles, at least with regard to the transmission of traditions about Eliezer.[33]

The formulary, "*m*ᶜ*śh b-* + R. Aqiva" occurs only two other times in T. (T. Shab. 7:9; T. Sanh. 2:8b). It does not occur in M.

IV.i.3

A. *m*ᶜ*śh b-*: R. Aqiva picked an etrog and acted with it (*nhg* ᶜ*lyw*) [following] the stringencies of the House of Shammai and the stringencies of the House of Hillel.

B. Why does [it state] [y. R.H. adds, *etrog*]? Even any other kind of fruit tree.

C. Teach [rather]: "According to the stringencies of R. Gamaliel and according to the stringencies of R. Liezer."

y. Bik. 2:5, 65b (y. R.H. 1:2, 57a)

A omits "on the first day of *Shevat*." According to B, the story about Aqiva is a precedent to illustrate consequences of the Houses' opinions concerning the New Year for fruit-trees generally; it therefore does not illustrate the consequences of the dispute between Gamaliel and Eliezer about the nature of the *etrog*. C does not mention Yosah b. Judah but does claim that the story about Aqiva has reference to the Gamaliel-Eliezer dispute.

---

32 *TK, Seder Zera*ᶜ*im*, pp. 545-46.

33 Neusner, *Eliezer*, Vol. II, pp. 143-44; but see also p. 126.

III.ii.1

A. *tnw rbnn*: *m^{c}śh b-*: R. Aqiva picked an *etrog* on the first [day] of *Shevat* and acted with it (*nhg bw*) [to give] two tithes, one according to the words of the House of Shammai and the other according to the words of the House of Hillel.

B. R. Yosé b. R. Judah says, "Not [according to the] practice of the House of Shammai and the House of Hillel did he act with it, but [according to the] practice of R. Gamaliel and R. Eliezer did he act with it, as it is taught (*dtnn*), "... [M. Bik. 2:6] ..."

b. R.H. 14a (b. Eruv. 7a; b. Yeb. 15a)

The *baraita* explains that Aqiva's actions in the story at T. Shev. 4:21 relate to two tithes.

I.ii.12

A. Testified R. Judah b. Isaiah the spice-maker before R. Aqiva in the name of R. Tarfon that *qtp* [is subject to the laws of the] Seventh-year (*šyš lqtp šby^{c}yt*).

T. Shev. 5:12 (Lieberman ed., p. 188 lines 28-29)

Judah b. Isaiah testifies before Aqiva concerning Tarfon's opinion on the status of *qtp*, which is interpreted either as balsam (Maim.) or as a kind of resin which flows from trees (Feldman).[34] The question is whether or not the laws of the Seventh-year apply to *qtp*, for it is inedible. Tarfon claims that *qtp* is subject to the restrictions of the Seventh-year. Aqiva's view is not given.

The same formulary, "Testified R. Judah b. Isaiah the spice-maker before R. Aqiva in the name of Tarfon," recurs at T. Hul. 3:7 (Zuckermandel ed., p. 504 lines 17-18) in connection with a different legal problem. Judah b. Isaiah does not occur elsewhere in M.-T.

v. *Terumot*

I.i.21

A. [Concerning] partners who gave Heave-offering one after the other:

B. R. Aqiva says, "[The] Heave-offering of both of them is Heave-offering."

C. But (*w*) sages say, "[Only the] Heave-offering of the first is Heave-offering."

D. R. Yosé says, "If the first [partner] gave Heave-offering in measure (*ks^{c}wr*) [then] the Heave-offering of the second [partner] is not Heave-offering; but if [the first parner] did not give Heave-offering in measure, [then] the Heave-offering of the second [partner] is Heave-offering."

M. Ter. 3:3

[34] *Flora of the Mishnah*, p. 314.

Deut. 18:4 mandates that Heave-offering must be separated from crops and given to priests. The pericope deals with a basic issue relating to Heave-offering: May separate gifts from the same field be combined? A specifies that two partners act independently. Aqiva, in B, holds that the gifts should be combined. Part of each gift, in proportion to the parters' respective shares of the field, is designated as Heave-offering, and the value of the balance of each gift is returned to the partners. (This interpretation first occurs at y. Ter. 3:2, 42d.) The unnamed sages, in C, hold that the gifts cannot be combined. A-C is in dispute-form.

In the pericope as redacted Yosé, in D, responds to the sages' opinion. The second gift is superfluous only if the first is "in measure," which is not defined here.[35] Yosé's language, however, differs from that which occurs in B-C. D, independent from B-C, could respond to the superscription in A.

III.ii.2

A. *dtnn*: [Concerning] partners who gave Heave-offering one after the other:

B. R. Eliezer says, "[The] Heave-offering of both of them is Heave-offering."

C. R. Aqiva says, "[The] Heave-offering of both of them is not Heave-offering."

D. And sages say, "If the first [partner] gave Heave-offering in measure, [then the] Heave-offering of the second [partner] is not Heave-offering; but if the first [partner] did not give Heave-offering in measure, [then the] Heave-offering of the second [partner] is Heave-offering."

b. Tem. 13a

The *baraita* reports the substance of M. Ter. 3:3, with slightly different language in C, but with different attributions for each of the opinions. b. assigns B to Eliezer, instead of to Aqiva, and C to Aqiva, instead of to unnamed sages. That is, b. attributes to Aqiva the opinion he disputes in M.

Y. N. Epstein cites this *baraita* to support his suggestion that y. Ter. 3:3 assumes a text that reverses Aqiva's and the sages' opinions in M:

A. What are we determining [in M. Ter. 3:3]? If [the discussion] concerns (*b*) [a case in which the partners] authorize [one another] (*mmḥyn*), even R. Aqiva agrees. And if [the discussion] concerns [a case in which the partners] do not authorize one another, even the sages agree.

35 Maim. notes that it is unclear whether D elaborates or contradicts the sages' view.

B. But we are determining the unspecified case: R. Aqiva says [that in] an unspecified case [the partners are] not [considered to] authorize [one another]; and the sages say [that in] an unspecified case [the partners are considered to] authorize one another...

y. Ter. 3:3, 42a

Following Maim., *Code* (H. Ter. 4:8), I have translated *mmḥyn* as a *hifil*: "to recognize as an authority, appoint, authorize" (Jastrow, p. 757, col. II). Epstein, however, interprets [36] *mmḥyn* as a *piel*: "to protest against" (Jastrow, *ibid*, col. I). The attraction of Epstein's suggestion is that, in reconciling the contradiction in the reports about Aqiva's opinion, it favors b., in which Eliezer's saying is at least consistent with a principle that is attributed to Eliezer elsewhere, namely, gifts of Heave-offering may be combined. [37]

D better suits the language of C in M. Ter. 3:3.

I.i.22

A. [Concerning] one who increases Heave-offering:

B. R. Eliezer says, "[He may give up to] one-tenth, as with Heave-offering of [First-]tithe."

C. [If he gives] more than this [i.e., one-tenth], let him designate it Heave-offering of [First-]tithe for [produce] elsewhere.

D. R. Ishmael says, "[He must keep at least one-]half as Heave-offering."

E. R. Tarfon and R. Aqiva say, "[He may give as much as he wants as Heave-offering] as long as he keeps some [produce] as common produce."

M. Ter. 4:5

As mentioned previously, no biblical prescription specifies how much produce must be given in order to fulfill the obligation of giving Heave-offering to the priests. The pericope discusses, What is the maximum amount of a crop that a man may designate as Heave-offering?

B, D and E each depends on A. C glosses B. G. Porton suggests that A+B+E form a dispute and D, which occurs by itself elsewhere, "does not belong in this context." [38]

In A Eliezer limits Heave-offering to ten percent of a crop. *Heave-offering of First-tithe* (mentioned in B and in C) is given by Levites

[36] *Mishnah*, p. 781.

[37] See J. Neusner, *Eliezer*, Vol. I, p. 46.

[38] *Ishmael*, pp. 44-5.

to priests from the produce that Levites receive as First-tithe from Israelites. Ishmael, in D, allows fifty percent of a crop to be designated as Heave-offering. And, in E, Tarfon and Aqiva allow a man to designate almost his entire crop as Heave-offering. Neusner notes that Eliezer must have a radically different concept of Heave-offering from that which Tarfon and Aqiva share. [39]

I.i.23
A. R. Joshua says,
1. "Black figs neutralize the white [figs],
2. "And the white [figs] neutralize the black [figs]."
B. [Concerning] round cakes (*ᶜgwly*) of pressed figs (*ᶜgwly dblh*)—
1. The large ones neutralize the small ones,
2. And the small ones neutralize the large ones;
3. The round ones (*hᶜgwlym*) neutralize the quadrangular ones (*hmlbnym*),
4. And the quadrangular ones neutralize the round ones.
5. R. Eliezer forbids.
C. And R. Aqiva says,
1. "When (*b-*) what fell [into the mixture] can be distinguished (literally, "when it is known") [from the rest of the mixture], one does not neutralize the other;
2. "But (*w*) when what fell in cannot be distinguished [from the rest of the mixture], one neutralizes the other."

M. Ter. 4:8 (y. Ter. 4:8, 43a)

I.i.24
D. How [could this happen]?
E. [Consider the case of a mixture containing] fifty black figs and fifty white [figs].
1. [If] a black fig [designated as Heave-offering] fell [into the mixture], the black [figs would be] forbidden and the white ones permitted.
2. [If] a white [fig] fell [into the mixture], the white [figs would be] forbidden and the black ones permitted.
3. When it is not known what fell [into the mixture], each neutralizes the other.
F. And in this R. Eliezer is stringent and R. Joshua is lenient.

M. Ter. 4:9

The context is a series of disputes between Eliezer and Joshua at M. Ter. 4:7-11. Restrictions apply to eating or otherwise using unconsecrated produce which has been mixed with Heave-offering. The

39 *Eliezer*, Vol. I, p. 48.

problem is that the latter might be eaten or used in error; and therefore, in a mixture with Heave-offering, all produce incurs a doubtful status. M. Ter. 4:8-9 focus on the question, When does Heave-offering which has been mixed with unconsecrated produce become neutralized? That is, in what circumstances may the produce in the mixture be used? I shall first discuss the literary traits of the pericope. Then I shall discuss the legal question at issue. And finally I shall take up the redactional problem.

A gives a complete sentence. Al and 2 balance; the topic is figs. B states a new topic, round cakes made from pressed figs. B1-4 give two syzygies, each of which corresponds to A1-2. "Quadrangular" cakes (B3-4) stands outside the topic specified in B, "round" cakes; a tighter dispute-form would give only B1-2—or a revised superscription. Eliezer's view (B5) occurs in indirect discourse. His prohibition applies to the case of fig-cakes (B); by extension it also applies to the figs (A). Properly, however, we can identify two separate units of tradition: (1) a sentence (A; form: X says...); and (2) a variation on the dispute-form (B; form: superscription + anonymous statement + X forbids).

Aqiva's opinion, like all of the foregoing except B5, is given in balanced sentences. By contrast to the foregoing, however, Aqiva does not focus specifically either on figs or on cakes. Instead C gives general statements. Aqiva in fact responds to a general question which does not explicitly occur in our pericope, namely, under what circumstances does Heave-offering become neutralized when mixed with unconsecrated produce? M. Ter. 4:9D-E elaborate on C. The question in D refers to Aqiva's saying. E states an illustrative case. E1, 2, and 3, each a complete sentence, give the three possible situations and the rules relevant to each. F glosses the foregoing, specifically A-B.

Underlying Joshua's opinion in A is the principle that a distinguishing feature, such as color, is irrelevant to determining whether or not Heave-offering becomes neutralized in a mixture. B1-4 assume the same principle. According to the preceding pericope, M. Ter. 4:7, Joshua holds that Heave-offering is neutralized in a mixture of which it comprises anything less than one per cent (1:99+). By contrast, Eliezer, who gives a slightly smaller ratio for a mixture in which Heave-offering become neutralized (1:100), holds that distinguishing features such as size and shape, and presumably also color, enter into the determination of whether or not Heave-offering becomes neutralized in a mixture. What is Aqiva's position? As Neusner notes, the view expressed in C is consistent with Eliezer's prohibition in B5. [40] If it is known what fell into the mixture, as, for example, in the case of a black fig designated as Heave-offering which falls into a mixture of black and white figs, then the Heave-offering will be neutralized only if the quantity of *black* figs is sufficient. The white figs, however, are permitted. The total quantity of mixed items is irrelevant. B5 and C1 assume that, to continue the same example, the quantity of black figs is insufficient; therefore none of the *black* figs in the mixture may be used. If, on the other hand, it is not known what kind of Heave-offering-fig fell into the mixture, whether black or white, then all the contents of the mixture become suspect. The positive formulation of C2 ("one neutralizes the other") assumes that the proportions of the mixture are adequate to neutralize Heave-offering (TYT, MS.). If the proportion of Heave-offering in the mixture is too large, then obviously the Heave-offering will not be neutralized, and the use of the entire mixture will be forbidden. The gloss in D-E elaborates on this. The situation in E, namely, one fig of Heave-offering falling into a mixture of one-hundred figs, constitutes the borderline-case on Eliezer's view concerning the neutralization of Heave-offering. This is a further suggestion that Aqiva, or at least Aqiva's glossator, assumes Eliezer's view of the law.

We now take up the redactional problem in the pericope. As noted above, several separate units of materials can be identified:

I. Joshua's saying (A)
II. Eliezer's dispute-form (B)
III. Aqiva's saying (C)
IV. Explanation of Aqiva's saying (D-E)
V. Observation concerning Eliezer's and Joshua's opinions (F)

To repeat my introductory comment, the context of the pericope is a series of Eliezer-Joshua disputes (M. Ter. 4:7-11) concerning Heave-offering. What is striking about our pericope is that, among the traditions brought together at M. Ter. 4:7-11, it alone does not report Joshua's and Eliezer's opinions in a dispute-form. Yet A and B do contrast opposing opinions of the two masters (A vs. B5). It is evident that A and B function in lieu of a dispute-form. It has been observed that the sequence of the masters in A-B breaks the pattern (i.e., Eliezer

[40] *Ibid.*, p. 50.

first, Joshua second) set in the series of dispute-forms.[41] But the ultimate authority behind A-B obviously had little choice if he wanted to give the dispute and yet was unwilling to tamper with the units of tradition (A, B) which had been transmitted to him. The discussion above, although it relates Aqiva's saying (C) and the Aqivan gloss (D-E) to Eliezer's opinion, does not help in determining at what stage in the redaction-process C and D-E became attached to B. B+C+D-E could have been produced by Aqiva's disciples as easily as by the ultimate redactor of M. Ter. 4:8-9. We note, however, that F probably assumes that A and B have been brought together; since it is not relevant to the Aqivan materials, which separate it from A and B, F seems to have been added on at the end and thus probably signals the very last stage in the redaction-process.

I.ii.13

A. "R. Eliezer says,

1. " 'When it can be distinguished (literally, "When it is known"), it will not neutralize;

2. " 'When it cannot be distinguished, it will neutralize.' "

B. "R. Joshua says,

1. " 'Whether it can be distinguished or whether it cannot be distinguished, it will not (so Lieberman, following E; V omits "not") neutralize,' "

C. words of R. Meir.

D. R. Judah says,

E. "R. Eliezer says,

1. " 'Whether it can be distinguished or whether it cannot be distinguished, it will not (so Lieberman, following E; V omits "not") neutralize.'

F. "R. Joshua says,

2. " 'Whether it can be distinguished or whether it cannot be distinguished, it will (so Lieberman, following E; V omits "not") neutralize.'

G. "R. Aqiva says,

1. " 'When it can be distinguished, it will not neutralize;

2. " 'When it cannot be distinguished, it will neutralize.' "

T. Ter. 5:10b (Lieberman ed., p. 133 lines 56-60; y. Ter. 4:9, 43a)

Despite the confusion in the manuscript-tradition concerning the opinions of Eliezer and Joshua, there is no confusion concerning Aqiva's opinion (G). G is in fact consistent with the saying attributed to Aqiva at M. Ter. 4:8. What is striking about the pericope, however,

41 *Ibid.*, pp. 52-53.

is the language attributed to the two other Yavnean masters. Unlike at M. Ter. 4:8 they do not focus on specific characteristics (black/white, large/small, round/square) of Heave-offering; instead Eliezer and Joshua, in that sequence, give generalizations formulated like Aqiva's saying. Clearly T. Ter. 5:10b reflects an effort to give the principles which stand behind the masters' opinions in M., not only at M. Ter. 4:8, but also in each of the other Eliezer-Joshua disputes in the series at M. Ter. 4:7-11. Different theories of redaction of legal materials underlie Meir's and Judah's traditions, on the one hand, and the unit of traditions about Eliezer and Joshua, M. Ter. 4:7-11, on the other hand. The latter give specific cases from which general principles can be inferred. By contrast, Meir and Judah attribute to the masters general principles which, once known, can be supplied to any particular case. We may add this observation to the other evidences, discussed above, which suggest that Aqiva's saying in M., formulated as a general principle, is out of phase with the other materials at M. Ter. 4:7-11. This may add weight to the view that the Aqivan material formed a unit with Eliezer's dispute-form at M. 4:8E-I prior to being transmitted to a conservative redactor who, although focusing on specific cases in the series of Eliezer-Joshua dispute-forms, preferred not to alter the traditions he used, neither deleting Aqiva's saying, for instance, nor, as observed above, forcing the sequence of the sages to correspond to that in all the other pericopae in the series.

Judah's tradition schematizes nicely according to both manuscript-traditions. Eliezer and Joshua give extreme positions, and Aqiva supplies a compromise. As has become familiar, Meir, by contrast to Judah, misses the opportunity to cite a relevant Aqivan saying. Strikingly, Meir attributes to Eliezer the opinion which Judah and M. (in a slightly different formulation) attribute to Aqiva. On the one hand, Meir's tradition corroborates our interpretation above, which equates Aqiva's opinion with that of Eliezer. On the other hand, it raises a serious question concerning the transmission of Eliezer's traditions. Taken together with the report at M. 4:8, Meir's tradition about Eliezer suggests that Judah transmits an altered version of Eliezer's opinion. M. Shev. 8:9-10, discussed above, provide two instances of Aqivan disciples' concern for establishing Eliezer's traditions. In view of such concern, it is appropriate that Eliezer's brief opinion at M. 4:8B draws a lengthy Aqivan explanation.

I.i.25

A. Said R. Yosé,

B. "A case came before (*m*ᶜ*śh b*ʾ *lpny*) R. Aqiva
C. "Concerning (*b*-) fifty bundles of vegetables
D. "In the midst of which fell a similar [bundle of vegetables], half of which was Heave-offering.
E. "And I said before him,
F. " 'It should neutralize—
G. " 'Not because the Heave-offering should neutralize in [a mixture of] fifty-one [parts], but because there were there [among the bundles] one-hundred-and-two halves.' "

M. Ter. 4:13 (A-F, y. Ter. 4:13, 43b)

The pericope gives a first-person report attributed to Yosé, an Ushan. Aqiva figures as a legal authority; the tradition is about Yosé's, and not Aqiva's, opinion.

The problem concerns Heave-offering previously mixed with unconsecrated produce. Since the Heave-offering had comprised half of the bundle, it had not been neutralized. What happens to the Heave-offering, however, if the mixture subsequently drops into a larger quantity of unconsecrated produce? Yosé assumes that Heave-offering becomes neutralized if it comprises less than one percent of the total mixture. He therefore rules that the Heave-offering in the case brought before Aqiva becomes neutralized when the bundle of which it comprises one-half falls in among fifty other bundles of vegetables. From the discussion of M. Ter. 4:8-9, above, it follows that Aqiva would agree with Yosé's view.

B, "a case came before R. Aqiva," implies that the master had the authority to make legal decisions. The pericope obviously relates nothing, however, concerning the enforcement of Aqiva's rulings.

I.i.26

[If a man ate Heave-offering in error, instead of giving it to a priest, he must repay its value and an Added-fifth... (M. Ter. 6:1)].

A. R. Eliezer says, "They pay back from one kind [of produce] for a different kind,
B. "Provided that he should pay back from a better instead of from a worse [kind]."
C. And R. Aqiva says, "They pay back only from one kind for its own kind."
D. Therefore if he ate cucumbers grown in (literally, "of") the year before the Seventh-year, he should wait for cucumbers grown in the year after the Seventh-year and pay back from [the latter; but he may not pay back from cucumbers grown in the Seventh-year, which are not liable for Heave-offering.]

E. From the place [in Scripture] on the basis of which R. Eliezer gives a lenient ruling, from that [same] place R. Aqiva gives a stringent ruling:

F. "As it is said, 'And he will give to the priest that which is holy' (Lev. 22:14): Whatever (*kl š-*) is appropriate to be holy (*rʾwy lhywt qwdš*) [K reads, *rʾwy lbᶜśwt qwdš*]," words of R. Eliezer.

G. And R. Aqiva says, " 'And he will give to the priest that which is holy': [whatever kind of] holy [thing] that he [actually] consumed."

M. Ter. 6:6

This pericope, like the other traditions given in 6:2-6, responds to an issue raised in 6:1: "If a man ate Heave-offering in error, instead of giving it to a priest, he must repay its value plus an Added fifth." 6:6 focuses on the nature of the produce which must be paid back. A-D can be separated from E-G, which provide scriptural warrant for the foregoing. A and C give two balanced sentences:

Eliezer: They pay back from one kind for a different kind.
Aqiva: They pay back only from one kind for its own kind

Each saying depends upon 6:1—and each could stand independent of the other. B limits Eliezer's opinion. "Therefore," in D, introduces a case which illustrates Aqiva's rule. It is assumed that sixth-year cucumbers are not available. Since the tithe-exempt Seventh-year cucumbers must be considered to be in a different legal category from cucumbers of other years, restitution can be made only when eighth-year cucumbers become available. The case in D in fact provides common ground for Aqiva and Eliezer in so far as the opinion of the latter is limited by B. If sixth-year cucumbers are available but not acceptable, as, for instance, if they have hardened, then, according to B, Eliezer would agree that they cannot be used (see Bert., TY.).

E announces the scriptural warrants in addition to introducing a concern about "leniency" and "stringency." The exegeses of Lev. 22:14 in F-G are straightforward: Eliezer interprets "that which is holy" broadly, that is, *anything* which is holy; and Aqiva follows a narrower construction, namely, restitution can be made only with that same kind of holy thing which was misappropriated.

Eliezer and Aqiva differ regarding a primary issue relating to Heave-offering, namely, the substitution of one category of produce for a different category. (By contrast, the context, M. Ter. chapter six, deals with a secondary issue, namely, restitution for misappropriated

Heave-offering.) Eliezer permits substitutions, and Aqiva does not. Eliezer's view in A is consistent with his opinion at M. Ter. 2:1; there he holds that clean produce may be offered as Heave-offering in place of unclean produce. Literary evidence at M. Ter. chapter two suggests that Eliezer's view differs from prior law. [42] Aqiva's opinion in our pericope is consistent with an anonymous saying at M. Ter. 2:4, "They do not give Heave-offering from one kind [of produce] for a different kind [of produce]." It is not clear whether Aqiva upholds prior law or whether, perhaps like Eliezer, Aqiva puts forward an innovation, a general rule regarding all cases of substitutions.

The limitation on Eliezer's view in B would not be inferred from the exegesis in F or from other statements about substitutions attributed to Eliezer elsewhere. Since B brings Eliezer over to Aqiva's opinion, it seems that Aqivan editors have transmitted this tradition. See M. Shev. 8:9-10.

I.ii.14

A. R. Liezer says, "They pay back from one kind [of produce] for a different kind,

B. "Provided that he should pay back from a better instead of from a worse [kind]."

C. 1. How so?
   2. He ate barley and repays wheat,
   3. Figs and repays dates—
   4. May a blessing come to him (C1-4 missing in E).

D. R. Aqiva says, "They pay back only from one kind for its own kind."

E. R. Le^cazar [E reads, Eliezer] said, "Just as they pay back from the new [crop] for the old [crop], so they pay back from one kind instead of from another kind."

T. Ter. 7:9 (Lieberman ed., p. 144 lines 29-33)

A+B+D give M. Ter. 6:6A-C. But instead of the saying at M. 6:6D, concerning substituting eighth-year cucumbers for sixth-year cucumbers, T.E attributes an additional statement for Eliezer: just as substitution is permitted between different (new/old) crops of the same species, so it is permitted between different categories of produce. As the following chart shows, T., by contrast to M., preserves the disagreement between the masters:

---

[42] *Ibid.*, p. 46.

M. Ter. 6:6A-D	*T. Ter. 7:9A-E*
1. R. Eliezer says,	1. R. Liezer says,
2. "They pay back from one kind for a different kind,	2. " " "
3. "Provided that he pays from a better instead of from a worse."	3. " " "
4. — — —	4. How so?
5. — — —	5. He ate barley and repays wheat,
6. — — —	6. Figs and repays dates —
7. — — —	7. May a blessing come to him.
8. R. Aqiva says,	8. " " "
9. "They pay back only from one kind for its own kind."	9. " " "
10. — — —	10. R. Eliezer says,
11a. Therefore if he ate cucumbers of the sixth year,	11. "Just as they pay back new for old,
b. He should wait for cucumbers of the eighth year.	
12. — — —	12. "So they pay back from one kind for a different kind."

M. and T. give the same opinions for Eliezer and Aqiva (nos. 1-3, 8-9). Nos. 4-7 gloss Eliezer's opinion. The significant part begins at no. 10: M. 11 introduces the specific case of sixth-year cucumbers; by contrast T. introduces a saying of Eliezer. As it happens, the first part of Eliezer's saying in T. (no. 11) gives a generalization covering the case specified in M. (nos. 11a-b). The new crop, the eighth-year cucumbers, should be used to make restitution for old crop, the sixth-year cucumbers. So far Eliezer and Aqiva agree. And that is where M. leaves the issue. In T., however, the conclusion of Eliezer's saying (no. 12) goes beyond the corresponding sub-unit in M. No. 12 in fact simply repeats Eliezer's principle (no. 2) permitting substitutions.

T. 10-12 provide a commentary on M. Ter. 6:6. The authority behind T. seems to troubled by "Therefore" in M. 11a. Why should Eliezer's and Aqiva's sayings (nos. 1-3, 8-9) necessarily yield the case of the eighth-year cucumbers, as "Therefore" in M. implies? The problem again centers on B, the limitation about paying back from better and not from worse produce (no. 3 in synopsis). That proviso sets up the special case at M.D (nos. 10-11 in synopsis). The authority behind the pericope in T. obviously had T.A—B+D (nos. 1-3, 8-9 in synopsis) in the formulation given by M. But significantly the limitation is not repeated in T.E, which gives only Eliezer's general view. Since the first part of Eliezer's saying in T.E is comparable to the case stated at M.D (nos. 10-11) it seems evident that the authority behind the pericope in T. wants to emphasize the disagreement between the two masters in the face of the better/worse proviso which occurs in the tradition that he finds before him. Very simply, a conservative tradent in T. corrects the redactional product of M. It is assumed that M.D is separate from what precedes it at M. 6:6. The evidence in T. further suggests that the limitation on Eliezer's opinion, M./T.B., is not integral to the master's saying.

The sophisticated redactional technique observed here sets the pericope at T. Ter. 7:9 in the generation of the ultimate redaction of Mishnah-Tosefta, beyond the activities of the disciples whom we can designate without ambiguity as "Aqivan circles" and to whom I have tentatively assigned the reshaping of Eliezer's tradition at M. 6:6.

I.ii.15

A. [Concerning] one who eats the untithed produce (*ḥtbl*)—

B. 1. "He pays back

2. "From the gleanings,

3. "From the Forgotten sheaf,

4. "From *peʾah*,

5. "And from produce which has not yet reached one-third [of its full growth],"

6. Words of R. Liezer (E omits).

C. R. Aqiva says, (E reads, "But sages say,),

1. "They do not pay back from them,

2. "For (*š*-) they do not pay back

3. "From that which has not reached the season [at which it incurs the obligation for giving] tithes."

T. Ter. 7:10a (Lieberman ed., pp. 144 lines 33-36)

T. Ter. 7:10a repeats the Eliezer-Aqiva dispute from T. Ter. 7:9. A states the topic. The problem concerns making restitution for the tithe-element in the produce eaten in error. B lists four kinds of produce, more precisely, four categories of produce, which are exempt from tithes. Eliezer holds that produce in each of the four categories can be substituted for untithed produce eaten in error. Aqiva's saying (C) depends upon Eliezer's. C1 corresponds to B1, although Aqiva's saying is formulated in the plural and not in the singular (C1: "They do not pay back" vs. B1: "He pays back"). The conjunction, "For," introduces C2, which repeats "They do not pay back." C3 uses a formula ("reaches the season of tithes") more inclusive, although no less common and stereotyped, than the formula in B5 ("reaches one-third [of full growth]"). The latter refers to produce which reaches its "season" when "one-third" grown. C2-3 thus seem to limit Aqiva's opposition to the last item in Eliezer's list B5. The conjunction and the repetition in C2 suggest, however, that C2-3 are added to C1. This in turn implies that the limitation of Aqiva's opposition only to B5 is not integral to Aqiva's saying. Certainly C1, without 2-3, would be assumed to refer to all four items listed in B.

Aqiva's view depends upon a fundamental distinction between, on the one hand, produce obligated for tithes and, on the other hand, produce not obligated. The latter cannot be substituted for the former, because produce not obligated for tithes lacks a tithe-element. Aqiva's view assumes that the tithe-element does not inhere in the produce but rather is a legal category, part of the calculus of the rules relating to agriculture. For C3, see M. M.S. 5:8.

II.i.1

A. From where [do they learn] that they pay back only from one kind for its own kind?

B. Scripture teaches, "And he will give to the priest that which is holy" (Lev. 22:14).

C. "Therefore if he ate cucumbers of the year preceding the Seventh-year, he should wait for cucumbers of the year following the Seventh-year and pay back from them," words of R. Aqiva.

D. R. Eliezer says, "They pay back from one kind for a different kind,

E. "Provided that he pays back from a better instead of from a worse [kind]."

F. How so? [If] he ate dry figs and repays dates—may a blessing come to him."

Sifra Emor 6:6 (Weiss ed., pp. 97b-98a)

Sifra, as to be expected, reorganizes the tradition at M. Ter. 6:6 so as to focus on the scriptural exegesis as the source for the law. As observed above, the varying exegeses attributed to Aqiva and to Eliezer in M. are obvious and straightforward; Sifra does not bother to give them. The authority behind the pericope in Sifra assumes that Aqiva's rule is normative; thus A, which states the question, gives Aqiva's formulation (= M.D/T.E.).

As Rabad notes, C-F report an artificial dispute. Eliezer does not disagree concerning the case of the cucumbers (= M. 6:6D). Eliezer's saying (D-E; = M. 6:6B-C/T. 7:9B-C) in fact challenges the statement of the law assumed in A. The gloss in F corresponds to Ter. 7:9D(2) + (4) + (5).

II.i.2

A. ..."They do not give tithes from [crop of one] year for [crop of] the next year," words of R. Aqiva.

Sifra B[c] 12,13 (Weiss ed., p. 115a)

Aqiva's view here is consistent with the position attributed to him at M. Ter. 6:6.

[If a field is sown with Heave-offering...M. Ter. 9:1]
I.i.27

A. [The field] is subject to [the laws of] gleanings, and Forgotten sheaf, and *pe*ʾ*ah*, [C and N add, "and Poorman's tithe"].

B. And the poor Israelites and the poor priests glean [the produce of the field].

C. And the poor Israelites sell their portion to the priest at the price of Heave-offering; but the money is theirs [i.e., the poor Israelites'].

D. R. Tarfon says, "Only the poor priests should glean."

E. Perhaps they [i.e., the poor Israelites] might forget and place [their gleanings] in their mouths.

F. Said R. Aqiva to him, "If so, only the clean should glean."

M. Ter. 9:2

I.i.28

G. [A field sown with Heave-offering] is subject (1) to [the laws of] tithes and (2) to Poorman's tithe.

H. And the poor Israelites and the poor priests take [the produce of the field].

I. And the poor Israelites sell their portion to the priests at the price of Heave-offering; but the money is [the poor Israelites'].

M. Ter. 9:3a

The pericope conflates two traditions, one an anonymous listing of obligations incurred by crop produced from Heave-offering (A+G+I), the other a debate between Tarfon and Aqiva concerning whether or not the privilege of gleaning such a crop is limited to poor priests (B-F). A takes up the problem raised in 9:1, namely, the status of a crop produced from Heave-offering erroneously planted in a field. Is it considered Heave-offering? A assumes that it is not: the crop incurs obligations for gleanings, Forgotten cheaf, *pe*ʾ*ah* and, according to variant readings, Poorman's tithe; none of these obligations applies to Heave-offering. B-F shift the focus to a different question: Who may glean? B gives the obvious answer: as with any other crop, any poor person may take gleanings. B assumes, however, a distinction between a priest and a layman. C picks up the distinction and specifies the procedure to be followed by Israelites who glean the crop: they sell their gleanings to a priest at the price of Heave-offering and pocket the money. This assumes that only priests eat crop produced from Heave-offering, although in every other respect the crop is considered like unconsecrated produce (T. Toh. 1:6). Tarfon, in D, presents a different view about who may glean; he alleges that only poor priests may do so. E, which explains Tarfon's opinion as a precaution against the misuse of the gleanings by an unwary Israelite, shares the assumptions of (A+B)—C; the crop is considered like unconsecrated produce, except that it may be eaten only by a priest. Aqiva, in F, responds to Tarfon's opinion. "Clean" (*ṭhrym*) corresponds to Tarfon's "poor priests" (*ᶜnyy khnym*), yielding a slightly unbalanced set of opposing terms. "Said... to him" evidences a debate-form. "If so" signals that Aqiva's argument is a *reductio ad absurdum*: if precautions are required, then gleaning the crop might as well be limited to "the clean," an unnecessary restriction even on the extreme view that the crop should be considered as Heave-offering. G shifts the focus back to the issue of A. It resumes the listing from A, adding tithes and Poorman's tithe. H responds to G2, Poorman's tithe. It corresponds to B, with one exception: H states that the poor Israelites and priests "take" the produce, B that they "glean." H obviously gives the more inclusive term. I repeats C *verbatim*.

Clearly a *reductio ad absurdum* is an argument suited for a debate. We have only a small number of Aqivan debates in M.-T. *Zeraᶜim*, and our pericope provides the only example of Aqiva's use of such an argument. If the debate is not the primary context for Aqiva's legal saying, what would a prior dispute-form look like? Stripping G of the marks of the debate ("Said... to him, 'If so...' "), Aqiva's and Tarfon's sayings, as noted above, almost balance:

Tarfon:	Only the	poor	priests	glean.
Aqiva:	Only the		clean	glean.

Mnemonic considerations suggest deleting "poor" from Tarfon's saying. The Hebrew yields a perfectly balanced apodosis hinging on *khnym* vs. *ṭhwrym* ("the priests" vs. "the clean"):"

Tarfon:	*lʾ ylqṭw ʾlʾ*	(*ᶜnyy*)	*khnym*
Aqiva:	*lʾ ylqṭw ʾlʾ*		*ṭhwrym*

What would be the topic of such a dispute-form? Since Tarfon declares that only the priests may glean and Aqiva that only the clean may, it seems that the topic must be, Who may glean? What is striking is that both masters, by contrast to the authority behind A-C, G-I, propose precautionary restrictions which assume that the gleanings are considered as Heave-offering. Tarfon limits gleaning to priests, who alone may eat Heave-offering. And Aqiva focuses on preserving the gleanings from contracting uncleanness, an unlikely possibility. Contrast, for instance, Aqiva's discussion on the preservation of the cleanness of tithes at M. M.S. 2:4 and T. M.S. 2:16 and of *ḥallah* at M. Hal. 2:3.

I.i.29

A. R. Yosé says,

1. "All [kinds of unconsecrated produce] that are boiled with beets are prohibited [to non-priests],

2. "because they [i.e., the beets] impart a flavor."

B. R. Simeon says,

1. "A cabbage from irrigated soil with a cabbage from rain-watered soil,—it is prohibited,

2. "because the one absorbs [the juices from the other]."

C. R. Aqiva (so K, P, M; most printed editions read, "R. Judah") says,

1. "All [kinds of foodstuffs, both permitted and prohibited,] which are cooked one with the other are permitted,

2. "except with (*ʾlʾ ʿm*) the meat."

M. Ter. 10:11a

The pericope gives the opinions of two Ushans, Yosé and Simeon, and then the opinion of a Yavnean, Aqiva. On the face of it, an editor has added an independent opinion of Aqiva on to the sayings of the two later masters. I shall first discuss the legal issue of the pericope, and then I shall relate the results of that discussion to the literary traits of the tradition.

The context is a series of traditions which focus on mixtures of consecrated and unconsecrated produce. The different elements in the mixtures presumably remain distinguishable (cp. M. Ter. 4:8, discussed above), and the question is, What happens to the status of the unconsecrated produce? Only priests may eat the consecrated produce; may laymen continue to eat the unconsecrated produce? The operative principle is that consecrated produce which Israelites are forbidden from eating renders unconsecrated produce forbidden when it imparts flavor to the unconsecrated produce (Maim., *Code*, H. Ter. 15:7; H. Prohibited Meals 15:1). The preceding pericope, M. Ter. 10:10, states that all kinds of unconsecrated produce, except for allia (e.g., onions, garlic, chives, leeks), continue to be permitted when pickled with produce designated as Heave-offering. MR notes that there are two traditions on the exegesis of our pericope. One, followed by Maim., explains the pericope by reference to 10:10. On this first view, Yosé, Simeon and Aqiva expand the theory of 10:10, which is limited to mixtures of picked produce. Yosé and Simeon, on this view, introduce items which, when boiled in a mixture, render unconsecrated produce prohibited. And Aqiva introduces the notion of *cooking* the different items in a mixture. In each case it is assumed that the prohibited produce in question is prohibited by virtue of being designated as Heave-offering, exactly as in 10:10. The second tradition of exegesis, followed by Sens, notes that, by contrast to the anonymous view put forward in 10:10, none of the masters in our pericope explicitly refers to Heave-offering. It is thus possible to infer that the prohibited produce in question may include categories of produce other than Heave-offering, e.g., Mixed-kinds of the vineyard. This is important in the interpretation of C, for Aqiva, by introducing the exclusion of meat, which canot be designated as Heave-offering, obviously stands outside a framework which deals primarily with Heave-offering. Maim. solves the problem by explaining that Aqiva refers to a mixture of permitted meat and Heave-offering produce; in such a mixture, on Maim.'s view, the meat absorbs the flavor of the Heave-offering produce and becomes prohibited. On Sens' view, however, Aqiva's saying refers to mixtures of similar kinds of produce, e.g., a mixture of unconsecrated beets with beets designated as Heave-offering. In such mixtures there is no question of imparting different flavors. On this view, the exclusion of "the meat" refers specifically to mixtures of permitted meat with prohibited meat.

Turning now to the literary traits of the pericope: A gives a complete sentence for Yosé. B1 corresponds to A1 and B2 to A2. B1, however, lacks a verb; as noted above, it is generally assumed that Simeon's saying depends upon "boiled" from A. Aqiva's saying, in C, differs strikingly from the foregoing: C introduces a new verb ("are cooked"), does not name specific items ("All... one with the other"), formulates the ruling in the positive ("are permitted"), and tags on its exception at the end ("except with the meat"). Although C gives a complete sentence, Aqiva's saying is in fact unintelligible on its own. Strikingly, Aqiva's saying is hardly more intelligible in its present context. Clearly Aqiva's opinion stands independent both of the discussions of mixtures of permitted produce with Heave-offering produce (10:10) and of the opinions attributed to the Ushan masters in A and B.

I.ii.16

A. R. Yosah says, "They pickle onions of Heave-offering in vinegar of unconsecrated produce, but they do not pickle onions of Heave-offering in vinegar of Heave-offering; and it is not necessary to say, onions of unconsecrated produce in vinegar of Heave-offering."

B. R. Aqiva says,
1. "All which are cooked one with the other are permitted,
2. "except with the meat."
C. Meat with meat is prohibited.
D. And [concerning] all of them that were (E adds, "mixed and") cooked one with the other—lo, they are prohibited.

T. Ter. 9:4 (Lieberman ed., p. 155 line 13—p. 156 line 17)

A shows that pickling was an issue for the Ushans. B gives Aqiva's saying as at M. Ter. 10:11. C and D supply T.'s comment on M. First, C explains the exception tagged on at the end of Aqiva's saying: according to C, B2 refers to permitted meat cooked with prohibited meat. D envisions the case of meat which is rendered prohibited in a mixture with prohibited meat and which subsequently gets cooked with another kind of foodstuff; the meat renders the latter prohibited. [43] The ultimate authority behind the pericope in T. obviously recognizes the difficulty in determining the reference of Aqiva's saying. On the one hand, C takes into account the exegetical requirement of restricting Aqiva's exception to a special case (one category of one kind of foodstuff being mixed with a different category of the same kind of foodstuff). And, on the other hand, D takes into account the sense of the words of Aqiva's saying ("All which are cooked one with the other"), which suggest that Aqiva refers to mixing different kinds of foodstuffs. C and D thus give two separate consequences of Aqiva's opinion.

IV.i.4
A. Said R. Abun,
B. "R. Aqiva asked R. Simeon b. Yoḥai,
C. " 'Expound [the case of] one [who] muzzled [his animal] outside [the field] and [then] brought [the animal] inside [the field to work].'
C. "He said to him, ' "[Drink no wine nor strong drink]... when (*b-*) you come into the tent of meeting (Lev. 10:9). [This means at any time] before (*m-*) you come into the tent of meeting.' "

y. Ter. 9:4, 46d

Abun is a late third-century Palestinian Amora. We have so far seen no example of a tradition in which Aqiva "asked" a disciple about a biblical exegesis.

The exchange in C-D focuses on the meaning of the prefix *b-*. Deut. 25:4 reads, "You shall not muzzle an ox when (*b-*) it treads out the grain." Does the verse refer only to muzzling while the ox is actually

[43] Contrast Lieberman, *TK, Zeraᶜim*, p. 445.

in the process of treading? Or does the prohibition include muzzling the animal even before it begins to tread? D answers by citing the uses of *b-* at Lev. 10:9; there the prefix refers to any time prior to entering the tent of meeting. By analogy, the prohibition concerning muzzling an ox also includes the case of a person who muzzles the animal prior to bringing it into the field.

vi. *Ma^caserot*

I.i.30

A. What type of courtyard is liable for tithes? [I.e., What type of courtyard makes produce brought into it liable for tithes?]

B. R. Ishmael says, 'A Tyrian style courtyard in which the vessels are watched."

C. R. Aqiva says, "Any [courtyard] that one opens and [another] one closes is exempt [i.e., produce brought into such a courtyard is ashamed to eat is liable."

D. R. Nehemiah says, "Any [courtyard] in which a man is not ashmad to eat is liable."

E. R. Yosé says, "Any [courtyard] which one may enter without someone asking him, 'What are you seeking?,' is exempt."

F. R. Judah says, "[Concerning] two courtyards, one inside the other: the inner is liable, but (*w*) the outer is exempt [i.e., produce brought into the inner courtyard is liable for tithes; produce brought into the outer courtyard is exempt from tithes]."

M. Ma. 3:5 (b. Nid. 47b)

A introduces a fundamental question concerning tithing. Bringing harvested crop into a house indicates an intention to eat the produce and thereby renders it liable for tithes (M. Ma. 1:1, 5). Each saying in the pericope assumes that produce brought into a courtyard that is closed to the public becomes liable, exactly as though it had been brought into a house (Maim., Sens).

"Courtyard" and "tithes" in A serve each of the independent sayings in B-E. Alone among the opinions of the masters, Ishmael's saying both responds to and also depends upon the question in A. Aqiva's saying, in C, does not disagree with Ishmael's, although both focus on a courtyard that serves more than one residence, or place of business, and one master declares "liable" while the other master declares "exempt." C states that a courtyard to which different people have independent access cannot be considered private domain (for the purposes of tithing). B implies that because "the vessels are watched," this particular kind of courtyard is not considered public domain.

D-F give the opinions of Ushan masters. Nehemiah's and Yosé's sayings conform to the principle of the Yavneans, but do not necessarily assume either Ishmael's saying or Aqiva's. D and E follow the same formulation as C ("Any that..."), but one declares "liable" and the other "exempt." Judah, in F, introduces a new topic.

I.ii.17

A. [y.: *tny*] R. Simeon b. Eleazar says in the name of R. Aqiva, "Any [courtyard] that one opens and [another] one closes [y. adds, "is exempt," i.e., produce brought into such a courtyard is exempt from tithes]."

T. Ma. 2:20a (Lieberman ed., p. 236 lines 68-69; y. Ma. 3:6, 50d)

Simeon b. Eleazar supplies a late Ushan report of the saying which also occurs in a more elaborate setting at M. Ma. 3:5, discussed above. T. fails to make clear that the saying relates to a courtyard. Indeed, the saying in T. lacks "is exempt" and is, by itself, unintelligible.

I.i.31

A. [Concerning] a vine which is planted in the courtyard:

B. 1. "One takes (*nwtl*) the entire grapecluster [without incurring liability for tithes];

2. "and so too with regard to the pomegranate,

3. "and so too with regard to the melon," words of R. Tarfon.

C. R. Aqiva says,

1. "One picks [the grapes] of the cluster one at a time (*mgrgr*)."

2. And one takes [the seeds] out of the pomegranate one at a time;

3. and one takes slices of melon one at a time.

M. Ma. 3:9a

Like M. Ter. 3:5, this pericope deals with a rule relating to a courtyard. Here produce has grown inside a courtyard, and the question is, Do the same laws apply to such produce as apply to produce grown in a field? I shall first discuss the literary traits of the pericope, and then I shall return to the legal issue.

The superscription in A specifies a "vine." B1 and C1 respond; B2-3 and C2-3 do not. Clearly the dispute between Tarfon and Aqiva focuses on *nwtl* vs. *mgrgr* in relation to grapeclusters. We could construct a dispute-form for the masters as follows:

Concerning a vine/grapecluster in a courtyard:
Tarfon: One takes the entire [grapecluster] (*nwtl* ᵓ*t hkl*).
Aqiva: One picks [grapes] one at a time (*mgrgr*).

The grapecluster, the pomegranate and the melon are linked together elsewhere, without attribution to Aqiva, in a discussion of tithes (M. Ma. 2:6); although such evidence is not decisive, it does suggest that C2-3 have been added on to Aqiva's saying in C1. B2-3 are in turn added on to Tarfon's opinion in order to balance the content, although obviously not the literary form, of C.

Now let us take up the legal issue relating to the grapecluster which grows in a courtyard. In a field a vine enters its "season of tithes" when its fruit becomes edible. Prior to the "season" the grapes may be used without incurring tithes. After they become edible the grapes may be eaten without liability only as "random" meals, e.g., by picking and eating one grape at a time. Picking a cluster, however, like bringing harvested crop into a house, signals the intention to eat the grapes as a "formal" meal and therefore causes liability for tithes to be incurred. Tarfon holds that this rule does not pertain to the courtyard. There one may take "the entire grapecluster" without liability. Aqiva disagrees; in the courtyard, as in a field, grapes may be picked without liability only for a "random" meal. We do not know whether Tarfon considers vines exceptional, or whether he extends his lenient rule to other produce planted in the courtyard. Aqiva, however, clearly enough applies the rule about produce grown in a field to produce planted in the courtyard.

I.i.32

A. Rabban Gamaliel says, "Stalks of fenugreek, and of mustard, and of white beans are liable for tithing."

B. R. Eliezer says, "The caperbush is tithed for stalks, and caperberries, and caper-flowers."

C. R. Aqiva says, "It is tithed only for caperberries

D. "Because they [alone] are fruit."

M. Ma. 4:6 (b. Ber. 3b)

The masters differ concerning a fundamental question of tithing: Do tithes apply only to produce in "normal use"?

A is independent from B-D. Gamaliel focuses on stalks of several different species. By contrast, Eliezer discusses a single, problematic species, which is not mentioned in A. Also, the formulations in the two sayings differ ("is tithed for" vs. "are liable for tithes").

The question in B-D is, What parts of the caperbush incur tithes? The caperberries obviously are food and are therefore liable. But what is the status of the stalks and the flowers? People sometimes eat the former, when soft, and pickle the buds of the latter. [44] Eliezer holds that they incur tithes, presumably because they are sometimes used as food.

Aqiva, in C, holds that the caperbush is tithed only for caperberries. D supplies a reason: only the berries "are fruit." Against Eliezer, Aqiva apparently holds that because people usually do not eat them, the stalks and flowers are not liable for tithing.

B-C is in a variation on the dispute-form. B includes the topic-statement, and C depends upon B.

Lieberman notes that the manuscript-tradition, with one exeption, [45] preserves difficult readings in A1b and 2b, below. Following Lieberman's example, I shall cite the pericope as most texts give it; then I shall discuss the legal issues at stake and spell out the wording changes that probably should be made; and finally I shall discuss the specific opinion ascribed to Aqiva. In view of the difficulties with the text, in this instance I prefer not to use quotation marks to designate Aqiva's opinion.

I.ii.18

A. [Concerning] one who buys a field of vegetables [from a gentile] in Syria:

1. a. [If the acquisition occurred] before [the crop] entered the season of tithes,

b. [the man] is exempt [from tithing].

2. a. [If the acquisition occurred] after [the crop] entered the season of tithes,

b. [the man] is liable.

B. 1. He gathers (*mlqṭ*; E reads: *lwqt*) in his usual fashion

2. and is exempt, words of R. Aqiva.

C. But (*w*) sages say,

1. Indeed (*ʾp*), after [the crop] entered the season of tithes

2. [the man] is liable according to calculation (*lpy ḥšbwn*).

D. Sages agree with R. Aqiva that if [a gentile] sold him grain for reaping, or (*w*) grapes for gathering, or (*w*) olives for picking,

1. that he gathers (*šlwqt*) in his usual fashion

2. and is exempt.

T. Ma. 3:14 (Lieberman ed., p. 241 lines 46-50)

---

[44] See Feliks, *Agriculture*, p. 153.

[45] In a Geniza-fragment "exempt" in A.1.b. is crossed out and "liable" is inserted, *TK, Zeraᶜim*, p. 241.

The legal problem focuses on the issue of ownership of crop at the moment at which the produce first enters "the season of tithes," that is, becomes edible and consequently must be tithed if used for a meal. A introduces the case of an Israelite who buys a gentile's field in Syria. What is the status of the vegetables in the field? A1b and 2b are problematic, for they allege (1) that if the vegetables become edible after the Israelite buys the field, the Israelite is exempt from tithing, and (2) that if the vegetables become edible before the Israelite buys the field, the Israelite is exempt from tithing. The first opinion would be impossible to apply to produce grown in the land of Israel, but it might be possible to hold it with regard to Syrian produce, given the anomalous legal status of Syria. If, however, Syrian produce which matures in the possession of an Israelite is exempt from tithes, then it makes no sense to allege, as A2b does, that Syrian produce which matured prior to being purchased by an Israelite is liable for tithes after the purchase. As Lieberman explains, A1b should read, "is liable." But what is the proper response to A2? Clearly the form demands, "is exempt." Since Aqiva's saying supplies that opinion, Lieberman suggests the revision of the pericope as follows:

A. [Concerning] one who buys a field of vegetables [from a gentile] in Syria:

1. [If the acquisition occurred] before [the crop entered the season of tithes

a. [the man] is liable [for tithing].

2. [If the acquisition occurred] after [the crop] entered the season of tithes—

a. 1) [The man] gathers in his usual fashion
2) and is exempt, words of R. Aqiva.

b. But sages say,
Indeed, after [the crop] entered the season of tithes
1) [the man] is liable
2) according to calculation.

c. Sages agree with R. Aqiva that if [a gentile] sold him grain for reaping, or grapes for gathering, or olives for picking, that
1) he gathers (*lwqt*) in his usual fashion
2) and is exempt.

According to this revision A1 specifies the obvious, that an Israelite is obligated to tithe vegetables which mature in his possession. A2, which quite clearly is tied to A1 and which depends upon the superscription in A, in turn supplies the superscription for a verbose dispute-form. The following would be sufficient:

After they entered the season of tithes:

"[The man] is exempt," words of Aqiva.
But sages say, "[The man] is liable."

The agreement-saying in 2c repeats all of Aqiva's language from 2a. This revision solves the legal problem, namely, the odd, yet consistent reversal of *liable/exempt* in the manuscripts. It does so, however, by setting Aqiva's saying into a somewhat elaborate literary context, viz., the superscription for the dispute-form matches the saying which precedes it, and the two together are unintelligible without a further preceding statement; 2a1) and b2) are superfluous to the apodoses but are obviously central to the respective opinions; and in the sages' opinion the repetition of "after [the crop] entered the season of tithes" is completely unnecessary. None of these items by itself is without parallel among traditions about Aqiva; all of them together in a single pericope is, however, unusual.

Let us return to the text preserved in the manuscripts. What is the smallest possible unit of tradition which can be ascribed to Aqiva? Clearly B1-2: "He gathers in his usual fashion and is exempt." The sages' opinion in C responds to Aqiva's saying; that is taken for granted in D, which repeats Aqiva's language (D1-2). C clearly implies that the issue pertains to crop acquired after the moment at which it entered its season of tithes. Aqiva declares an Israelite exempt from tithing such crop. The sages hold that, regardless of the moment at which he acquired it, the man is obligated for a percentage of the growth of the produce proportionate to the time that he owns the crop. D alleges that the sages except ripened produce which an Israelite buys for immediate harvesting; this implies that the sages disagree with Aqiva concerning the purchase of a field of ripened vegetables from a gentile. Missing from the dispute obviously is any concern about Syria, which is explicitly mentioned in A. How is the Aqivan tradition, which I take to be B-D, linked to A?

At this point we must turn to the following tradition at M. Ma. 5:5:

A. [Concerning] one who buys a field of vegetables [from a gentile] in Syria:

1. a. [if the acquisition occurred] before [the crop] entered the season of tithes,

b. [the man] is liable [for tithing].

2. a. But (*w*) [if the acquisition occurred] after [the crop] entered the season of tithes,

b. [the man] is exempt [from tithing],

c. and he continues to gather (*wlwqt...whwlk*) in his usual fashion.

B. R. Judah says, "Indeed (ʾ*p*), he should hire laborers to gather [the crop]."

C. Said Rabban Simeon b. Gamaliel,

1. "To what do these words apply? To when he bought the land.

2. "But when he did not buy the land [i.e., when he bought only the crop]:

a. "if [the acquisition occurred] before [the crop] entered the season of tithes,

b. "[the man] is exempt [from tithing]."

D. Rabbi says, "Indeed (ʾ*p;* K, C omit), according to calculation."

M. Ma. 5:5

The superscription in A of M. corresponds to the superscription in A of our pericope in T. M.A, however, gives the expected rulings: if before (then) liable; if after (then) exempt. The language at M.A2c echoes Aqiva's lemma in T. (M, "and he continues to gather in his usual fashion"; T., "He gathers in his usual fashion and is exempt"). By contrast to T., M. cites only post-Yavnean masters: Judah, an Ushan, and the two patriarchs, Simeon b. Gamaliel and Rabbi. The issue in C of M. (the purchase of produce rather than of land) is similar to the issue touched on in the agreement-saying in D of T. (produce purchased for immediate harvesting). Rabbi's opinion in D of M. corresponds to the sages' saying in C of T. Can we speculate on the relationship between these pericopae in M. and T.? My remarks in this regard refer to the following synopsis of the two traditions:

M. Ma. 5:5	*T. Ma. 3:14*
1. [Concerning] one who buys... in Syria:	1. ,, ,, ,,
2. Before entered the season of tithes,	2. ,, ,, ,,
3. Is liable.	3. Is exempt [Lieb., "Is liable"].
4. *But* after entered season of tithes,	4. ,, ,, ,,
5. Is exempt,	5. Is liable [Lieb. omits].
6. and he continues to gather (*wlwqt...whwlk*)	6. He gathers (E, *lwqt*)
7. in his usual fashion.	7. ,, ,, ,,
8. — — —	8. and is exempt,
9. — — —	9. words of R. Aqiva
10. R. Judah says, "Indeed, he should hire..."	10. — — —

M. Ma. 5:5	*T. Ma. 3:14*
11. Said Rabban Simeon b. Gamaliel, "To what..."	11. — — —
12. Rabbi says,	12. But sages say,
13. "Indeed	13. " " "
14. — — —	14. after entered the season of tithes,
15. — — —	15. is liable
16. according to calculation	16. " " "
17. — — —	17. Sages agree with R. Aqiva... [cp. no. 11]
18. — — —	18. that he gathers
19. — — —	19. in his usual fashion
20. — — —	20. and is exempt.

I suspect that the ultimate authority behind the pericope in T. has taken over the superscription (no. 1) and the response (nos. 2-5) which he found in front of him in the tradition given in M. I cannot explain the change, "exempt" for "liable," which Lieberman's revision rectifies in no. 3. If the language in nos. 6-7 is primary to the tradition in M., then clearly the editor of the pericope in T., acting as a commentator, supplies Aqiva's lemma as the source for the opinion quoted in M. This would explain how the Aqivan tradition, which does not refer to Syrian property, has been inserted into the context of T. Ma. 3:14. The view that the Aqivan tradition focuses on land with ripened produce acquired from a gentile and does not necessarily relate to Syria is supported by the following tradition in y.

III.i.1

A. *tny*: [Concerning] a field [the crop in which] brought forth one-third [i.e., had reached one-third of its full growth and was therefore considered edible] while it was in the possession of (literally, "before") a gentile and which an Israelite bought from [the gentile]:

B. R. Aqiva says, "[Concerning] the Addition (*twspt*): [the Israelite] is exempt [from tithing]."

C. But (*w*) sages say, "[Concerning] the Addition: [the Israelite] is liable."

y. Ma. 5:4, 51d (y. Hal. 3:3, 59a; y. Orlah 1:1, 60d)

The Addition is the growth of the crop after it becomes edible. The setting is a discussion of M. Ma. 5:5. y. uses an expression for incurring liability for tithing different from that used at T. Ma. 3:14 (y., "brought forth one-third"; T., "entered the season of tithes"). y. does not state that the field in question is in Syria. T. does not use the term Addition, which, except for "exempt" and "liable," is all that y.

gives in the masters' opinions. Aqiva's and the sages' opinions are consistent with the positions attributed to them in T.

IV.ii.2

A. [Concerning] an Israelite who bought a field in Syria from a gentile: [if the acquisition occurred] before [the crop in the field] brought forth one-third, [the Israelite] is liable [for tithing].

B. [If the acquisition occurred] after [the crop] brought forth one-third,

C. R. Aqiva declares [the Israelite] liable for [paying tithes for] the Addition.

D. But sages exempt.

b. Hul. 136a

b. specifies "Syria" and reverses Aqiva's and the sages' opinions, which it reports in indirect discourse.

II.iii.1

["You shall seek the place which the Lord your God will choose out... there you shall bring your burnt offerings and your sacrificies, your tithes... (Deut. 12:5-6)."]

A. "Your tithes": R. Aqiva says, "Scripture refers to two tithes: one is the tithe of grain, and the other is the tithe of cattle."

Sifré Deut. 63 (Finkelstein, ed., p. 130 lines 11-12)

The exegesis responds to the plural-form of "tithes" in the verse. Aqiva's comment supplies two references for "your tithes."

IV.i.5

A. [Concerning] an *etrog* which is in the first stages of ripening (*hbwsr*):

B. R. Aqiva says, "It is not a fruit."

C. But (*w*) sages say, "[It is a] fruit."

y. Ma. 1:4, 49a

The tradition is in dispute-form. The context is a discussion of the moment at which the *etrog* becomes liable for tithing. Aqiva and the sages differ with regard to the status of an *etrog* which is in the first stages of ripening. Aqiva holds that the half-ripened *etrog* is not yet a "fruit" and thus remains exempt from tithes. The sages allege the opposite. Both B and C assume, however, that the progress of the ripening process is critical to the determination of the status of the *etrog*. This agrees with Eliezer's view, reported at M. Bik. 2:6, that an *etrog*, like a fruit-tree, becomes liable for tithing from the moment that its fruit is formed; by contrast, Gamaliel alleges that an *etrog*, like a vegetable, does not incur liability until it is picked.

III.ii.4

A. [Concerning] an *etrog* which is in the first stages of ripening:

B. R. Aqiva declares [the *etrog*] unfit.

C. But (*w*) sages declare [it] fit.

b. Suk. 36a

y. reported the opinions in direct discourse. b. shifts to indirect discourse and substitutes *unfit* vs. *fit* for y.'s *not a fruit* vs. *fruit* The dispute in b. concerns whether or not the partially ripened *etrog* is fit for ritual use. Lev. 23:40 states that only "the fruit of goodly trees" may be used, and the question is whether an *etrog*, if only partially ripened, is excluded by the biblical verse.

Can we say that one of the versions, whether y.'s or b.'s is prior? The evidence is hardly decisive. The tradition occurs twice in b., first in the context of an anonymous discussion concerning when an *etrog* becomes disqualified for ritual use, and second at the beginning of a discussion in which Rabbah and Abaye, fourth-century Babylonian Amoras, relate Aqiva's opinion to the view of another master concerning liability of a less-than-fully-grown *etrog* for tithing. b.'s language, *unfit* vs. *fit*, is appropriate in the first context, but not in the second. y.'s language, *not a fruit* vs. *fruit*, would be more appropriate in the second context, the discussion of tithing. Conceivably y.'s language is prior, and the wording-changes in b. reflect, first, an effort to make the dispute fit the first context in b., concerning the ritual use of *etrogs*, and second, an editorial effort in b. to make the two reports consistent. As it happens, the issue of tithing recurs in traditions in M. and T. in connection with masters both chronologically prior to and chronologically after Aqiva. By contrast, the issue of the ritual use of the *etrog* occurs only in traditions about masters who post-date Aqiva. Obviously, however, there is no attestation to either version of the Aqivan tradition prior to the fourth century.

vii. *Ma^caser Sheni*

I.i.33

A. Vetches of Second-tithe

1. should be eaten [when] they are buds,

2. and they are brought into Jerusalem, and [subsequently they may] take them out.

B. [If the vetches] contracted uncleanness:

1. R. Tarfon says, "They should be divided among lumps of dough."

2. But (*w*) sages say, "They should be redeemed."

C. And [concerning vetches] of Heave-offering:
1. House of Shammai say,
a. "They soak and grind in cleanness,
b. "and they give as food in uncleanness."
2. But (*w*) House of Hillel say,
a. "They soak in cleanness,
b. "and they grind and give as food in uncleanness."
3. Shammai says, "They should be eaten dry (*ṣryd*)."
4. R. Aqiva says, "Whatever concerns them [may be done] in uncleanness."

M. M.S. 2:4 (C = M. Ed. 1:8; y. Hal. 4:11, 60b)

The pericope gives several cases concerning vetches, a kind of plant, generally used as fodder. Aqiva's saying relates to the last case in the pericope, vetches designated as Heave-offering (C). The question is, What precautions must be taken to guard the plants from contracting uncleanness? Only priests may eat Heave-offering, and only in cleanness. But generally vetches are not eaten by people; and priests are free to use unclean Heave-offering of any kind of produce for fodder, the usual use to which vetches are put. To what extent, then, must Heave-offering vetches be protected against contracting uncleanness? The House of Shammai allege that the vetches must be protected until they are fed to livestock; thus soaking and grinding, which are preparatory actions, may be performed only by a person who is in a state of cleanness. The House of Hillel hold that only soaking need be performed by a person in a state of cleanness. MS suggests that the opinion of the House of Hillel assumes the following: plants eaten by human beings frequently are soaked but usually are not ground up; grinding therefore marks off vetches as fodder, thus obviating the necessity that they be handled in cleanness. On this view, the issue concerns giving the appearance of making Heave-offering unclean; the vetches in fact are not considered produce fit for human consumption. Shammai, in C3, introduces an extreme position: it is assumed that uncleanness can be contracted only when the plants are wet; Shammai's view, that the vetches should be kept dry at all times, implies that the plants, once designated as Heave-offering, must be protected from contracting uncleanness regardless of whether or not people might eat them. Aqiva's position in C4 stands at the other extreme: vetches may be handled in uncleanness at all times, presumably because they are not considered fit for human consumption. Aqiva does not take into account the possibility that in an unusual situation a person might eat vetches. Aqiva's ruling seems to rely on usual practice with regard to vetches, which are commonly defined as an inedible plant. For the principle of adhering to usual practice, cp. M. Shev. 1:8, 4:6.

C1-2 are in dispute-form. The pattern of A1+C1-2 (X of Second-tithe should be eaten as buds + X of Heave-offering + Houses' dispute) corresponds to the pattern in the preceding pericope, which focuses on fenugreek, an anomalous kind of clover. C3 and 4 depend upon the Houses' dispute; C3 and 4 in fact expand the foregoing by adding the logical opinions at the extremes. In any case, the combination of disputants is odd. On the transmission-process behind Shammai's saying, see Neusner, *Phar.,* Vol. I, p. 190.

I.ii.19

A. Vetches of Second-tithe
  1. should be eaten [when] they are buds.
B. [Concerning vetches] of Heave-offering:
C. 1. "House of Shammai say,
    a. " 'They soak in cleanness,
    b. " 'and they rub and give as food in uncleanness.'
  2. "But (*w*) House of Hillel say,
    a. " 'They soak and grind in cleanness,
    b. " 'and they give as food in uncleanness,' " words of R. Judah.
D. R. Meir says,
  1. "House of Shammai say,
    a. " 'They soak and grind in cleanness,
    b. " 'and they give as food in uncleanness.'
  2. "But (*w*) House of Hillel say, "Whatever concerns them in uncleanness.' "
E. Said R. Yosé, "This is the teaching (*zw mšnt*) of R. Aqiva."
F. Therefore [Aqiva] says, "They may be given to any priest" [= M. Hal. 4:9].
G. But (*w*) sages did not agree with him.

T. M.S. 2:1b (Lieberman ed., p. 249 lines 6-10)

T. supplies Ushan attributions for the Houses' dispute and for Aqiva's opinion at M. M.S. 2:4. The Tarfon-tradition does not interrupt the pattern in T., as it does in M. In C Judah's version of the Houses' dispute switches the attributions for the two opinions. Meir's version agrees with that in M. with regard to Shammai's position (D1). What is of interest here is that Meir, in D2, ascribes to the House of Hillel the same postion which in M. is ascribed to Aqiva, "Whatever concerns them in uncleanness." Yosé, in E, seems to comment on the last statement in Meir's saying, which Yosé identifies as "the teaching of R. Aqiva." M. thus is consistent with Yosé's view regarding Aqiva's opinion. The phrase, "teaching (*mšnt*) of R. Aqiva" recurs at T. M.S. 2:12, discussed below.

For F-G, see discussion on M. Hal. 4:9, below.

I.i.34

A. House of Shammai say, "A man should not change his *selas* [i.e., silver coins of Second-tithe money for] gold *denars*."

B. But House of Hillel permit.

C. Said R. Aqiva, "I changed Rabban Gamaliel's and R. Joshua's silver [coins] for gold *denars*."

M. M.S. 2:7

Second-tithe produce may be exchanged for money, which is then brought to, and spent in, Jerusalem. The Houses, in A-B, disagree as to whether or not silver coins, once they have been obtained in exchange for Second-tithe produce, can subsequently be exchanged for gold coins. C supplies a precedent to show that the law follows the ruling of the House of Hillel.

C implies that even after the destruction of the Temple Gamaliel and Joshua observed laws relating to Second-tithe. Aqiva acts as the agent of the two older masters.

I.i.35

A. [Concerning] one who changes a *sela* of Second-tithe [money] in Jerusalem:

B. House of Shammai say, "[He changes the] whole *sela* for [copper] coins."

C. But (*w*) House of Hillel say, "[He may take] a *sheqel* of silver and a *sheqel* of [copper] coins."

D. Those who make argument before sages say,

1. "For (*b*-) three *denars* of silver
2. and for a *denar* of [copper] coins."

E. R. Aqiva says,

1. "For (*b*-) three *denars* of silver
2. and for (*b*-) a quarter of [copper] coins."

F. R. Tarfon say, "Four *aspers* of silver."

G. Shammai says, "He should deposit it [i.e., the *sela* of Second-tithe money] in a shop, and he should [gradually] consume its value [in produce]."

M. M.S. 2:9

The pericope is the last in a series of three, beginning with M. M.S. 2:7, discussed above, which give Houses' disputes concerning the exchanging of Second-tithe money. 2:7 focuses on changing coins of silver for coins of gold (Aqiva alleges that he exchanged silver for gold for Gamaliel and Joshua); 2:8 focuses on exchanging copper coins for silver coins; and 2:9 focuses on exchanging silver coins for copper. The legal problem relates to the protection of the sanctity which is attached to the particular coins which are brought to Jerusalem to substitute for Second-tithe produce. The preceding pericope, 2:8, discusses the precautions to be taken for the journey to Jerusalem: the House of Shammai hold that a pilgrim changes all copper coins to the value of a *sela* to silver; the House of Hillel hold that a pilgrim exchanges only half of a *sela* for silver and keeps the other half in copper coins. 2:9 takes up the question, What precautions should be taken within Jerusalem? The House of Shammai, which holds that on the journey copper coins should be exchanged for silver, alleges that once a pilgrim reaches the capital a silver *sela* may be exchanged for copper coins. The House of Hillel takes an intermediate position, as it does with regard to coins on the journey to Jerusalem: a *sela* is exchanged for a *sheqel* of silver (1 *sela* = 2 *sheqels*) and one *sheqel* of copper coins. Aqiva and the other masters in E-G allege that further precautions must be taken within Jerusalem. Aqiva (E) holds that more than three-quarters of a *sela* remains in silver coin. Against the unnamed debaters in D, who argue that one-quarter of a *sela* (1 *sela* = 4 *denars*) is exchanged for copper coins, Aqiva states that only "a quarter" is exchanged for copper coins. On the view that E2 responds to D2, Aqiva holds that a quarter of a *denar*, that is, merely one-sixteenth of the *sela* of silver, is changed for copper coins (Sens, ag. Maim.). On the view that "four *aspers* of silver" (F) responds to D2, Tarfon also puts forward a small proportion for copper coins. [46] At the far extreme, Shammai, in G, holds that the *sela* of silver should not be exchanged for any copper coins at all; instead the pilgrim should use it to open an account with a shopkeeper who will provide consumable produce.

A-C are in dispute-form. B-C recur *verbatim* as the apodosis in the dispute-form at the beginning of 2:8. There the superscription reads, "[Concerning] one who changes a *sela* of [copper] coins of Second-tithe [money]." The two Houses' disputes belong to the same unit of tradition, although reconstructing that unit is problematic. [47] D-E

[46] Maim. notes that the relation between an *asper* and a *denar* is not clear. If, as Sens suggests, 5 *aspers* = one denar, then Tarfon holds that merely one-twentieth of the *sela* of silver is exchanged for copper coins. Recently D. Sperber has supported the suggestion that one *asper* = 1/5 *denar*; see "Palestinian currency during the Second Commonwealth," *Jewish Quarterly Review* 56, 1966, pp. 292-93.

[47] *Pharisees*, Vol. II, pp. 96-99.

respond to the superscription in A but stand outside the framework of the Houses' dispute. The attributive formulary, "Those who make argument before sages," does not recur elsewhere in Aqivan traditions on agriculture. D introduces *denar* as a measure; A-C give only *sela* and *sheqel*. Aqiva's saying, in E, also mentions *denars*. E, like D, uses *b-* to introduce the specific sums. D-E are a unit; the difference between D and E hinges on *denar* vs. *a quarter*. D-E could be reformulated in a dispute form in which the master's opinion looks like a gloss, as, for example,

> Those make argument before sages say, "For three *denars* of silver and for a *denar* of coins."
>
> R. Aqiva says, "A quarter."

Tarfon's and Shammai's opinions bear no formal relation to the foregoing. [48]

---

[48] *Ibid.*, Vol. I, p. 191.

In my comment on this pericope, as in comments on other pericopae, I have preferred to say little or nothing concerning the value of the source for economic history. Clearly traditions in M.-T. provide valuable evidence for the economic history of the periods in which they were formulated. D. Sperber's comment on the value for monetary history of third and fourth-century rabbinic sources applies, however, also to the value for economic history of traditions in M.-T.: "the full picture ... only emerges with clarity when seen against the backdrop of the second century [sic] legal position," *Roman Palestine, 200-400. Money and Prices*, (Ramat Gan, 1974), p. 19. In this study of Aqiva's traditions the fundamental traits of "the second century [sic] legal position" constitutes the main focus of attention. It is hoped that the basic sort of work carried out in this study, e.g., the delineation of Tannaitic legal concerns and the investigation of the literary nature of the sources, will prove helpful for the future work of economic historians of the period. Too often in the past mishnaic evidences have been appropriated without due regard for the limits of their usefulness. The "sociological" approach to *halakhic* literature, suggested by L. Ginzberg in "The Significance of the *Halachah* for Jewish History," reprinted in *On Jewish Law and Lore*, (Phila., 1955), pp. 77-124, applied by L. Finkelstein in *Akiba. Scholar, Saint and Martyr*, (Phila., 1936), and in *The Pharisees. The Sociological Background of Their Faith*, (Phila., 1962[3]), and criticized by G. Alon in "The Sociological Approach for the Investigation of the *Halakhah*" (Heb.), reprinted in *Studies in Jewish History in the times of the Second Temple, the Mishna and the Talmud*, (Tel Aviv, 1970[2]), Vol. II, pp. 181-227, is a case in point. In view of the history of the "sociological" approach, however, the following remark by Sperber is puzzling.

> Even now, one cannot help but feel that students of Jewish legal history place too little emphasis on the socio-economic forces acting on the *halacha* and shaping its development. (*Roman Palestine*, p. 21).

Where possible social and economic considerations obviously must be related to contemporary developments internal to the *halakhah*. Legal, social, and economic history ideally move forward together. It must be noted, however, that the systematic, critical investigation of the literary sources for Tannaitic legal history, although it follows, and depends upon, important previous studies by Lieberman and by Y. N.

I.i.36

A. Said R. Judah, "Formerly (*br*ʾ*šwnh*) they used to send [the following instructions] to landowners in the provinces: 'Hurry and take care of your produce (*mhrw whtqynw* ʾ*t prwtykm*) before the time for removal [of tithes] arrives.'

B. "Until R. Aqiva came and taught that all produce which did not enter into the season of tithes is exempt from the removal

M. M.S. 5:8

Second-tithe, and all other kinds of tithes, must be disposed of by Passover of the fourth and seventh years of the Sabbatical-cycle. At the "time for removal" all tithes still in the possession of an Israelite must be disposed of, after which the Israelite declares, "I have removed the sacred portion out of my house..." (Deut. 26:13ff.).

According to Judah, "formerly" (A) notices were sent to the provinces to remind landowners to tithe their produce before the "time for removal." [49] Then (B) Aqiva "came and taught" that produce prior to its season of tithes, that is, not yet liable for tithing, is not liable for removal. Aqiva's view is clear. Removal relates to tithes which a person separates from his produce but which he never gives away. A person is not obligated to separate tithes from crop which has not yet reached its season of tithes. Removal does not apply, therefore, to produce which has not yet reached its season of tithes. After the crop reaches its season, however, the tithes must be removed or else the Israelite's declaration, "I have removed...," is vitiated.

The redactional formula, "Formerly... Until X came and taught," implies that Aqiva's teaching revises the procedure described in A. Following this implication Bertinoro explains that A assumes the opposite from Aqiva's opinion, namely, that produce not yet liable for tithing is nonetheless liable for removal. [50] This view assumes that

---

Epstein, among others, has begun only in the past decade. At this stage, prior to the determination of the nature of the literary sources, it would be rash to speculate on an issue as momentous as that of the economic and social "forces" shaping *halakhic* development. Such a discussion can well be postponed until "students of Jewish legal history" present results based not on logical theories but rather on hard data and sophisticated methods comparable to those to which present-day economic historians presumably lay claim.

[49] *Mid. Tan* (ed., Hoffmann [Berlin, 1909], pp. 175-76) reports a tradition concerning how Rabban Simeon b. Gamaliel [the Elder?] and Rabban Yoḥanan b. Zakkai sent such instructions to the provinces. See Epstein, *Tannaim,* p. 75.

[50] Bertinoro seems to stand alone here. MR completely rejects Bertinoro's explanation. MR holds that A cannot assume that the obligation for removal can precede the obligation for separating tithe; MR therefore suggests that Aqiva refers to a special case, namely, to crop less than one-third grown at Passover which, "formerly," a landowner was required to bring to Jerusalem immediately upon its maturity. Aqiva,

the "tithe element" in the crop is "holy" at all times, not merely after liability for tithing has been incurred. [51] Aqiva thus holds that holiness is not inherent in the produce given as tithe but is rather to be understood as a legal category, an element in the calculus of the system of agricultural laws. If this interpretation of the pericope is correct, then Aqiva's view represents a fundamental revision in the understanding of the nature of tithes.

"Taught" (*lmd*) contrasts strikingly with the more common formulary, "says/said." In Mishnah *lmd,* in the sense of "to teach," most frequently occurs in connection with exegesis of Sripture (16 times; 19% of total); with pedagogy, including artisans' crafts, literature, childrens' lessons, priestly duties (22 times; 26% of total); and, as a technical term, with courtroom procedure (29 times; 35% of total). Less frequently anonymous sages "instruct" people to perform certain actions or to speak certain words (8 times; 9% of total) or disciples are "instructed" by the conduct of their masters (5 times; 6% of total). Aqiva's teaching, as reported by Judah, neither relates to the exegesis of Scripture nor speaks to the question of the enforcement of Aqiva's personal opinions. The introduction, "Formerly, ...," recalls similar descriptions in traditions about Gamaliel concerning the histories of particular laws. For instance, M. Git. 4:2 reports:

> Formerly (*brʾšwnh*) a man appointed a court...
> [But] Rabban Gamaliel decreed (*htqyn*) that they should not do so...

Gamaliel's traditions consistently report that the patriarch "decreed" the changes from the laws observed "formerly." [52] Appropriately the patriarch decrees, but the rabbinic sage teaches, legal innovations.

Only Aqiva's name occurs in the "Formerly... Until/taught" formulation in M. and T. (M. M.S. 5:8; T. Pes. 1:7, T. M.K. 2:10; M. Ned. 9:6; T. Ned. 5:1). The specific innovations attributed to Aqiva are in line with tendencies observed in the traditions of other masters. For instance, Eliezer's lenient views at M. Ned. 9:1-2 concerning releasing people from their vows imply, as Ṣadoq states explicitly at 9:1, that "there should be no vows," surely a change from prior Pharisaic law. [53] M. Ned. 9:6 reports a tradition about Aqiva in the "For-

---

according to MR, merely abrogates the obligation to bring such crop to Jerusalem immediately. Maim. states that A refers to crop which had already entered its season.

[51] See y. M.S. 5:6, 56c, and B. Bokser's discussion, *Samuel*, p. 115-16.

[52] See Kanter, *Gamaliel*, p. 36-40.

[53] Neusner lists M. Ned. 9:1-2 among Eliezer's "best" traditions. See *Eliezer*, Vol. I, pp. 110, 311, 328.

merly... Until/taught" formulation that is consistent with the tendency of Eliezer's views:

> Formerly they used to say, "[On] those days [i.e., festivals and Sabbaths] [vows, e.g., to fast] are not binding; but [on] all other days [vows] are binding."
> Until R. Aqiva came and taught that a vow which is not binding in part is not binding at all.

The tradition which Judah reports at M. M.S. 5:8 thus reflects Yavnean legal issues and occurs in an unusual formulation which emphasizes the authoritativeness of Aqiva's legal teachings.

I.i.37

A. *m^c^śh b-*: Rabban Gamaliel and the elders were travelling on a ship. Said Rabban Gamaliel, "[The] tithe (*^c^śwr*) which I am going to measure is given to Joshua, and the land it grows on [literally, "its place"] is rented to him. Another tithe (*^c^śwr*) which I am going to measure [as Poorman's tithe] is given to Aqiva ben Joseph (P omits "ben Joseph") that he may possess it on behalf of the poor (*šyzkh bw l^c^nyym*), and the land it grows on [literally, "its place"] is rented to him."

C. Said R. Joshua, "[The] tithe (*^c^śwr)* which I am going to measure is given to Eleazar ben ^c^Azariah, and the land it grows on [literally, "its place"] is rented to him."

D. And they received from each other rent.

M. M.S. 5:9b (b. Qid. 26b-27a, b. B.M. 11a-b; y. Pe. 4:6, 18c, y. M.S. 5:6, 56c)

Aqiva plays a subordinate role in A of this pericope. The legal problem concerns the plight of a landowner who must dispose of tithes for his crop: the time limit for removal [54] is at hand, but the landowner is far away from his field. An anonymous statement which immediately precedes our pericope at M. M.S. 5:9a alleges that a person who is at a distance from his field should designate tithes from his crop. Our pericope gives a story in which Gamaliel, in A, assigns people to whom his tithes are to be given. [55] Kanter observes that the point of the story is that ownership of the produce must be transferred; that transfer is accomplished by collecting rent for the property on which the crop grows (C). [56]

---

[54] See M. M.S. 5:8, discussed above.

[55] On whether Gamaliel's action falls within the definition of "designation" according to the preceding anonymous statement, see Maim.

[56] *Gamaliel*, p. 53.

The story assumes that Aqiva is an Israelite, as opposed to a priest or a Levite. No explanation is given for his assignment as the agent of the poor.

B raises the question, To whom should tithes be paid? Num. 18:21-32 and M. Git. 3:7 state that tithes are given to Levites. B alleges, however, that Joshua assigns tithe to Eleazar, a priest. Maimonides explains that Joshua is a Levite and is in fact assigning Heave-offering of tithe, which a Levite does owe to a priest. This issue recurs at y. M.S. 5:5, 56b-c, to which we now turn.

IV.i.6

[The greater part of this tradition is in Aramaic; Hebrew sections are italicized.]

A. R. Ba used to tell the following story:

B. R. Leazar b. ᶜAzariah used to take tithes from a certain garden.

C. *That garden had two exits, one to a place of uncleanness* [i.e., a graveyard], *the other open to a place of cleanness.*

D. R. Aqiva came along [and] said to [the owner of the garden], "Open this [i.e., an entrance to the neighboring cemetery] and close off this [the previous entrance] (*ptḥ hhn wstwm hhn*). If [someone] comes, tell him 'Come in on this path [through the cemetery].' "

E. "If so, send his [Eleazar's] disciples."

F. "Say to him, 'You [plural] is written.' " [Num. 18:31 gives part of the charge to the Levites: "*You* shall eat [tithe] in any place..."]

G. *R. Leazar b. ᶜAzariah heard, and he said, "By Aqiva's acumen* (so Jastrow, p. 846 col. II, no. 2, reading *bmrṣᶜh*, literally, "by the awl of"; alternatively, *bmrṣᶜh*, "by the strap of.") [matters] *have come to this.*"

H. *In that hour R. Leazar b. ᶜAzariah returned all the tithes which he had taken.*

y. M.S. 5:5, 56b-c

The context is a discussion of whether first-tithe should be given exclusively to Levites or whether it may also be given to priests. Immediately prior to our pericope, y. reports a debate between Joshua, who limits first-tithe to Levites, and Eleazar b. ᶜAzariah, who holds that priests too may receive first-tithe. According to Ba's story, Aqiva agrees with Joshua: first-tithe should be given exclusively to Levites. The problem raised in the story is that Eleazar, himself a priest, has been taking tithes from "a certain garden." By leaving open only the entrance from the cemetry, through which a priest may not pass, the owner of the garden prevents Eleazar from taking more of the crop in the garden.

E assumes an exegesis of Num. 18:31 which y., in the debate preceding our pericope, attributes explicitly to Joshua. The verse, addressed to the Levites, states, "You may eat in any place, you and your households"; "you" is interpreted to exclude all others, such as priests.

In the Aramaic section of the story, B+D can be distinguished from E+F. In the former, B sets the problem, and D introduces Aqiva's position. It is evident that E-F are given in order to introduce the biblical warrant for Aqiva's opinion. In E the respective identities of the speaker and of the auditor, who is to send the disciples, are not clear. The imperative "say" in F is in the singular and presumably is therefore not addressed to Eleazar's disciples. (The story, and especially the reference in F, obviously depends for intelligibility upon the preceding accounts in y., which discuss priestly perquisites with regard to tithes.)

By contrast to the Aramaic sections, which could stand together as a unit (whether B+D or B+D+E+F), the Hebrew sections, C, G, and H, add discrete details which develop the story. C notes that the garden previously had no exits and makes explicit the status of two areas adjoining the garden (one unclean, the second clean). D obviously assumes the latter, the status of the adjoining areas, but not the former, the initial number of exits. Aqiva's statement in D could mean that a new entrance, to an adjoining cemetery, should be opened up and that a (single) previous entrance, to a place of cleanness, should be closed off. G and H give Eleazar's reaction. But whereas in G Eleazar merely acknowledges his frustration, H implies that in the end he accepts Aqiva's, and Joshua's, view on priestly perquisites, a very different situation from conceding to the wiles of Aqiva in one specific case. G could properly cap the story given in the Aramaic sections. H, by contrast to G, adds a new development to that story.

III.ii.3

[Hebrew sections in this pericope are italicized.]

A. *tnw rbnn*;

B. 1. *"Heave-offering* [should be given] *to the priest*

2. *"and first-tithe to the Levite,"* words of R. Aqiva.

C. *R. Eleazar b. ᶜAzariah says, "To the priest."*

D. *To the priest but not to the Levite?* Say rather: *also to the priest.*

E. What is R. Aqiva's reason? Because Scripture states, *"Speak to the Levites and say to them...* (Num. 18:26)." Scripture [explicitly] refers to Levites.

F. And the other? [What reason stands behind Eleazar's opinon?] [He reasons] as does R. Joshua b. Levi [in the following statement]:

G. *As said R. Joshua b. Levi, "In twenty-four places priests are called Levites, and this is one of them: 'And the priests, the Levites, sons of Zadok'* (Ez. 44:15)."

H. And R. Aqiva? [How does he respond to the allegation that Levite means priest? Aqiva holds that] you do not find [that Levite means priest] in this case, for Scripture states, "*You shall eat* [the tithe] *in any place*" (Num. 18:31). [This implies] *one who is able to eat it in any place; a priest is excluded for he cannot eat it in a cemetery.*

I. And the other [i.e., Eleazar b. ᶜAzariah; how does he explain "in any place"]? Any place that one desires, for it is not required [that it be eaten within the confines of the] wall [i.e., within Jerusalem]; or (*w*) if [someone] in a state of uncleanness eats it, that person is not [subject to the punishment of] lashes.

b. Yeb. 86a-b

IV.ii.3

J. 1. There was a certain garden from which R. Eleazar b. ᶜAzariah used to take first-tithe.

2. R. Aqiva went [and] moved the exit [so that the garden] opened onto a [neighboring] cemetery.

3. Said [Eleazar], "Aqiva with his leather pouch, and I *ḥyy* (Slotki suggests, "but I must live")."

b. Yeb. 86b

b. presents two traditions about the difference between Aqiva and Eleazar. B-C are in a variation on the dispute-form. J gives in Babylonian Aramaic a variant of the story which occurs at y. M.S. 5:5, 56b-c, discussed above. The masters' positions are consistent in the two traditions, with Aqiva in each instance limiting first-tithe exclusively to Levites. By contrast, D-I present a different order of inquiry, namely, that of the agendum of *gemara*. Thus D notes that Eleazar's lemma, C, seems to be defective.[57] E-I inquire into the reasons (here scriptural exegeses) which stand behind the opinions of the two Yavneans. And J broadens the inquiry by reference to comparable materials.

The link between (1) B-C+D-I and (2) J is clear enough: the explanations of the master's opinions lead to a cemetery (H) and to eating first-tithe in a state of uncleanness (I). The story in J explicitly mentions the former and, by implication, includes the latter. What is not clear, however, is the relation between the story in J and the sayings

---

[57] Parallel passages at b. Ket. 26a and at b. B.B. 81b give B-D with C corrected as suggested in D.

in B-C, other than the consistency of the masters' positions. It is not possible to suggest, for instance, that one generated the other.

What can be said of the relation between the two versions of the story about Aqiva and Eleazar? The following is a synopsis of the stories:

y. M.S. 5:5, 56b-c	*b. Yeb. 86a-b*
1. R. Leazar b. Azariah used to take tithes from a certain garden.	1. There was a certain garden from which R. Eleazar b. ᶜAzariah used to take first-tithe.
2. *That garden had two exists...*	2. — — —
3. R. Aqiva came along.	3. R. Aqiva went
4. He said, "Open this and close off that."	4. and moved the exit so that it opened onto a cemetery.
5. "If so, send his disciples."	5. — — —
6. "Say to him, ' "You" is written' "	6. — — —
7. *R. Leazar b. Azariah heard,*	7. — — —
8. And he said,	8. He said,
9. *"By Aqiva's acumen matters have come to this."*	9. "Aqiva with his leather pouch, and I *ḥyy*."
10. *In that hour R. Leazar b. Azariah returned all the tithes which he had taken.*	10. — — —

b. lacks the Hebrew specification of two initial exits (no. 2) and instead explicitly states that Aqiva moved one exit, presumably the single initial exit, so that it opened onto a cemetery (no. 4). b. also omits both the reference to Scripture (no. 6) and the description of Eleazar's rectification (no. 10). The phrases in y. and in b. in no. 9 are equally enigmatic, although the purposes of both are clear: Eleazar protests his exclusion from the garden. b. leaves off with that protest, thereby preserving the masters' disagreement, which has been spelled out at length in b.E-I. By contrast, y., in no. 10, adds a further development to the story, as discussed above. The evidence suggests the freedom with which a *baraita*-editor could develop a story about Tannaitic masters.

Consistent with his position here, Aqiva elsewhere also takes positions which considerably expand the roles of non-priests in activities which require priestly participation (e.g., y. Bik. 1:7, 64a, discussed below); for a similar position expressed outside of laws on agriculture, see Neusner's discussion of Aqiva's view on the priestly inspection of plagues, HMLP, Vol. VIII, pp. 197-99.

I.ii.20

A. [Concerning] cakes of saffron:

B. Said R. Yosah,

C. "R. Yoḥanan b. Nuri approached R. Ḥalafta [and] said to him, 'What is the status of saffron-cakes? May they be purchased with [Second-]tithe money? [That is, can money received in the sale of Second-tithe produce be used in turn to purchase saffron-cakes?]'

D. "He said to him, '[Saffron-cakes] may not be purchased [with Second-tithe money].'

E. "He said to him, 'I am of the same opinion, but (ʾ/ʾ š-) Aqiva said, "They may be purchased." ' "

T. M. S. 1:13b (Lieberman ed., p. 246 lines 41-43)

Yosah reports a story in which Yoḥanan b. Nuri claims to be puzzled about an opinion of Aqiva. Underlying the pericope is a basic problem concerning what can be done with Second-tithe produce. If such produce cannot be brought to Jerusalem, it is sold and the proceeds of the sale are brought to the capital and exchanged there for consumable produce. May one use the proceeds to buy food-coloring? The pericope assumes that saffron-cakes are used to color food; they do not themselves constitute food. For that reason Yoḥanan and Yosah agree that saffron-cakes cannot be purchased with Second-tithe money; the holiness of the Second-tithe produce had been transferred to the money, and the two masters hold that that holiness can be transferred in turn only to something fully comparable to the original produce. Aqiva, by permitting the purchase of coloring, takes a broader view of what may be done with Second-tithe money. His position reflects an effort to define the dynamic of holiness by reference to a process, here the eating of a meal, rather than by reference to manipulation of specific objects, such as specific types or categories of produce.

The issue of the status of food-coloring and condiments recurs at M. Uks. 3:5:

A. "Costus, amomum, and the principal spices, crowfoot and asafoetida, black pepper and saffron-cakes

(1) "are purchased with Second-tithe money

(2) "and do not convey food-uncleanness," words of R. Aqiva.

B. Said to him R. Yoḥanan b. Nuri,

(1) "If they are purchased with Second-tithe money, why do they not convey food-uncleanness?

(2) "And if they do not convey food-uncleanness, [then] they also (ʾp) should not be purchased with Second-tithe money."

M. Uks. 3:5

Here Aqiva makes a distinction regarding food-coloring: on the one hand, since it is used to prepare food for eating, it may be purchased with Second-tithe money; on the other hand, since it itself is not food, it does not convey food-uncleanness. Yoḥanan b. Nuri, as we have seen in our pericope at T. M.S. 1:13b, does not permit the purchase of coloring with Second-tithe money; for Yoḥanan, if the items may be purchased with Second-tithe, then logically they must be considered as food. This view is expressed in B(1). B(2) adds nothing to Yoḥanan's argument; it does, however, provide a final counter-point to Aqiva's position. Both traditions, T. M.S. 1:13b and M. Uks. 3:5, occur in a dialogue-form, rather than in dispute-form.

IV.i.7

A. R. Ishmael interpreted (*drš*),

(1) "And you shall give the money however much as you want," [as] a general statement (*kll*);

(2) "In cattle or in sheep or in wine or in liquor," [as] a limitation (*prṭ*);

(3) "And in anything which you want" (Deut. 14:26), this too is another general statement.

(4) General statement—limitation—general statement: you reason in terms of the limitation.

(5) That is to say, just as the limitation is interpreted as something which is (a) produce or (b) the product of produce of the land, so too it can be only something which is (a) produce or (b) the product of produce of the land.

B. R. Aqiva interprets (*mprš*),

(1) Just as the limitation is interpreted as something which is (a) produce or (b) a product of produce or (c) is connected with acts preliminary to eating produce,

(2) So too I have only something which is (a) produce or (b) the product of produce or (c) something connected with acts preliminary to eating produce.

y. M.S. 1:4, 52d-53a

y. provides a scriptural exegesis for Aqiva's opinion permitting the use of Second-tithe money to purchase items, such as saffron-cakes (T. M.S. 1:13, discussed above), which are used in the preparation of a meal but which themselves are not considered food. Ishmael's explanation of Deut. 14:26 is straightforward. (It recurs, without attribution to Ishmael, at b. B.Q. 54b, 63a, and b. Naz. 35b.) By contrast, Aqiva's exegesis, specifically the connection between the "limitation" in Deut. 14:26 ("cattle, or sheep or wine or liquor") and condiments (B(1)c) is less obvious. Aqiva's interpretation of Deut. 14:26 does not recur elsewhere in this stratum of the literature.

I.ii.21

A. [Concerning] olive presses
1. a. the exits of which are inside Jerusalem
b. and the contained space [of which] is outside [the city],
2. a. [or] the exits of which are outside (the city],
b. and the contained space of which is inside [the city]:

B. House of Shammai say,
1. "They do not redeem Second-tithe [produce] in such [olive presses],
a. "as though [the places] were inside [the city];
2. "nor do they eat lesser sanctified things in such [places],
a. "as though [the places] were outside [the city]."

C. But (*w*) House of Hillel say,
1. "[The area] from the wall and inwards is regarded as inside [the city],
2. "and from the wall and outwards is regarded as outside [the city]."

D. Said R. Yosah, "This is the teaching of R. Aqiva. The prior teaching (*mšnt r*ʾ*šwnh*) [was as follows]:
1. "House of Shammai [say],
a. " 'They do not redeem Second-tithe [produce] in such [places],
2. "But (*w*) House of Hillel say, 'Lo, [such places] are like the chambers [of the Temple]:
a. "whatever the exit of which is to the inside [is regarded] as inside;
b. " 'and whatever the exit of which is to the outside [is regarded] as outside.' "

T. M.S. 2:12b (Lieberman ed., p. 253 line 65—p. 254 line 72; y. M.S. 3:7, 54b)

The pericope focuses on the anomalous case of rooms which contain olive-presses and which are built in, or attached to, the wall of the city of Jerusalem. Conceivably the press could be built such that access is gained only by passing through the city, although most of the enclosed area of the room actually is outside the city; or the reverse, namely, most of the enclosed area is actually inside the city, but the only exit available opens outside the wall. The issue is, Does the sanctity of the city pertain to such an olive-press? The opinions in the pericope assume different positions regarding the nature of the holiness attached to Jerusalem. I shall first discuss these different views on the nature of holiness, and then I shall discuss the literary traits of the pericope.

Yosah, in D, ascribes the opinion given in C to Aqiva. My discussion accepts Yosah's statement; the tradition at T. M.S. 2:16, discussed below, attributes to Aqiva the same basic position, namely, the holiness of Jerusalem functions in the specific place defined by the boundaries of the city. With respect to the problem of the olive-press, Aqiva rules that the enclosed area should be divided as if by a line running parallel to the wall of the city. The section of the room on one side of the boundary-line is inside the city, and the sanctity attached to the city pertains to that section. Obviously the sanctity of the city does not pertain to the section of the room which lies on the other side of the boundary-line.

A different view of holiness underlies the opinion which Yosah refers, as "prior teaching," to the House of Hillel. According to D2 the opening to the olive-press is crucial. This position assumes that the holiness attached to Jerusalem, here explicitly compared to the Temple, flows into connected space. The sanctity of the city will therefore apply to an olive-press the exit of which opens into the city even though most of the enclosed space of the room actually is outside the wall of the city. On the other hand, if the only exit from the olive-press opens outside the city, the sanctity of Jerusalem does not pertain to the room even though most of the contained space may actually be inside the city's boundary. By contrast to Aqiva's position, which identifies the area in which the holiness of Jerusalem operates as a function of the boundaries of the city, this second position seems to identify the holiness attached to the city as active, with a potential for movement. It assumes that a physical barrier, here the wall of the room of the olive-press, can delimit the area in which the sanctity of the city operates. On Aqiva's view, the mere abstraction of a boundary-line, associated with but obviously separable from the wall of the city, interposes between the realm to which the rules of the holiness of the city pertain and the realm to which those rules do not pertain.

A-C are in a variation on the dispute-form. The form is complex and, taken together with the statement of Yosah, suggests discretion in dating the Houses' dispute to earlier than Usha. The form of Aqiva's "teaching" cannot be specified. In passing we should note that at M. M.S. 3:7 a different version of the Houses' dispute is given: the House of Shammai rule that the olive-press is in every circumstance considered inside the city; the House of Hillel is quoted as in B of our pericope; and Aqiva is not cited. M. keeps, however, the connection with the Temple; the next pericope, 3:8, digresses from the topic of Second-tithe produce and focuses solely on exits to and from the chambers in the Temple court. See discussion at Neusner, *Phar.*, vol. II, pp. 102-3, 112-13.

The phrase, "teaching of R. Aqiva," is attributed to Yosé at T. M.S. 2:1, discussed above. There it is not contrasted with a "prior teaching," as it is in this pericope. If we take "prior" in a temporal sense, then Yosah's statement alleges that the second position, with its view of holiness as active, predates Aqiva's position. Obviously such a view of holiness has a long history in Judaism.[58] It is striking, however, that Yosah attributes to Aqiva a contrary position, which sees holiness as subject to the interposition of an abstraction, such as a boundary-line.

I.ii.22

A. [Concerning] Second-tithe [produce] which entered Jerusalem and contracted uncleanness:

B. 1. a. Whether it contracted uncleanness by a Father of uncleanness

b. or whether it contracted uncleanness by an Offspring of uncleanness,

2. a. Whether inside [Jerusalem or]

b. whether outside,

C. 1. "House of Shammai say,

a. " 'All should be redeemed and eaten inside.'

2. "But (*w*) House of Hillel say,

a. " 'All should be redeemed and eaten inside,

b. " 'except that which contracted uncleanness

(1) by a Father of uncleanness

(2) outside,' "

words of R. Meir.

D. R. Judah says,

1. "House of Shammai say,

a. " 'All should be redeemed and eaten inside,

b. " 'except that which contracted uncleanness

(1) by a Father of uncleanness

(2) outside.'

2. "But (*w*) House of Hillel say,

a. " 'All should be redeemed and eaten outside

b. " 'except that which contracted uncleanness

(1) by an Offspring of uncleanness

(2) inside.' "

E. R. Leazar says,

1. "What contracted uncleanness by a Father of uncleanness,

a. "Whether inside [or] whether outside,

b. "Should be redeemed and eaten outside;

---

[58] See B. Levine, *In the Presence of the Lord* (Leiden, 1974); J. Neusner, *The Idea of Purity in Ancient Judaism* (Leiden, 1973), Part I: "The Biblical Legacy," pp. 7-31.

2. "What contracted uncleanness by an Offspring of uncleanness,
   a. "Whether inside [or] whether outside,
   b. "Should be redeemed and eaten inside."

F. R. Aqiva says,
   1. "What contracted uncleanness outside,
      a. "whether by a Father of uncleanness [or] whether by an Offspring of uncleanness,
      b. "should be redeemed and eaten outside; [59]
   2. "What contracted uncleanness inside,
      a. "whether by a Father of uncleanness or whether by an Offspring of uncleanness,
      b. "should be redeemed and eaten inside."

G. Said R. Simeon b. Leazar,
   1. "The House of Shammai and the House of Hillel did not dispute
      a. "that that which contracted uncleanness
         (1) by a Father of uncleanness
         (2) outside
         (3) should be redeemed and eaten outside
      b. "or (*w*) that that which contracted uncleanness
         (1) by an Offspring of uncleanness
         (2) inside
         (3) should be redeemed and eaten inside.
   2. "About what did they dispute? [They disputed] concerning
      a. "That which contracted uncleanness
         (1) by a Father of uncleanness
         (2) inside
         (3) or (*w*) by an Offspring of uncleanness
         (4) outside:
      b. "House of Shammai say,
         (1) " 'It is redeemed in the [same] place [that it contracted uncleanness],
         (2) " 'and it is eaten in the [same] place.
      c. "But (*w*) House of Hillel say,
         (1) " 'It is redeemed in the [same] place,
         (2) " 'but (*w*) it is eaten in all places.' "

T. M.S. 2:16 (Lieberman ed., p. 255 line 87—p. 256 line 101)

Like T. M.S. 2:12, discussed above, this pericope deals with the holiness of the city of Jerusalem. It is assumed that Second-tithe produce is to be brought to Jerusalem in a state of cleanness and eaten

[59] Ms. Vienna omits X-Z; Lieberman gives the reading of E, which includes X-Z, because of the parellel texts at M. Sheq. 8:7 and at Sifra Ṣav Pereq 8:7 (Weiss ed., p. 33a), discussed below.

in the city. If the produce contracts uncleanness it must be redeemed for its value in money, and the money is brought to the capital city and used to purchase consumable goods. (As noted above, at any time prior to entry into Jerusalem an Israelite has the option of redeeming Second-tithe produce for money even if the produce does not contract uncleanness.) The pericope focuses on Second-tithe produce which, once inside Jerusalem, is discovered to have contracted uncleanness. It is assumed that Second-tithe produce, once brought inside Jerusalem, is not subsequently taken outside the city. Obviously the produce must be redeemed for its value in money. The question is, Is it redeemed and subsequently eaten inside the city or outside? At issue is the relation, if any, between the holiness of the city and the uncleanness of the produce. I shall first discuss the opinions attributed to Aqiva and to Eliezer, the two Yavnean masters in the pericope; then I shall take up the opinions put forward by the Ushans, Meir, Judah, and Simeon b. Leazar; and finally I shall comment on the literary traits of the pericope.

Consistent with his position at T. M.S. 2:12, Aqiva in this pericope (F) holds that the place at which uncleanness is contracted is crucial. F envisions a line at the city's boundary: produce which contracts uncleanness on one side of the line, inside the city, should be redeemed and eaten inside Jerusalem; produce which contracts uncleanness on the other side of the line should be redeemed and eaten outside.

Eliezer, in E, alleges that the place at which uncleannes is contracted is irrelevant. Instead Eliezer holds that the virulence of the uncleanness is crucial. Second-tithe produce which is made unclean by a Father (e.g., a dead body or a reptile), the most virulent degree of uncleanness, should be removed from the city, regardless of whether it contracts the uncleanness inside or outside Jerusalem. The produce is to be redeemed and eaten outside the city. On the other hand, Second-tithe produce which is made unclean by an Offspring, a lesser degree of uncleanness, should be kept inside the city, again regardless of whether the uncleanness is contracted inside or outside Jerusalem. Clearly on Eliezer's view the uncleanness contracted by the produce can be measured against the holiness attached to the city of Jerusalem; thus, for instance, uncleanness contracted from the most virulent kind of source, a Father, overrides the holiness of the city. By contrast, on Aqiva's view it is not relevant to relate the degree of uncleanness to the nature of the holiness of the city. Aqiva's position does not envision that the uncleanness of the produce and the holiness of the city can affect one another. As at T. M.S. 2:12, Aqiva seems to assume that the holiness of Jerusalem is passive in the sense that it operates within a sphere defined by an abstraction, the boundary of the city. (It is not clear whether or not Eliezer assumes the view, again familiar from the pericope at T. M.S. 2:12, that the holiness of the city is itself potentially active, that it is affective and that it can be affected.)

Meir (C), Judah (D), and their younger contemporary, Simeon b. Leazar (G), formulate Houses' disputes. They do not refer to Aqiva and Eliezer. (M. M.S. 3:9 gives Judah's version of the Houses' dispute and does not mention the Yavnean masters.) Where for Aqiva the issues of the nature of the source of uncleanness and the site at which the uncleanness is contracted are quite distinct, for the Ushans the two issues must be brought together. The question is, How does the holiness of the city relate to the respective degrees of uncleanness communicated by the Father and by the Offspring? Two points here are noteworthy. First, the Ushans spell out every position logically consistent with the possible relationships between the virulence of the sources of uncleanness and the holiness of thhe city, except for one. No master rules that, regardless both of the source of the uncleanness and of the site at which the uncleanness is contracted, the produce must be redeemed and eaten outside the city. The Ushans clearly assume that the nature of the source of the uncleanness and the holiness attached to the city are categories that can be compared. The comparison of the two categories resembles the tack taken by Eliezer, in E. Clearly, however, most of the particular combinations attributed by the Ushans to the Houses are inexplicable by reference to a theory of the active nature of the holiness of the city. For example, in one case (Meir's Hillelites, in C2, and Judah's Shammaites, in D1) it is alleged that all produce should be redeemed and eaten inside the city, except for that which contracted uncleanness from a Father outside. The ruling distinguishes between a Father inside and a Father outside the city. But on what basis? In either case the source of uncleanness is the same, a Father. Regardless of the source of uncleanness the Second-tithe produce in question is inside the city, and if the holiness of the city mitigates the uncleanness transmitted by the one Father, why does it not mitigate the uncleanness transmitted by the other Father? It is apparent that the Ushans can make the two categories, the source of uncleanness and the holiness of the city, comparable, because, as on Aqiva's view of the nature of the latter, neither the uncleanness of the produce nor the holiness of the city is considered to be an active entity. Indeed, the

Ushans' opinions assume a third criterion against which to measure the correspondence between the two categories. That criterion is the intention of the pilgrim. The Ushans obviously disagree as to how the criterion applies to the situation. Thus, for example, according to Meir's Shammaites, in C1, all produce, regardless of the source of uncleanness and the place at which uncleanness is contracted, should be redeemed and eaten inside the city, presumably because the pilgrim had brought the produce into Jerusalem with the proper intention. According to Judah's Hillelites, in D2, however, all produce should be redeemed and eaten outside, except for that which contracts uncleanness from an Offspring inside; this position assumes, (1) proper intention never mitigates the affects of uncleanness contracted from a Father; (2) proper intention does not affect the status of produce which contracts uncleanness from an Offspring outside the city, for regardless of the intention of the pilgrim the produce is in fact unclean when it is brought into Jerusalem; and (3) proper intention does affect the status of the produce which contracts uncleanness from an Offspring inside the city, for the produce is clean at the moment that it is brought into the city. If we understand that the Ushans assume the applicability of the criteron of intention, then we can also understand why no master rules that all produce, regardless of the source of uncleanness or site of contraction, should be eaten outside the city. To such a rule intention is an irrelevant category.

It seems to me that the Ushans develop Aqiva's position. [60] Their positions assume that the holiness of the city and the uncleanness of the source are not active; for the Ushans this means that they can be manipulated as comparable legal categories. More decisively, however, the question of intention arises from Aqiva's position. Once entry into the city is accepted as a primary criterion for judgment, how the intention of the pilgrim at the moment of entry affects the status of the tithe follows as an obvious issue.

The second noteworthy point is that development may be observed from the opinions of the early Ushans, Meir (C) and Judah (D), to the opinion of the later Ushan, Simeon b. Eliezer (G). Simeon introduces for the first time a distinction between redeeming the produce and eating it (G2b-c). By this distinction Simeon manages to give an account of the Houses' dispute in which the Hillelites' position agrees with all of the disparate views attributed to the previous Yavnean and Ushan masters, with the sole exception of Meir's Shammaites.

[60] Cp. Neusner, HMLP, Vol. III, pp. 335-36.

The literary traits of the pericope confirm the view of the development of the law, as discussed above. As in the pericope at T. M.S. 2:12, the versions of the Houses' dispute in our pericope are complex in form. The discrepancies between the versions, the attributions to Meir, Judah, and Simeon b. Eliezer, and the formal literary evidence indicate that the Ushans have formulated the Houses' disputes to serve their own purposes. [61] Like the Houses' opinions, Eliezer's and Aqiva's sayings, in E and F, are elegantly formulated. Both E and F depend upon A.

As presently formulated the two opinions balance in structure. That structure is complicated, however, and the specific differences between the two opinions are not striking:

Eliezer: Father/outside — Offspring/inside
Aqiva: Outside/outside — Inside/inside

Eliezer's and Aqiva's opinions could stand independent of one another.

We should note that Eliezer's and Aqiva's (and the various Houses') opinions do not necessarily relate exclusively to problematic Second-tithe produce. M. Sheq. 8:6-7 relate the respective opinions to sacrifices brought to the Temple:

A. [Concerning] the flesh of the most holy things which contracted uncleanness,
B. 1. Whether [it contracted uncleanness]
  a. by a Father of uncleanness
    (1) or whether by an Offspring of uncleanness
  b. Whether [it contracted uncleanness]
    (1) inside [the Temple-court]
    (2) or whether outside:
C. House of Shammai say,
  1. "All should be burned inside,
  2. except that which contracted uncleanness
    a. by a Father of uncleanness
    b. outside."
D. But (*w*) House of Hillel say,
  1. "All should be burned outside,
  2. except that which contracted uncleanness
    a. by an Offspring of uncleanness
    b. inside."

M. Sheq. 8:6

---

[61] Neusner, *Phar.*, Vol. I, pp. 113-16.

E. R. Eliezer says,
1. "That which contracted uncleanness by a Father of uncleanness,
a. "whether inside [or] whether outside,
b. "should be burned outside;
2. "and that which contracted uncleanness by an Offspring of uncleanness,
a. "whether inside [or] whether outside,
b. "should be burned inside."

F. R. Aqiva says,
"Wherever it contracted uncleanness it should be burned [literally, "The place place of [contracting] its uncleanness-*there* is its burning."]."

M. Sheq. 8:7

Here *inside/outside* refers to the Temple-court and not to the city of Jerusalem, as in the pericope at T. M.S. 2:16. Formulaic usage of *inside/outside* frequently occurs in contexts relating to the Temple and usually refers in those contexts to the Temple-court. [62] By contrast, in M. formulaic usage of *inside/outside* with reference to Jerusalem is unusual. [63] That does not necessarily mean, however, that the discussion concerning the "flesh of the most holy things," and not the discussion concerning Second-tithe produce, provides the primary context for the apodoses attributed to the Houses, to Eliezer and to Aqiva. The *inside/outside* formula serves equally well (or poorly) in both contexts.

Strikingly in contrast to Judah's Houses' and Eliezer's, Aqiva's opinion occurs in different formulations at T. M.S. 2:16 and at M. Sheq. 8:6-7. As the following synopsis shows, the superscription (nos. 1-6), Judah's Houses' dispute (nos. 14-19), and Eliezer's opinion (nos. 20-28), recur almost *verbatim* in the two texts, except for changes absolutely necessary to the different contexts (nos. 1, 15, 18, 24, 28). 24, 28).

T. M.S. 2:16	*M. Sheq. 8:6-7*
1. [Concerning] Second-tithe — [produce] which entered Jerusalem	1. [Concerning] the flesh of the most holy things
2. *and* contracted uncleanness,	2. *which* contracted uncleanness,
3. whether *it contracted uncleanness* by a Father of uncleanness,	3. whether by a Father of uncleanness,
4. *or* whether *it contracted uncleanness* by an Offspring of uncleanness,	4. whether by an Offspring of uncleanness,
5. whether inside,	5. " " "
6. whether outside:	6. " " "

62 E.g., M. Zev. 2:1, 3:2, 7:5; M. Men. 7:3, 11:4.
63 See M. Men. 11:2.

	T. M.S. 2:16		*M. Sheq. 8:6-7*
7.	"House of Shammai say,	7.	— — —
8.	" 'All should be redeemed and eaten inside.'	8.	— — —
9.	"But the House of Hillel say,	9.	— — —
10.	" 'All should be redeemed and eaten inside,	10.	— — —
11.	" 'except that which contracted uncleanness by a Father outside,' "	11.	— — —
12.	words of R. Meir.	12.	— — —
13.	R. Judah says,	13.	— — —
14.	"House of Shammai say,	14.	” ” ”
15.	" 'All should be *redeemed and eaten* inside,	15.	"All should be *burned* inside,
16.	" 'except that which contracted uncleanness by a Father outside.'	16.	” ” ”
17.	"But the House of Hillel say,	17.	” ” ”
18.	" 'All should be *redeemed and eaten* outside,	18.	"All should be *burned* outside,
19.	" 'except that which contracted uncleanness by an Offspring inside."	19.	” ” ”
20.	R. Leazar says,	20.	R. Eliezer says,
21.	"What contracted uncleanness by a Father,	21.	” ” ”
22.	"whether inside,	22.	” ” ”
23.	"whether outside,	23.	” ” ”
24.	"should be *redeemed and eaten* outside;	24.	"should be *burned* outside;
25.	"what contracted uncleanness by an Offspring	25.	” ” ”
26.	"whether inside,	26.	” ” ”
27.	"whether outside,	27.	” ” ”
28.	"should be *redeemed and eaten* inside."	28.	"should be *burned* inside."
29.	R. Aqiva says,	29.	” ” ”
30.	"What contracted uncleanness outside,	30.	— — —
31.	"whether by a Father,	31.	— — —
32.	"whether by an Offspring,	32.	— — —
33.	"should be redeemed and eaten outside;	33.	— — —
34.	"what contracted uncleanness inside,	34.	— — —
35.	"whether by a Father,	35.	— — —
36.	"or whether by an Offspring,	36.	— — —
37.	"should be redeemed and eaten inside."	37.	— — —
38.	— — —	38.	"Wherever it contracted uncleanness it should be burned."

The editor of M. Sheq. 8:7 has attributed to Aqiva language which recalls Simeon's revision of the Houses' dispute at T. M.S. 2:16.

T. M.S. 2:16: Simeon b. Leazar	*M. Sheq. 8:7: Aqiva*
"House of Shammai: It is redeemed in the [same] place and eaten in the [same] place. "House of Hillel: It is redeemed and eaten in all places."	"The place of contracting its uncleanness—*there* is its burning."

We should expect that a different formulation of Aqiva's opinion, comparable to the formulation of Eliezer's opinion at M. Sheq. 8:7, also circulated. And in fact Sifra gives that formulation:

A. R. Eliezer says, "...[= M. Sheq 8:7E]..."
B. R. Aqiva says,
  1. "That which contracted uncleanness outside,
    a. "whether by a Father of uncleanness [or] whether by an Offspring of uncleanness,
    b. "should be burned outside;
  2. "that which contracted uncleanness inside,
    a. "whether by a Father of uncleanness [or] whether by an Offspring of uncleanness,
    b. "should be burned inside."

Sifra Ṣav Pereq 8:7 (Weiss ed., p. 33a)

Aqiva's position concerning the nature of holiness, whether it pertains to the city of Jerusalem or to the Temple, remains the same.

II.iii.2

A. Scripture states, "[Then you shall turn {the tithe-product} into money,] and you shall bind up the money (*wṣrth hksp*) [in your hand and go to the place...]" (Deut. 14:25).

B. "["Bind up" refers to] a thing which is usually bound up [in the way that money is bound up]," words of R. Ishmael.

C. R. Aqiva says, "[*wṣrth* refers to] a thing upon which there is a figure (*ṣwrh*)."

D. This excludes a token on which there is no figure [imprinted]."

Sifré Deut. 107 (Finkelstein ed., p. 167 line 19—p. 168 line 21)

The legal problem concerns the nature of the currency for which Second-tithe produce may be exchanged. Ishmael's exegesis of Deut. 14:25 draws on the obvious meaning of the words of the verse; Ishmael defines "money" as whatever is handled like money. By contrast, Aqiva builds on the similarity between two different words, *wṣrth* ("bind up") and *ṣwrh* ("figure"), to limit the definition of the type of money for which Second-tithe produce may be exchanged. Aqiva holds that only minted currency may be exchanged for Second-tithe produce. (The issue recurs at M. M.S. 1:2, M. Ed. 3:2 and T. M.S. 1:4 without attribution either to Aqiva or to Ishmael.) The masters' opinions balance in syllables:

Ishmael: *d-br š-dr-kw ly-ṣ-rr*
Aqiva: *d-br š-yś ʿlyw ṣw-rh*

D notes that Aqiva's position excludes tokens, that is, unminted pieces of metal which function as currency.[64]

viii. *Ḥallah*

I.i.38

A. Produce from abroad which entered the land [of Israel] is liable for dough-offering.

B. [Concerning produce which] went out from here to there:

1. R. Eliezer declares liable.
2. And R. Aqiva declares exempt.

M. Hal. 2:1

Priests receive a share of all dough prepared for baking (Num. 15:17-21). The gift is called "dough-offering." The masters assume that the obligation for dough-offering is incurred when produce is made into dough.

Once again we encounter a dispute concerning the nature of holiness. Here Eliezer and Aqiva differ regarding the liability of produce exported from the land of Israel for dough-offering. Aqiva exempts the produce from dough-offering, because at the moment that it is made into dough it is outside the land. The fact that the produce grew inside the land of Israel is irrelevant. The element of holiness associated with the gift of dough-offering, on Aqiva's view, is a function of abstract, logical rules; it comes into play only at the moment specified by those rules. By contrast, Eliezer assumes that the element of holiness associated with dough-offering is inherent in the produce. Eliezer therefore rules that exported produce is liable for dough-offering.

B is in dispute-form. The masters do not respond to A1, although it would be easy enough to spell out their opinions on the liability of imported produce for dough-offering. Eliezer would exempt such produce from dough-offering, for it lacks, on his view, the element of holiness inherent in produce which grows inside the land of Israel. Aqiva would make imported produce liable, so long as it is inside the land at the moment at which it is made into dough.

---

[64] See Lieberman, *TK, Seder Zeraʿim*, p. 715.

II.ii.1

A. "When I bring you there" (Num. 15:17). From this you say,

B. 1. "Produce from abroad which they imported into the land is liable for dough-offering.

2. "[Concerning produce which] they exported from here to there:

a. "R. Eliezer declares [it] liable [for dough-offering].

b. "And R. Aqiva exempts [it from dough-offering]."

C. R. Judah says,

1. "[Concerning] produce from abroad which they imported into the land:

a. "R. Eliezer declares [it] exempt.

(1) "As it is said, 'When you eat of the food of the land'" (Num. 15:19). [This is said] to exclude produce from outside the land.

b. "And R. Aqiva declares [it] liable [for dough-offering].

(1) "As it is said, 'There' (15:18). [Dough-offering is due] whether [the produce is] of the land or from outside the land.

2. "[Concerning produce which] they exported from here to there:

a. "R. Eliezer declares [it] liable.

(1) "As it is said, 'And when you eat of the food of the land' (15:19). [That is], whether [you eat the food] in the land or outside the land.

b. "And R. Aqiva exempts [it].

(1) "As it is said, 'There' (15:18). There you are liable; outside from there you are exempt."

Sifré Num. 110 (Horowitz ed., p. 113 lines 8-13)

Sifré provides an Ushan attribution for Aqiva's and Eliezer's opinions on the liability of imported and exported produce for dough-offering. As to be expected, the innovation of Sifré is to provide scriptural warrants for the masters' views.

B is M. Hal. 2:2, almost *verbatim*. In C Judah spells out Aqiva's and Eliezer's opinions with regard to both imported and exported produce. The scriptural exegeses are based on the opening words of the injunction regarding the dough-offering at Num. 15:18-21: "When you come into the land to which I bring you (literally, "the land to which I bring you *there*"), and when you eat of the food of the land, you shall present an offering to the Lord..." (15:18b-19). Sifré alleges that Eliezer derives his opinion from the phrase, "the food of the land" (vs. 19). That is, Eliezer holds that dough-offering must be given even for produce grown in Palestine and subsequently exported. The crucial point is the physical connection with the land. Aqiva's exegesis depends upon the significance of the extra word, *there*, in vs. 18. The emphasis on presence in the land, signified by the repetition, "the land to which I bring you *there*," means, on Aqiva's view, that the offering spoken of in the verses is required only for produce actually inside the land of Israel.

IV.i.8

A. "Abroad, etc." It is written: "to the land to which (*šmh*, literally, "there") I bring you" (Num. 15:18). "There" you are liable. You are not liable outside the land. This teaching is according to the words of R. Meir.

B. But the words of R. Judah [are as follows]:

1. "[Concerning] produce [from] abroad which they imported into the land:

a. R. Eliezer exempts [it from dough-offering],

b. and R. Aqiva declares [it] liable."

2. What is the reason of R. Eliezer? "Food of the land" (Num. 15:19). Not food from abroad.

3. What is the reason of R. Aqiva? "To the land to which I bring you" (15:18). "There" you are liable [for dough-offering], whether the produce [which you use to prepare dough] is from the land or whether the produce is from abroad.

y. Hal. 2:1, 58b

A credits to Meir the exegesis which Judah credits to Aqiva (B3; also Sifré Num. 110, discussed above). As at T. Ter. 5:10 and T. M.S. 2:1, Meir does not mention Aqiva's views.

B gives Aqiva's and Eliezer's views on imported produce and not, as in M., the masters' views on exported produce. Perhaps this is because the scriptural exegeses attributed to the masters refer to food in the land and are obviously more germane to imported produce than they are to exported produce. If this is the case, it suggests that the selection of imported produce by the editor of the pericope in y. represents an effort to adapt to the exegetical interpretation connected with the master's opinions. It also suggests that the formulation of the dispute in M., which focuses on exported produce, stands independent of the exegetical tradition.

I.i.39

A. One who cannot prepare his dough in cleanness should prepare small clumps the size of a *qab*; but (*w*) he should not prepare it [i.e., his dough] in uncleanness.

B. But (*w*) R. Aqiva says, "He should prepare it in uncleanness; but he should not prepare small clumps the size of a *qab*."

1. For (*š*) in the same way that he designates what is clean [as dough-offering] he should also designate what is unclean;

2. for (*š*) the one [i.e., dough which has not contracted uncleanness] he designates dough-offering, and for the other [i.e., dough which has contracted uncleanness] he designates dough-offering; but dough-offering is not designated for clumps the size of a *qab.*

M. Hal. 2:3b (y. Hal. 2:4, 58a, y. Hal 3:2, 59a)

Like Heave-offering, dough-offering is given to priests; if it contracts uncleanness, it cannot be eaten by priests and must be burned. What if a person cannot prepare his dough-offering in cleanness? Both opinions in this pericope assume that the obligation for dough-offering does not apply to small clumps the size of a *qab.* [65] According to B, the person should prepare small pieces of dough, each the size of a *qab*, and thus avoid liability. Aqiva holds, however, that the person should not prepare the small pieces of dough, which presumably is an irregular procedure; the person should not avoid the obligation even though the offering will be vitiated. This position obviously bothers the glossator (B1-2). Aqiva's position here is consistent with that assigned to him at M. Pes. 1:6; he stands with Joshua—and against Eliezer— in maintaining that in certain circumstances one may take actions which are certain to result in making unclean something which is clean. [67]

A-B are in a variation on the dispute-form. A is a complete sentence. Aqiva's opinion, in B, seems to gloss A. B1-2 depend upon Aqiva's saying.

I.ii.23

A. One who cannot prepare his dough in cleanness should prepare small clumps the size of a *qab*; but (*w*) he should not prepare it [i.e., his dough] in uncleanness.

B. But (*w*) R. Aqiva says, "He should prepare it [i.e., his dough] in uncleanness; but he should not prepare small clumps the size of a *qab*."

1. For (*š*) in the same way that he designates what is clean [as dough-offering] he should also designate what is unclean;

2. for (*š*) the one [i.e., dough which has not contracted uncleanness] he designates dough-offering, and for the other [i.e., dough which has contracted uncleanness] he designates dough-offering (Lieberman: *qwrʾ...lšm*); but dough-offering is not designated for clumps the size of a *qab.*

---

[65] For the issue of the minimum size which obligates for dough-offering, see discussion on M. Hal. 4:4-5, below.

[66] *Eliezer*, Vol. I, pp. 63-66, 117-19; II, pp. 104-5.

C. 1. They said before R. Aqiva,
2. "They don't say to a man,
3. " 'Get up and commit a transgression in order to gain some benefit (*ʿmwd wḥt bšbyl štzkh*).'
4. "[or] 'Get up and spoil something so that it may be repaired.' "

T. Hal. 1:9 (Lieberman ed., p. 277 lines 25-30)

A-B are M. Hal. 2:3b. C1 recurs several times in M.-T. Here, however, it introduces an unrebutted criticism of Aqiva's position, and that is unusual. Elsewhere (e.g., M. Shev. 8:9, 10; M. Kel. 25:4) it introduces a question to which Aqiva responds.

C3 and 4 seem to be stock-phrases. C1 corresponds somewhat more closely than C2 to the situation in A-B. Eliezer's view, namely, that a person should not perform an action that will definitely cause something clean to become unclean, stands behind C.

I.i.40

A. [Concerning] someone who had become a proselyte and who [subsequently] had dough in his possession;
[If the dough] was prepared
1. before he converted, it is exempt [from dough-offering];
2. and [if] after he converted, it is liable;
3. but (*w*) if there is doubt [as to when the dough had been prepared], it is liable for dough-offering,
a. but [because there is doubt as to whether or not the dough-offering is due, people who misappropriate the offering] are not liable for the [added] fifth [i.e., the penalty for misusing consecrated property].

B. R. Aqiva says, "Everything [i.e., the obligations relating to dough-offering] follows from the forming of a light crust in the oven."

M. Hal. 3:6

The problem concerns the moment at which dough becomes liable for dough-offering. Aqiva, in B, alleges that dough becomes liable when a light crust forms during the baking. Prior to that time small bits may be broken off and eaten as a snack without obligation for giving dough-offering; the situation may be understood on analogy with crop during its "season of tithes" (Bert.; cp. discussion on T. Ma. 3:14, above). An alternative view is that dough becomes liable at the moment at which it is rolled out (if the flour is made from wheat) or kneaded (if the flour is made from barley). This latter view is stated at M. Hal. 3:1 and is assumed in all of the cases given in 3:1-5. The pericope which immediately precedes ours, 3:5, focuses on the liability of dough which a gentile gives to an Israelite. A of our pericope presumably gives the next case in sequence, the dough of a proselyte, and assumes that liability is incurred at the moment that the dough is rolled out or kneaded. Thus if the proselyte had converted prior to rolling out his dough, when it is finally rolled out the dough becomes liable; but if the person converted after rolling out his dough, the dough remains exempt from dough-offering, for the dough of a gentile is exempt and at the crucial moment the person was still a gentile.

Aqiva's view that dough becomes liable at the moment at which a light crust forms during the baking could be applied to each of the cases in the preceding pericopae, as well as to the case of the dough of a proselyte (Maim.). In this connection MR notes, first, that the language of B, "Everything," suggests a general statement, and second, that 3:6 concludes the series of cases begun at 3:1. 3:7 turns to a different topic. We may note that, on Aqiva's view, liability for dough-offering is incurred after the yeast cells have died during the process of baking; at that time the bread is a fit offering. [68]

By contrast to the complex form of the statements in A, B gives a simple declarative sentence. Aqiva's saying neither specifies *liable/exempt* nor responds directly to the superscription which serves A. As it stands, however, B cannot be understood apart from the foregoing.

For other instances in which Aqiva focuses on issues of *gmr ml'kh*, that is, fixing the moment at which liability for tithing is incurred, see discussions on M. Pe. 1:6 and on M. M.S. 5:8, above.

I.ii.24

A. [Concerning] someone who had become a proselyte and who [subsequently] had dough in his possession:

B. "Before a light crust had formed, [the dough] is liable; but after a light crust had formed, it is exempt;" words of R. Aqiva.

C. R. Yoḥanan b. Nuri says, "Before he rolled it out if the flour was made from] wheat or (*w*) [before] he kneaded it into a lump [if the flour was made from] barley, [the dough] is liable; [but if he had previously] rolled it out or (*w*) kneaded it into a lump, it is exempt."

D. In the name of R. Judah b. Bethryra they said, "[The obligation for dough-offering is incurred] from [the moment] that the dough can be divided into lumps."

T. Hal. 1:12 (Lieberman ed., p. 278 lines 41-45)

---

[67] This was suggested to me by Rabbi Richard A. Marker.

T. gives a different formulation of the problem which occurs at M. Hal. 3:6. Aqiva's opinion is set in a dispute-form. In T. Aqiva does not specify "in an oven," as at M.B. In context Aqiva's saying relates directly to the case of dough of a proselyte. The view which is assumed throughout M. Hal. 3:1-6A, namely, that liability is incurred at the moment that the dough is rolled out or kneaded, is attributed in T. to Yoḥanan b. Nuri. D introduces a third view concerning liability for dough-offering: Judah b. Bethyra, another Yavnean master, holds that liability is incurred when the dough can be made into small cakes, or "twists" (Lieberman). D stands outside the dispute-form of A-C.

II.ii.2

A. When is the obligation for dough-offering incurred [literally, "What is its *gmr mlᵓkth*"]?

B. "The light crust forming in the oven," words of R. Aqiva.

C. R. Yoḥanan b. Nuri says, "From when he rolled it out [if the flour is made from] wheat or (*w*) [from when] he kneaded it [if the flour is made from] barley."

Sifré Num. 110 (Horowitz ed., p. 114 lines 5-7)

Sifré explicitly focuses on defining the action which completes the process of preparing dough. By contrast to M. and T., Sifré does not refer to the case of the proselyte's dough. Aqiva's and Yoḥanan's opinions are consistent with those attributed to them in T.

A-C are in dispute-form. The dispute-formulation and the attribution to Yoḥanan b. Nuri echo T. But the phrase, "the light crust forming in the oven," resembles M.'s, "Everything from *the light crust forming in oven.*" Sifré may conflate the versions of Aqiva's saying as they occur in M. and T.

I.i.41

A. [Concerning] one who takes dough-offering from [one] *qab* [of dough]:

B. R. Aqiva says, "It is a [valid] dough-offering."

C. But (*w*) sages say, "It is not a [valid] dough-offering."

M. Hal. 4:4

I.i.42

D. [Concerning] two *qabim* [of dough] from which dough-offering has been taken,

E. [One dough-offering having been taken] for one [*qab*] by itself and [another dough-offering having been taken] for the other [*qab*] by itself,

F. [If] one subsequently made [the two *qabim* into] a single [piece of] dough:
G. R. Aqiva exempts [the piece of dough from dough-offering].
H. But (*w*) sages declare [it] liable [for dough-offering].
I. It turns out that his stringency is a leniency.

M. Hal. 4:5 (y. Hal. 3:1, 59a; y. Hal. 4:5, 59d-60a)

Aqiva's statements in this pericope assume that dough-offering can be given from one *qab*; this view seems to contradict Aqiva's opinion at M. Hal. 2:3b, discussed above. I shall first consider the literary and legal traits of this pericope; then I shall refer to a related Houses' dispute at M. Ed. 1:2; and finally I shall take up the problem of the discrepancy in the reports about Aqiva's opinion on the minimum measure for dough-offering.

The pericope gives two separate dispute forms (A-C; D-H). The apodoses in both cases balance nicely (*dough-offering* vs. *not dough-offering*; *exempts* vs. *declare liable*). D-F, a lengthy apodosis, make it clear that the second dispute-form builds upon the first: D follows the language of A (A: *takes/dough-offering*; D: *dough-offering/taken*); E explicates what perhaps should be obvious; and F specifies the new problem. The gloss in I refers to Aqiva's views.

The legal issue concerns the status of an offering taken from a single *qab* of dough. The first dispute focuses directly on that issue. The second dispute, building on the first, gives a simple conundrum: what of a piece of dough made from two one-*qab* pieces, for both of which offerings have previously been taken? Aqiva rules consistently that an offering taken from one *qab* is valid. Although this leads to the stricter position in the first dispute, it leads to the more lenient position in the second dispute, as noted by I.

Aqiva's view recalls Shammai's opinion at M. Ed. 1:2:

Shammai says, "[Dough made] from one *qab* [is liable] for dough-offering."
But (*w*) Hillel says, "From two *qabim*."
And sages say, "It is not according to the opinion of either.
But one *qab* and a half [is] liable to dough-offering."
And when the weights were made greater,
They said, "Five quarters of a *qab* are liable."
R. Yosé says, "Five [quarters only] are exempt; but five and aught are liable."

M. Ed. 1:2

Neusner notes that this tradition is one of several which "are highly credible and may well be authentic traditions of the masters!" Shammai is no mere foil but is represented as of equal importance as Hillel. Also, the issue was of primary concern to the Pharisaic *ḥavurah.* [68] This suggests that Aqiva's position might reflect prior tradition. On the other hand, Neusner points out that the dispute between the ancient masters is first attested by Yosé, an Ushan.

We now take up the problem of the discrepancy between this pericope and M. Hal. 2:3b. There are two possibilities. Either the two reports about Aqiva's opinion on the minimum quantity for dough-offering contradict each other. Or the issue of our pericope is not the specification of a minimum measurement. Lieberman prefers the latter. On this view, A pertains to the status of an offering given from a small quantity of dough *not obligated* for dough-offering. Aqiva and the sages assume, as at M. Hal. 2:3b, a minimum obligatory measure greater than one *qab.* But Aqiva focuses here on the donor's intention. Lieberman observes [69] that the sages' view in the following tradition is comparable to the opinion attributed to Aqiva in our pericope:

> Said R. Eliezer b. Jacob, "[Concerning] one who takes dough-offering from [one] *qab* [of dough]: To what is he comparable? To [one who] gives as Heave-offering produce which has not yet reached one-third of its full growth, for [just as in the case of giving Heave-offering] the gift is not considered a valid offering, [so too in the case of one who gives a piece from one *qab* of dough, the gift is not a valid offering]."
>
> But sages say, "[One who takes dough-offering from one *qab* is comparable] to [one who] gives as Heave-offering produce which has not yet been completely processed (*gmr mlʾkh),* for [just as] if a person gave [the produce] as Heave-offering the gift is a valid offering, [so too if a person gives a piece from one *qab* of dough, the gift is a valid offering]."
>
> T. Hal. 2:5 (Lieberman ed., p. 279 line 13—p. 280 line 16)

The sages compare the problematic gift of dough-offering to Heave-offering taken from crop which has entered its season of tithes but which has not yet been processed. The Heave-offering is valid, for once crop reaches its season it is considered potentially liable for tithes, although liability is not necessarily incurred until the crop is completely processed. By contrast to the sages, Eliezer compares the gift of dough-offering to Heave-offering designated from produce which has not yet

---

[68] *Phar.*, Vol. I, pp. 305-7, 338.

[69] *TK, Seder Zeraᶜim*, p. 808.

entered its season of tithes; such an offering is invalid. *Both* Eliezer and the sages assume that the minimum quantity of dough which incurs liability for dough-offering exceeds one *qab*. The topic-statement in T., "Concerning one who takes dough-offering from [one] *qab*," is the same as the topic-statement in A of our pericope in M. Eliezer's view corresponds to the sages' in M., and the sages' opinion in T. corresponds to Aqiva's.

Eliezer b. Jacob is an Ushan.

I.i.43

A. And these are given to any priest:
(1) the devoted things; and
(2) the firstlings; and
(3) the redemption-price of a [first-born] son; and
(4) the redemption-price of the first-born of an ass; and
(5) the shoulder, and
(6) the two cheeks, and
(7) the maw [of animal sacrifices]; and
(8) the first of the fleece; and
(9) the oil [designated as Heave-offering which happens to contract uncleanness and which consequently must be] burned; and
(10) the holy things of the Temple; and
(11) the first-fruits.

B. R. Judah prohibits with regard to (*b*) first-fruits.

C. [Concerning] vetches of Heave-offering:

D. R. Aqiva permits [giving them to any priest].

E. But (*w*) sages prohibit.

M. Hal. 4:9

A lists eleven items which "are given to any priest." That is, any priest is trusted to protect these items from contracting uncleanness. Judah, in B, disputes the last item on the list; he holds that, because first-fruits are not necessarily consumed within the Temple precincts but are only distributed there, they can be entrusted only to a priest who is also a *ḥaver*.

The question in C-E concerns to whom vetches of Heave-offering can be given. Aqiva, in D, permits giving vetches to any priest. This follows from his opinion at M. M.S. 2:4, "Whatever concerns [vetches designated as Heave-offering] may be done in uncleanness." This opinion is based on the observation that vetches serve as animal fodder, and people usually do not eat them. Aqiva permits giving vetches of Heave-offering to any priest because he believes it immaterial whether or not the vetches contract uncleanness. By contrast, the list in A and

Judah's saying in B focus on items that can be given to any priest only when it is clear that, whether or not he is a *ḥaver*, he will protect them from contracting uncleanness.

The sages, in D, reject the distinction that Aqiva draws between produce usually given as Heave-offering and produce given as Heave-offering only in exceptional circumstances. The sages assume that, if the vetches have been designated as Heave-offering, they must be protected from contracting uncleanness; this entails giving them only to a priest who is also a *ḥaver*.

C-E are in dispute-form. Without the phrase, "And these are given to any priest," which introduces the list in A, the opinions in D and in E are unintelligible.

The dispute between Aqiva and the sages does not concern dough-offering. It occurs at M. Hal. 4:9 because it has been attached to A-B. A-B, in turn, occurs here because of the statement at the end of the preceding pericope, "and [dough-offering] may be given to any priest."

IV.i.9

A. The teaching [at M. Hal. 1:3 concerning the residue of the *omer*] is not according to the view of R. Aqiva,

B. For R. Aqiva held [them] liable [both] for dough-offering and [also] for tithes.

y. Hal. 1:4, 57d

The context in y. is a discussion of M. Hal. 1:3, which lists items liable for dough-offering but not for tithes. Among the items listed is "the residue of the *omer*," that is, the portion of flour that remains left over, unused, in the preparation of the meal-offering for Passover. y. notes that Aqiva holds a contrary opinion: the residue should be liable for both dough-offering and tithes. M. Men. 10:4b gives the statement to which y. presumably refers:

A. They spread out the grain in the Temple courtyard and the wind winnows it. They set it in a gristmill. Then they removed a tenth [of an *ephah* of flour], which [in turn was] sifted through thirteen sieves. And the residue is redeemed and may be eaten by any person. And it is liable for dough-offering, but (*w*) it is exempt from tithes.

B. R. Aqiva declared [it] liable for dough-offering and for tithes.

M. Men. 10:4b

The anonymous statement, which Aqiva disputes, is consistent with the anonymous list at M. Hal. 1:3.

ix. ᶜ*Orlah*

I.i.44

("If a man had bunches of fenugreek that were Mixed-kind of the vineyard, they must be burned; if they were confused with others, all must be burned," words of R. Meir. But sages say, "They are neutralized in two-hundred and one."

M. Or. 3:6)

A. For R. Meir used to say, "Whatever one usually counts [as, for example, bunches of fenugreek are counted when they are sold] renders [other produce] prohibited [when combined in a mixture with that produce; the mixture must be burned]."

B. But sages say, "Only six things render [other produce] prohibited [when they are combined in a mixture]."

C. And R. Aqiva says, "Seven."

D. And these are they: (1) nuts of Perech, and (2) pomegranates of Badan, and (3) sealed jars [of wine], and (4) beet-root-tops, and (5) cabbage- stalks, and (6) Greek gourds.

E. R. Aqiva says, "Also (ᵓ*p*) the loaves of a householder."

F. What is fitting for ᶜ*orlah* is ᶜ*orlah* [and what is fitting] for Mixed-kinds of the vineyard is Mixed-kinds of the vineyard. [Danby, p. 93: "To such among these as may come from ᶜ*orlah*-fruit the law of ᶜ*orlah* applies; and to such among these as may come from Mixed-seeds of the vineyard the law of Mixed-seeds of the vineyard applies."]

M. Or. 3:7 (b. A.Z. 74a, b. Bes. 3b)

The issue is the status of items mixed with consecrated produce. The preceding pericopae, M. Or. 3:1-6, give particular cases of doubtful mixtures. Our pericope, 3:7, gives, first, Meir's summary (A) and, second, the list, with Aqiva (B-E). The ultimate authority behind the pericope implies that the two units address the same issue, the doubtful status of items in a mixture. Meir's opinion, however, seems to relate to the cases in the foregoing pericopae which focus on problems of mixtures of items with ᶜ*orlah*-produce. In three of those pericopae, 3:1, 2, and 6, Meir disputes with unnamed sages; Meir claims that all items in the respective mixtures should be burned, and the sages claim that the ᶜ*orlah*-produce is neutralized in a mixture of two-hundred and one. By contrast to Meir's opinion, which the context suggests relates to ᶜ*orlah*-produce, the list of items in B-D obviously does not relate, at least exclusively, to ᶜ*orlah*-produce. The laws of ᶜ*orlah* do not apply to beet-root tops (no. 4) or to cabbage-stalks (no. 5). This draws the gloss in F which asserts that the list pertains both to ᶜ*orlah*-produce and also to produce of Mixed-kinds of the vineyard. What is absolutely clear, however, is that the chronological relationship suggested in the pericope (Meir disputes with sages whose opinion is glossed by Aqiva) is impossible.

It would be easy enough to construct an Aqiva-dispute-form from the lemmas in B-E. Most probably it would be the variation in which a master, here Aqiva, seems to gloss an anonymous rule, as in the following:

> Six things, if consecrated, render other produce prohibited when combined in a mixture: nuts of Perach; pomegranates of Badan; sealed jars [of wine]; beet-root tops; cabbage-stalks; and Greek gourds.
> Aqiva says, "Also the loaves of a householder."

If such a form stands behind B-E, then E has generated C.

Problematic is the identification of the context of the Aqivan tradition and the circumstances which would have brought the tradition into connection with Meir's opinion. Sens, following the suggestion of the Palestinian Amora, R. Yonah, suggests that the list may pertain to Heave-offering produce. This suggestion provides a category, Heave-offering, which accounts for the language of the tradition, "renders consecrated" (B). It also provides a category which could include each of the items on the list. But what marks off these six, or seven, items in relation to Heave-offering? Each of the items elsewhere in M.-T. is designated as in some way unusual; the only item on the list which is explicitly mentioned in M.-T. Ter., namely, beet-root tops, occurs in a context which might be relevant. At T. Ter. 5:10, Judah b. Baba, Aqiva's younger contemporary, states,

> I am one of those fit to teach that if they should bring to me [the case of] beet-root tops, I would say that they are neutralized in one-hundred and one.

The context is a discussion of whether all items in a mixture with consecrated produce become prohibited or whether in certain circumstances the consecrated produce can be neutralized. Except for Judah b. Baba, the masters cited are Ushans (Judah, Simeon, and Meir). Eliezer, Joshua and Aqiva are cited at the end of the long, composite pericope, but the Yavneans focus on a different issue (see discussion on T. Ter. 5:10b, above). In M.-T. Ter. Aqiva, as seen above, does not discuss the special nature of any particular kind of produce.

> II.i.3
> ["When you come into the land and plant all kinds of trees for food, then you shall count their fruit as forbidden {alternatively, 'you shall make their fruit ᶜ*orlah*'}" (Lev. 19:23).]

A. ...It is possible that I might include [among the items liable for ᶜ*orlah*] undeveloped grapes and half-ripened fruit. Scripture [therefore] states, "Their fruit."

B. "[Which means] their fruit [i.e., excluding items like undeveloped grapes which are not yet considered to be fruit]," words of R. Yosé the Galilean.

C. R. Aqiva says, " 'Then you shall make their fruit ᶜ*orlah* (*w*ᶜ*rltm* ᵓ*t* ᶜ*rltw*).' [The word] ᶜ*orlah* is repeated (literally, "ᶜ*orlahs*" [ᶜ*rlym*, the plural of ᶜ*orlah*]) [in the verse] in order to include everything."

Sifra Qid. III, 3b (Weiss ed., p. 90a)

Aqiva's view, that the prohibitions of the laws of ᶜ*orlah* apply to fruit that is defective or less than fully developed, occurs without attribution at M. Or. 1:8.

x. *Bikkurim*

I.i.45

A. R. Simeon b. Nanos says, "They bedeck the first-fruits [with produce] other than the seven species."

B. R. Aqiva says, "They bedeck the first-fruits only [with produce] of the seven species."

M. Bik 3:9

A landowner brings his first-fruits to Jerusalem. First-fruits are produce from the seven species specified at Deut. 8:8: wheat, barley, grapes, figs, pomegranates, olive-oil, and date-honey. M. Bik. 2:3 notes that pilgrims, when close to Jerusalem, "bedecked their first-fruits." M. Bik. 3:8 describes the baskets in which the rich and the poor brought their first-fruits. Our pericope focuses on the decorations of the baskets (Sens). The question, surely a theoretical one in Aqiva's time, is, Can produce other than the seven species be used in decorating the pilgrims' baskets? Simeon b. Nanos, in A, holds that produce other than the seven species can be used. Aqiva, in B, states that only produce from the seven species can be used. y. suggests the following reason for Aqiva's opinion: if people see the pilgrims' baskets decorated with produce other than the seven species, it will be thought that the produce brought as first-fruits is itself not of the seven species. Aqiva rules as he does in order to prevent such suspicions.

The opinions of the two masters match:

Simeon b. Nanos:	*m*ᶜ*ṭryn* ᵓ*t hbkwrym ḥwṣ mšb*ᶜ*t hmynym*
Aqiva:	ᵓ*yn m*ᶜ*ṭryn* ᵓ*t hbkwrym* ᵓ*l*ᵓ *mšb*ᶜ*t hmynym*

A and B differ only in contrasting *ḥwṣ* with *ʾyn...ʾlʾ*. The pericope thus is in a variation of the dispute-form. A more standard formulation, separating the topic-statement from the opinions of the masters, would resemble the following:

Concerning produce other than the seven species:

Simeon b. Nanos,	They bedeck,
Aqiva,	They do not bedeck.

The pericope obviously depends on a context dealing with first-fruits.

III.i.2

A. We learn, "One who eats first-fruits prior to the declaration designating them [...is liable for lashes] (M. Mak. 3:3)."

B. R. Hoshaya [b.] R. Judah [said] in the name of Samuel, "These are the words of R. Aqiva."

C. R. Yosé asked, "What is R. Aqiva's [opinion]?"

D. Said R. Mana, "My father heard [the following] tradition:

E. "*tny*: Setting delays. Declaring does not delay.

F. "R. Aqiva says, 'Declaring delays.' "

y. Bik. 1:7, 64a

IV.i.4

G. [M. Mak. 3:3] Said Rabbah bar bar Ḥannah, said R. Yoḥanan, "These are the words of R. Aqiva given anonymously."

H. "But sages say, '[Concerning] first-fruits: setting delays them, declaring does not delay them."

b. Mak. 17a

Aqiva holds, according to both y. and b., that first-fruits become the property of priests only after two conditions mentioned in Deut. 26 have been satisfied: first, the priest sets the offering on the altar (26:4); and second, the Israelite makes a personal declaration describing his action. Against Aqiva's view, the anonymous statements cited in E and H allege that the priestly action alone is essential: first-fruits may be eaten, obviously only by priests (Maim.), at any time after the priestly task has been performed; the Israelite's declaration is irrelevant. Aqiva's position emphasizes the role of the layman.

PART TWO

CHAPTER TWO

THE TRADITION AS A WHOLE

i. *Introduction*

In Part One I commented on ninety (90) pericopae related to Aqiva. This corpus deals with sixty-three (63) separate legal topics related to agricultural issues. In succeeding chapters I shall focus on the literary formulations in which the Aqivan traditions occur (Chapter Three), the attributions to specific masters which are attached to a number of the traditions (Chapter Four), and the substance of the legal positions in the statements in the pericopae (Chapter Five). This chapter contains a statistical summary of the ninety (90) pericopae. These items occur, as discussed previously, in several distinct corpora of literature: M.-T.; Tannaitic Midrashim; *beraitot* in y. and in b. which are introduced by *tny* or *tny*ᵓ; [1] Amoraic traditions in y. and in b. I shall first list all of the pericopae in a chart. A substantial majority of the pericopae (66 out of 90, or slightly more than 73% of the entire tradition) occur in M.-T., the primary literary stratum. I shall therefore next discuss the traits of the pericopae in this stratum, particularly with reference to the distribution of Aqivan traditions throughout the tractates in M.-T. We shall observe both that Aqivan pericopae are relatively evenly distributed throughout M.-T. and also that this fact contrasts markedly with the distribution of pericopae related to agriculture in the major traditions assigned to two other Yavnean masters, Eliezer and Joshua. Finally the twenty-four (24) pericopae which occur in the Tannaitic Midrashim, in y., and in b. will be considered. These comprise 26.5% of the whole tradition. I shall distinguish between those pericopae which deal with legal topics that also occur in M.-T. and those which do not.

---

1 I distinguish between the two latter categories in order to preserve the distinction made in the *gemarot*. The terms *tny* and *tny*ᵓ are sometimes taken to designate Tannaitic traditions. In the materials in *gemarot* which I investigate there is no significant distinction between statements introduced by either of the two terms and statements which lack the introduction.

ii. *The Entire Tradition*

The following chart, organized by reference (a) to the legal topics addressed in the pericopae and (b) to the different literary strata, summarizes the entire tradition and shows the predominance of pericopae in M.-T.:

Item	I M.-T.	II Tannaitic Midrashim	III *Beraitot* in *gemarot* introduced by *tny* or *tny*ʾ	IV Other tradition in *gemar*
1. Exemptions from *peʾah* prior to stacking	M. Pe. 1:6			
2. *Peʾah* given from separate sections of a single field	M. Pe. 3:2			y. Pe. 3:2
3. Obligations of land of any size	M. Pe. 3:6			
4. 3 searches daily	M. Pe. 4:5			
5. Produce over the top of harvester's hand	M. Pe. 4:10			
6. Vineyard of defective clusters	M. Pe. 7:7			
7. Quantities consigned to poor	M. Pe. 8:5			
8. Landowners give fallen ears of corn to poor	T. Pe. 2:21			
9. Law of Forgetting applies to olive trees				y. Pe. 7:1
10. Regulating bean-market in Meron	T. Dem. 4:13			
11. Tithes Samaritans' vegetables	T. Dem. 5:24			
12. Pairs that are Mixed-kinds	M. Kil. 1:3/ T. Kil. 1:2			
13. 6 handbreadths separate rows of vegetables	M. Kil. 3:3			
14. Rows of gourds among onions	M. Kil 3:6/ T. Kil. 2:12			
15. Shoots from seeds planted inadvertantly	M. Kil. 5:7			
16. Tillage of vine	M. Kil. 6:1			
17. Mixed-kinds of 7th-year produce	M. Kil. 7:5			
18. Do not allow Mixed-kinds to grow	T. Kil. 1:15			b. Mak. 21
19. Untangling greens from vines	T. Kil. 4:10			
20. Seedling is as its name implies	M. Shev. 1:8			
21. Neither clutter nor straighten public domain	M. Shev. 3:10/ T. Shev. 3:5			
22. Cut reeds in usual way in 7th-year	M. Shev. 4:6			
23. Everything permitted in Israel is permitted in Syria	M. Shev. 6:2/ T. Shev. 4:12			
24. Will not reveal Eliezer's opinion on hide anointed with 7th-year oil	M. Shev. 8:9			
25. Will not reveal Eliezer's opinion on Samaritans' bread	M. Shev. 8:10			

Item	I M.-T.	II Tannaitic Midrashim	III *Beraitot* in *gemarot* introduced by *tny* or *tny*ʾ	IV Other traditions in *gemarot*
Use 7th-year produce until second rainfall	M. Shev. 9:6			
Reversed to ben Azzai's (Joshua's) opinion on tithing Egyptian beans	T. Shev. 2:13			
Picked an *etrog* on first day of *Shevat*	T. Shev. 4:21		b. R.H. 14a	y. Bik. 2:5
qtp is subject to 7th year	T. Shev. 5:12			
Combine Heave-offering given by partners	M. Ter. 3:3		b. Tem. 13a	
No limit on Heave-offering gift	M. Ter. 4:5			
Neutralize Heave-offering	M. Ter. 4:8-9/ T. Ter. 5:10			
102 halves neutralize Heave-offering	M. Ter. 4:13			
Pay back only from same kind	M. Ter. 6:6/ T. Ter. 7:9	Sifra Emor 6:6 Sifra Bᶜ 12,13		
Don't pay back from unripe	T. Ter. 7:10			
Poor glean crop from Heave-offering seed	M. Ter. 9:2			
All mixtures with Heave-offering permitted except meat	M. Ter. 10:11/ T. Ter. 9:4			
Muzzle ox prior to plowing				y. Ter. 9:4
Courtyard liable for tithes	M. Ma. 3:5/ T. Ma. 2:20			
Vine in a courtyard	M. Ma. 3:9			
Liability of caperbush	M. Ma. 4:6			
Vegetables in field bought from gentile	T. Ma. 3:14		y. Ma. 5:4	b. Hul. 136a
Exegesis on 2 tithes		Sifré Deut. 63		
Newly ripened *etrog* exempt from tithes				y. Ma. 1:4
Vetches of Heave-offering handled in uncleanness	M. M.S. 2:4/ T. M.S. 2:1			
Changed silver for gold Second-tithe money	M. M.S. 2:7			
Change silver for copper coins	M. M.S. 2:9			
Unripe produce exempt from tithes	M. M.S. 5:8			
Assignment of first-tithe to Levites	M. M.S. 5:9		b. Yeb. 86a	y. M.S. 5:5 b. Yeb. 86b
Saffron-cakes purchased with Second-tithe money	T. M.S. 1:13			y. M.S. 1:4
Boundary of Jerusalem: olive press	T. M.S. 2:12			
Boundary of Jerusalem: contracting uncleanness	T. M.S. 2:16			
Only minted currency as Second-tithe money		Sifré Deut. 107		

Item	I M.-T.	II Tannaitic Midrashim	III *Beraitot* in *gemarot* introduced by *tny* or *tny*ᵓ	IV Other tradition in *gemar*
54. Exported produce exempt from dough-offering	M. Hal. 2:1	Sifré Num. 110		y. Hal. 2:1
55. Do not prepare *qab*-sized pieces	M. Hal. 2:3/ T. Hal. 1:9			
56. Obligation for dough-offering depends on forming of crust	M. Hal. 3:6 T. Hal. 1:12	Sifré Num. 110		
57. Offering from one *qab* valid	M. Hal. 4:4-5			
58. Heave-offering vetches to any priest	M. Hal. 4:9			
59. Residue of *omer* liable for both dough-offering and tithes				y. Hal. 1:4
60. 7 render produce prohibited	M. Or. 3:7			
61. Defective fruit subject to ᶜ*orlah*		Sifra Qid. III,3		
62. Bedeck first-fruits of 7 species	M. Bik. 3:9			
63. Declaring delays			y. Bik. 1:7	b. Mak. 17a

The following table, organized by tractate, gives the specific numbers of pericopae in the respective strata.

Table A

Total number of pericopae in the tradition, by tractate (figures in parenthesis give percentage of total number of pericopae represented by each item in the table).

Tractate	Total	I M.-T.	II Tannaitic Midrashim	III *Beraitot* in *gemarot* introduced by *tny* or *tny*	IV Other traditions in *germarot*
Pe.	10 (11.1%)	8 (8.9%)			2 (2.2%)
Dem.	2 (2.2%)	2 (2.2%)			
Kil.	11 (12.2%)	10 (11.1%)			1 (1.1%)
Shev.	14 (15.6%)	12 (13.3%)		1 (1.1%)	1 (1.1%)
Ter.	15 (16.7%)	11 (12.2%)	2 (2.2%)	1 (1.1%)	1 (1.1%)
Ma.	8 (8.9%)	5 (5.6%)	1 (1.1%)	1 (1.1%)	1 (1.1%)
M.S.	14 (15.6%)	9 (10.0%)	1 (1.1%)	1 (1.1%)	3 (3.3%)
Hal.	11 (12.2%)	7 (7.8%)	2 (2.2%)	1 (1.1%)	1 (1.1%)
Or.	2 (2.2%)	1 (1.1%)	1 (1.1%)		
Bik.	3 (3.3%)	1 (1.1%)		1 (1.1%)	1 (1.1%)
Total	90 (100 %)	66 (73.3%)	7 (7.8%)	6 (6.7%)	11 (12.2%)

M.-T. account for nearly three-quarters of all pericopae in the tradition, 66 out of 90 items, or slightly more than 73%. Seven pericopae, 7.8% of the total corpus, occur in Tannaitic Midrashim. The *gemarot* present seventeen (17) pericopae, or 18.9% of the total tradition. Of these six, or 6.7% of the total, are introduced by *tny* or *tny*ᵓ. The other eleven (11) pericopae, 12.2% of the total, give other traditions. The predominance of pericopae from M.-T. in this sample of legal traditions is comparable to the predominance of pericopae from M.-T. in the major legal traditions assigned to Eliezer, [2] to Joshua, [3] and to Gamaliel. [4]

iii. *The Primary Stratum*

I shall first focus on the sixty-six (66) pericopae, or slightly more than 73% of the total tradition, in M.-T. As the following chart shows, no single tractate contains more than 18.2% of the total number of Aqivan pericopae in the sample from M.-T.:

TABLE B

Distribution of Aqivan pericopae in M.-T. Pe.-Bik.

Tractate	Number	Percentage of total number of Aqivan pericopae in M.-T. Pe.-Bik.
Pe.	8	12.1
Dem.	2	3.0
Shev.	10	15.2
Kil.	12	18.2
Ter.	11	16.7
Ma.	5	7.6
M.S.	9	13.6
Hal.	7	10.6
Or.	1	1.5
Bik.	1	1.5
Total	66	100.0

Each of six of the ten tractates contains more than 10% of the total corpus. In fact the distribution of these pericopae within M.-T. corresponds fairly closely to the relative sizes of the tractates, with one exception. It is convenient to illustrate this distribution by reference

---

[2] J. Neusner, *Eliezer*, Vol. II, pp. 1-2.
[3] W. Green, *Joshua*.
[4] S. Kanter, *Gamaliel*, pp. 367-74.

to a central unit of organization in the ten tractates, the chapter. M. Pe. through Bik. contain sixty-two (62) chapters. Forty-two (42) Aqivan pericopae in M. are distributed through thirty (30), more than 48%, of these chapters. The following table shows that with the exception of M. Dem. the proportion of Aqivan pericopae in any one tractate approximates the size of the tractate as measured by reference to the number of chapters.

TABLE C

Distribution of Aqivan pericopae in M. by reference to chapters.

Tractate	(a) No. of chaps. (% of total no. of chaps. in M. Pe.-Bik.)	(b) No. of chaps. in which Aqivan pericopae occur (% of total no. of chaps. in which Aqivan traditions occur)	(c) Deviation of % of (b) from (a)	(d) No. of Aqivan pericopae in a tractae without regard to chaps. (% of total no. of Aqivan pericopae in M.)	(e) Deviation of % of (d) from (a)
Pe.	8 (13%)	5 (16.5%)	+ 3.5%	7 (16.5%)	+ 3.5%
Dem	7 (11%)	0	— 11%	0	— 11%
Kil.	8 (13%)	5 (16.5%)	+ 3.5%	6 (14%)	+ 1%
Shev.	10 (16%)	6 (20%)	+ 4%	6 (16.5%)	+ 0.5%
Ter.	11 (18%)	5 (16.5%)	— 1.5%	7 (16.5%)	— 1.5%
Ma.	4 (6.5%)	2 (6.5%)	—	3 (7%)	+ 0.5%
M.S.	5 (8%)	2 (6.5%)	— 1.5%	5 (12%)	+ 4.0%
Hal.	4 (6.5%)	3 (10%)	+ 3.5%	5 (12%)	+ 5.5%
Or.	2 (3%)	1 (3.5%)	+ 0.5%	1 (2.5%)	— 0.5%
Bik.	3 (5%)	1 (3.5)	— 1.5%	1 (2.5%)	— 2.5%
Totals	62	30		42	

The data in columns (a) through (c) show that the distribution of Aqivan pericopae in chapters in M. closely approximates the relative number of chapters in each of the tractates. This holds true regardless of the size of the tractates. No single tractate contains more than 20% of the Aqivan pericopae in M., and only in M. Dem. does the proportion of Aqivan pericopae in a single tractate relative to the total number of Aqivan pericopae in M. deviate by more than 4% from the proportion of chapters in that same tractate relative to the total number of chapters in M. Pe.-Bik. The pattern of Aqivan traditions in the tractates in M., if measured in absolute numbers, shows a similar correspondence to the pattern of distribution of chapters among the tractates (columns a, d, and e). Aqivan pericopae are most numerous in the largest tractates (Ter., Shev., Pe., Kil.). Only in M. Dem. is the deviation significantly larger than 4%. The important fact here is that in only two cases (M. Ter. Chapter Four and M. M.S. Chapter Two) does a single chapter in M. contain as many as three Aqivan pericopae; eight chapters include only two Aqivan pericopae. Twenty (20) chapters contain only a single Aqivan tradition.

The following table shows that Aqivan pericopae are only slightly less well distributed among the chapters in T. Pe.-Bik.

Table D

Distribution of Aqivan pericopae in T. by reference to chapters.

Tractate	(a) No. of chaps. (% of chaps. in M. Pe.-Bik.)	(b) No. of chaps. in which Aqivan pericopae occur (% of total no. of chaps. in which Aqivan traditions occur)	(c) Deviation of % of (b) from (a)	(d) No. of Aqivan pericopae in a tractate without regard to chaps. (% of total no. of Aqivan pericopae in M.)	(e) Deviation of % of (d) from (a)
Pe.	4 (8.5%)	1 (5.5%)	— 3%	1 (4%)	— 4.5%
Dem.	8 (16.5%)	2 (11%)	— 5.5%	2 (8.5%)	— 8%
Ter.	10 (21%)	3 (16.5%)	— 4.5%	4 (16.5%)	— 4.5%
Shev.	8 (16.5%)	4 (22%)	+ 5.5%	4 (16.5%)	+ 4.5%
Kil.	5 (10.5%)	3 (16.5%)	+ 6%	4 (16.5%)	+ 6%
Ma.	3 (6.25%)	2 (11%)	+ 4.75%	2 (8.5%)	+ 2.25%
M.S.	5 (10.5%)	2 (11%)	+ 0.5%	4 (16.5%)	+ 6%
Hal.	2 (4%)	1 (5.5%)	+ 1.5%	2 (8.5%)	+ 4.5%
Or.	1 (2%)	0	— 2%	0	— 2%
Bik.	2 (4%)	0	— 2%	0	— 2%
Total	48	18		24	

Aqivan pericopae occur in eighteen (18) out of the forty-eight (48) chapters in T. Pe.-Bik., or 37.5% of the total. Unlike M., T. does include Aqivan pericopae in tractate Dem. Since the number of items in the sample of traditions from T. is considerably fewer than the number of items in the sample of traditions from M., the slightly wider deviations for T. reported in columns (c) and (e) of Table C are not significant. Instead it is striking that, as in M., the tractates with the most chapters have proportionately the most Aqivan pericopae.

Two other Yavnean masters, Eliezer and Joshua, have significant corpora of traditions in M.-T. Pe.-Bik. Fifty-four (54) pericopae in this literature include attributions to Eliezer, only eight fewer than the number of attributions to Aqiva, and thirty-eight (38) pericopae contain attributions to Joshua. The distribution of the Aqivan pericopae differs markedly, however, from the distribution of Eliezer's and Joshua's pericopae. In M., for instance, slightly more than one-half of all of Eliezer's pericopae (20 out of 38, or 53% of the total) occur in a single tractate, M. Ter. Three-quarters of all of Joshua's pericopae in M. (18 out of 24) occur in two tractates, M. Ter. and M. Shev. (Although they are the largest tractates in M. Pe.-Bik., M. Ter. and M. Shev. together contain only 21 chapters, or only 34% of all 62 chapters; see Table C, above, p. 128.) Laws related to Heave-offering and to the Seventh-year, the primary topics in M. Ter. and M. Shev., respectively, play disproportionately large roles in Eliezer's and Joshua's legal agenda as compared to the place of such laws in Aqiva's agenda—and in the agenda of M.-T. The statistical correspondence between Aqiva's agenda and that of M.-T. obviously does not show that Aqiva is the authority behind the agenda of M.-T. That correspondence is unique among the major traditions assigned to Yavnean masters, however, and must be explained. It possibly can be accounted for by reference to the redaction of most of the traditions in M.-T. Pe.-Bik. by circles which looked to Aqiva as the most authoritative of the Yavnean masters; [5] Aqiva's pericopae are the most numerous among those ascribed to Yavneans and also most closely correspond to the distribution of legal topics, for Aqiva's work set the agenda for subsequent masters. Internal evidence, as in the pericopae in which Aqiva is asked about Eliezer's opinions on two issues related to laws of the Seventh-year (M. Shev. 8:9-10; nos. 24-25 in chart, above), suggests that Aqiva himself played a role in the shaping of Yavnean traditions other than his own. This view, of course, is in accord with the role assigned to Aqiva by later rabbinic tradition. Of primary concern to us, however, is the substance of Aqiva's legal opinions, and particularly the relation of those opinions to other relevant opinions, both named and unnamed, which are given in the earliest strata of the literature. In Chapter Five, when we focus specifically on the substance of Aqiva's legal opinions, we shall look for evidence internal to his legal positions regarding Aqiva's role in the formation of early rabbinic traditions.

---

[5] "Most authoritative" here is inferred solely from the unique size and scope of Aqiva's tradition as compared to the traditions of other Yavnean masters. If, for instance, we credit the final redaction of M. to circles associated with Judah the Patriarch at the end of the second century, it remains a fact that the traditions on agricultural issues ascribed to Gamaliel, Judah's grandfather and predecessor as patriarch, are too few in number (12 in M.; only only 4 more in T.) to be meaningfully compared with the corpus of Aqiva's—or even of Eliezer's or Joshua's—pericopae.

iv. *Strata Other Than M.-T.*

Of the twenty-four (24) pericopae which do not occur in M.-T., or slightly less than 27% of the total sample of items in the tradition, the following introduce legal topics which do not have counterparts in pericopae in M.-T. (the numbers in parenthesis refer to the chart above which lists the entire tradition):

A. Tannaitic Midrashim
   1. Sifré Deut. 63—tithe for grain and tithe for cattle; scriptural exegesis (no. 43).
   2. Sifré Deut. 107—only minted currency as Second-tithe money; scriptural exegesis, dispute with Ishmael (no. 53).
   3. Sifra Qid. III,3—defective fruit are subject to laws of ᶜ*orlah*; scriptural exegesis, dispute with Yosé the Galilean (no. 61).

B. Pericopae in *gemarot* introduced by *tny* or *tny*ᵓ
   1. y. Bik. 1:7—first-fruits cannot be eaten prior to declaration by Israelite (no. 63).

C. Other traditions in *gemarot*
   1. y. Pe. 7:1—law of Forgetting applies to olive trees; scriptural exegesis (no. 9).
   2. y. Ter. 9:4—ox muzzled prior to entering field cannot be used; scriptural exegesis requested of Simeon (no. 38).
   3. y. Ma. 1:4—newly ripened *etrog* exempt from tithes; dispute with sages (no. 44).
   4. y. Hal. 1:4—residue of *omer* liable for both dough-offering and tithes (no. 59).

Eight topics out of a total of sixty-three (63), or more than 12.5% of the total, are introduced in strata other than M.-T. By contrast, only one of thirty-two (32) topics dealt with in Eliezer's legal traditions in M. Pe.-Bik., or 3% of the total number of topics, is introduced in a stratum other than M.-T. The three pericopae in the Tannaitic Midrashim which introduce new Aqivan topics represent about one-half of all pericopae in that stratum which contain Aqivan traditions on agriculture (3 out of 7). The sample of items obviously is not large. The sample of items in the *gemarot* similarly is not large. C2, y. Ter. 9:4 (no. 38), gives Simeon's, and not Aqiva's, opinion. The remaining four pericopae in the *gemarot*, as listed in B and C, above, represent slightly less than one-quarter of all the Aqivan tradition in the sample (4 out of 17, or 23.5%). Two of the three pericopae in the Tannaitic Midrashim give scriptural exegeses; one of the four Aqivan traditions in the *gemarot* also gives a scriptural exegesis (as does Simeon's tradition). By contrast, only two scriptural exegeses occur in all of the sixty-six (66) pericopae on fifty-five (55) individual topics which occur in M.-T., the primary stratum—and both of these exegeses are obviously generated by dispute-forms (M. Pe. 7:7, no. 6 on chart, above; and M. Ter. 6:6, no. 34 on chart, above).

Exclusive of *verbatim* reports of Aqivan traditions on agriculture in M.-T., of the fifty-five (55) individual topics which are discussed in M.-T. ten, or slightly more than 18% of the total, are dealt with in other strata. These ten topics occur in the following pericopae (numbers in parenthesis refer to the topics listed in the chart on the entire tradition, pp. 124-26);

A. Tannaitic Midrashim
   1. Sifra Emor 6:6—Pay back Heave-offering only from same kind; scriptural exegesis, dispute with Eliezer (no. 34) [cp. M. Ter. 6:6].
   2. Sifra Bᶜ 12, 13—same topic as in A1.
   3. Sifré Num. 110—Exported produce exempt from dough-offering; dispute with Eliezer (no. 54) [cp. M. Hal. 2:1].
   4. Sifré Num. 110—Obligation for dough-offering depends upon forming of crust; dispute with Yoḥanan b. Nuri (no. 56) [cp. M. Hal. 3:6 and T. Hal. 1:12].

B. Pericopae in *gemarot* introduced by *tny* or *tny*ᵓ
   1. b. R.H. 14a—Acted with an *etrog* on first day of *Shevat* in accord with the Houses and/or with Eliezer and Gamaliel (no. 28) [cp. T. Shev. 4:21].
   2. b. Tem. 13a—Combine Heave-offering given by partners; dispute with Eliezer (no. 30) [cp. M. Ter. 3:3: dispute with sages, not Eliezer, and Aqiva's position reversed].
   3. y. Ma. 5:4—vegetables in field bought from gentile; dispute with sages.
   4. b. Yeb. 86a—assignment of first-tithe to Levites; dispute with Eleazar b. ᶜAzariah (no. 49) [cp. M. M.S. 5:9].
   5. y. Hal. 2:1—exported produce exempt from dough-offering; dispute with Eliezer (no. 54) [cp. M. Hal. 2:1].

C. Other pericopae in *gemarot*

1. y. Pe. 3:2—*pe*ʾ*ah* given from separate sections of a single field (no. 2) [cp. M. Pe. 3:2].
2. b. Mak. 21b—do not allow Mixed-kinds to grow (no. 18) [cp. T. Kil. 1:15].
3. y. Bik. 2:5—same as B1.

4-5. y. M.S. 5:5/b. Yeb. 86b—assignment of first-tithe to Levites; narrative, with Eleazar b. ᶜAzariah (no. 49) [cp. M. M.S. 5:9].

6. y. M.S. 1:4—inedible items used to prepare food may be purchased with Second-tithe money; scriptural exegesis, dispute Ishmael (no. 50) [cp. T. M.S. 1:3: report by Yoḥanan b. Nuri to Ḥalafta that Aqiva permits purchase of saffron-cakes with Second-tithe money].

The total sample of legal items in Tannaitic Midrashim, as noted above, is small, merely seven pericopae on six individual topics. The four pericopae on three topics listed in A represent one-half of the sample of items in Tannaitic Midrashim. The number of pericopae from the *gemarot* provides a somewhat larger sample of items—seventeen (17) pericopae in all. Of these eleven (11), or 65% of the total, deal with topics which are also dealt with in pericopae in M.-T., as listed in B and C. These eleven (11) pericopae in the *gemarot* deal with eight separate legal topics (14.5% of all topics in M.-T.). These topics are discussed in pericopae which occur in seven different tractates in M.-T. (Pe., Kil., Shev., Ter., Ma., M.S., and Hal.). There is no obvious statistical pattern among these pericopae. In Chapter Five I shall return to the question of the substance of the legal positions expressed in these pericopae.

Finally, we note that forty-five (45) out of fifty-five (55) topics, or 82% of all topics discussed in Aqivan traditions in M.-T., do not recur in Aqivan traditions in other strata of the literature. This again demonstrates the predominant importance of traditions in M.-T. for the investigation of Aqiva's legal positions.

v. *Summary*

Items from M.-T. predominate in Aqiva's traditions on agriculture. Almost three-quarters of the ninety (90) pericopae in the tradition occur in M.-T. And more than four-fifths of all legal topics discussed in the pericopae in M.-T. (45 out of 55) do not recur in the other strata of the literature.

The sample of items from Tannaitic Midrashim is small. It includes only seven pericopae on six different legal topics, half of which occur in M.-T. and half of which are new. The number of items from the *gemarot*, although somewhat larger (17 pericopae on 13 different legal topics, of which 8 also occur in M.-T.), is still statistically insignificant. Nonetheless it is striking that proportionately so many new legal topics do occur in the Tannaitic Midrashim and in the *gemarot*; by contrast, in Eliezer's traditions on agriculture thirty-one (31) out of thirty-two (32) topics are already accounted for in M.-T.

It is also striking that Aqiva's pericopae are fairly well distributed throughout M.-T. Pe.-Bik. Eliezer and Joshua are the only other Yavneans with significant numbers of traditions in this literature (with 54 and 38 pericopae, respectively), and those traditions are concentrated in only one or two tractates. By contrast, Aqiva's pericopae are distributed in numbers almost directly proportionate to the size of the different tractates. The largest tractates have the most traditions. More impressively, the distribution of Aqiva's pericopae also approximates the distribution through the ten tractates of chapters, which are important units of organization in the ten tractates. Aqivan pericopae occur, for instance, in more than 48% of the total number of chapters in M.-T. Pe.-Bik. (30 out of 62); and in any single tractate the number of chapters containing Aqivan pericopae relative to the number of such chapters in all of M.-T. Pe.-Bik. corresponds to the total number of chapters in that same tractate relative to the total number of chapters in all ten tractates.[6] The two proportions in fact never deviate by more than 4%, with one exception. That exception is M. Dem., which contains no Aqivan pericopae. Given the size of the Aqivan corpus (42 pericopae in M. Pe.-Bik.), which is without peer among traditions of Yavnean masters, this fact about its distribution is remarkable. Obviously Aqiva does not stand behind the agenda of M., which goes considerably beyond the problems discussed in his tradition. Nonetheless these statistical data indicate that Aqiva plays a special role, unique among Yavneans, in setting the agenda on agricultural issues later taken up in the redaction of M.-T.

---

[6] These proportions could be expressed as follows:

$$\frac{\text{Number of chapters containing Aqivan pericopae in tractate X}}{\text{Number of chapters containing Aqivan pericopae in tractates Pe.-Bik.}} \approx \frac{\text{Total number of chapters in tractate X}}{\text{Total number of chapters in tractates Pe.-Bik.}}$$

CHAPTER THREE

FORMS AND FORMULARY PATTERNS

i. *Introduction*

A form is an arrangement of words in a fixed and consistent structure independent of content. It is exemplified by the standard dispute-form:

Statement of legal problem:
X says,...
Y says,...

A form may be either elaborate, like the dispute-form, or simple, like the particle *b-* used for a single, fixed purpose. As Neusner notes, what is essential is that a form be recurrent and that it have no relation to the legal content of the rules being expressed. [1]

Previous studies have shown that traditions about early rabbinic masters are predominately cast in a limited number of forms. More than two-hundred fifty traditions about the Houses, for instance, occur almost exclusively in the standard dispute-form and its variations. [2] Similarly, approximately two-hundred legal traditions about Eliezer occur in only six different formulations; Neusner notes, however, that four of these formulations are in fact variations on the dispute-form. [3] In more than one-hundred twenty-five legal traditions of Ishmael, Porton has discovered only one form which does not also occur in the Houses' and Eliezer's corpora—and that form occurs only a few times in y. [4] Because of the uniformity of formulations in the traditions of the various early masters, it has been observed that the forms of early rabbinic literature have no history. [5] That is, particular forms cannot be identified with particular masters or with specific circles of tradents. In general it is not possible to argue that the use of one particular kind of form evidences that a pericope was necessarily formulated by, or transmited among, a specific circle of tradents.

1 HMLP, Vol. III, p. 194.
2 *Phar.*, Vol. III, pp. 5-16, 64.
3 *Eliezer*, Vol. II, pp. 19-31, 60-61.
4 G. Porton, "According to R. Ishmael. A Palestinian Amoraic Form," in *Approaches to Ancient Judaism: Theory and Practice* (ed., W. Green; Missoula, forthcoming).
5 HMLP, Vol. III, p. 236.

In previous studies the identification of forms has been helpful primarily for the exegesis, and not the history, of law.

Aqiva's traditions on agriculture include the use of only one form which is not familiar from the traditions of the Houses and of the other Yavnean masters,—and that form, the witness-form (*X said before Y + legal statement*), occurs only six times in the entire tradition. In the materials under investigation here I have identified the following sorts of formulations: the standard dispute-form and its variations; sayings simply attached to an attributive formulary such as, *X says*; narratives; and witness-sayings. In this discussion I assume a distinction between a "form" and a "formulary pattern." The latter, by contrast to a form, is an arrangement of *different* words in a consistent pattern, as, for example, in the question-and-answer pattern (*Question + Several independent answers*). In function, however, there is no necessary distinction between a form and a formulary pattern; the question-and-answer pattern, to continue the example, commonly functions as a variation on the dispute-form.

ii. *Forms and Formulary Patterns*

A. Dispute-form: *Legal statement + X says,...Y says,...* (or *Legal statement + ...words of X. Y says,...*)

1. M. Pe. 3:2

> Concerning one who harvests his field selectively:
> Aqiva: He gives *pe*ʾ*ah* from every one [of the sections].
> Sages: From one for all.

Both sayings respond to the superscription. The sages' lemma depends upon Aqiva's and balances the words in the last part of Aqiva's saying: *from every one* vs. *from one for all.* As noted in the comment on this pericope, two manuscripts, P and K, omit "He gives *pe*ʾ*ah*," thus making the apodosis balance perfectly.

2. M. Pe. 4:10

> [What falls over]...the top of the [harvester's] hand or sickle:
> Ishmael: To the poor.
> Aqiva: To the landowner.

Both short sayings in the apodosis respond to the superscription; "the poor" and "the landowner" constitute a syzygy only by reference to the law of gleanings, the legal problem at issue in the pericope.

3. M. Pe. 7:7

Vineyard wholly of defective clusters:
Eliezer: To the landowner.
Aqiva: To the poor.

Same as no. 2, except Aqiva's position is switched and Eliezer occurs instead of Ishmael.

4. M. Kil. 3:3

If one seeks to plant one kind of vegetable in a field already sown with a different kind of vegetable:
Ishmael: [Must first dig] a furrow across the field.
Aqiva: [Area to be planted must be] six handbreadths in length and fully as wide (*rḥb mlwʾw*).

The masters' sayings respond to the superscription but are totally independent of one another.

5. M. Kil. 3:6

If one seeks to plant rows of gourds in the midst of a field previously planted with onions:
Ishmael: Uproot 2 rows and plant 1; leave 2; uproot 2 and plant 1.
Aqiva: Uproot 2 rows and plant 2; leave 2; uproot 2 and plant 2.

The dispute is perfectly balanced. The masters' sentences differ only regarding the number of new rows to be planted: 1 vs. 2.

6. T. Kil. 2:12

qṣr, words of both of them:
Ishmael: 10 *amot.*
Aqiva: 8 *amot.*

Same as no. 5. The difference is 10 vs. 8.

7. T. Kil. 4:10

Concerning greens which stretch into the midst of a vine:
Abba Saul says—
Aqiva: One returns [the greens to their place].
Ben Azzai: He trims [them].

The attribution to Abba Saul interrupts the development of the form. Aqiva's and ben Azzai's sayings do not balance; both sayings respond to the superscription.

8. M. Shev. 4:6

> If one cuts reeds during the 7th-year:
> Yosé the Galilean: He keeps at least one handbreadth away from the ground.
> Aqiva: He cuts in the usual way.

The masters' sayings respond to the superscription but are independant of one another.

9. M. Ter. 3:3

> Concerning gifts of Heave-offering from partners:
> Aqiva: The Heave-offering of both of them is Heave-offering.
> Sages: The Heave-offering of the first is Heave-offering.

The sayings in the apodosis balance perfectly; they differ only regarding *both of them* vs. *the first.*

10. M. Ter. 4:5

> Concerning one who increases Heave-offering:
> Eliezer: [Up to] 1/10...
> Ishmael: 1/2 as common produce and 1/2 as Heave-offering.
> Tarfon and Aqiva: As long as he keeps some as common produce [he may give as much as he wants].

Each of the masters' sayings responds to the superscription, but the lemmas are independent of one another. The attribution of a single statement to two masters, here Tarfon and Aqiva, is unique in this sample of traditions. Indeed, it is unusual to include more than two masters in a dispute-form.

11. M. Ma. 3:9

> Concerning a vine planted in a courtyard:
> One takes the entire grape-cluster [without incurring liability for tithing], words of Tarfon.
> Aqiva: One picks grapes one at a time.

Again each of the masters' sayings responds to the superscription, but the lemmas are independent of one another.

12. T. Ma. 3:14

> Concerning one who buys a field of vegetables from a gentile in Syria:...
> If acquisition occurred after the produce entered season of tithes—

He gathers in his usual way and is exempt, words of Aqiva.
Sages: After entered season, he is liable according to calculation.

As discussed in the comment on this pericope, the reference of Aqiva's saying is not clear. In any case, Aqiva's saying does not balance that of the sages.

13. y. Ma. 5:4

Concerning produce in a field which was more than one-third grown before purchased from a gentile:
Aqiva: Addition is exempt [from tithes].
Sages: Addition is liable.

Unlike in the pericope in no. 12, the sayings of the masters in this pericope both respond to the superscription. The difference between them is *exempt* vs. *liable.*

14. b. Hul. 136 [cp. no. 13]

Concerning produce which was more than one-third grown...
Aqiva declares liable for Addition.
Sages exempt.

b. reverses the opinions attributed to Aqiva and the sages and gives slightly different verbs for the fixed difference, *declares liable* vs. *exempt.*

15. y. Ma. 1:4

Concerning *etrog* in the first stages of ripening:
Aqiva: Not a fruit.
Sages: Fruit.

The masters' sayings respond to the superscription and differ only in that Aqiva says *not.*

16. M. M.S. 2:4

Concerning vetches of Heave-offering:
House of Shammai: Soak and grind in cleanness; give as food in uncleanness.
House of Hillel: Soak in cleanness; grind and give as food in uncleanness.
Shammai: Should be eaten dry.
Aqiva: Whatever concerns them in uncleanness.

All of the sayings in the apodosis respond to the superscription, but only the Houses' sayings balance in word-choice. Shammai's and Aqiva's lemmas are independent of each other and of the Houses' sayings. This is properly only a Houses' dispute-form.

17. M. M.S. 2:9

> Concerning changing a *sela* of Second-tithe money in Jerusalem:
>
> House of Shammai: Whole *sela* for [copper] coins.
>
> House of Hillel: *Sheqel* of silver and *sheqel* of [copper] coins.
>
> Those who make argument before sages: For 3 *denars* of silver and for a *denar* of [copper] coins.
>
> Aqiva: For 3 *denars* of silver and for a quarter of [copper] coins.
>
> Tarfon: 4 *aspers* of silver.
>
> Shammai: He should deposit it in a shop and consume its value [in produce].

Each of the sayings in the apodosis responds to the superscription. Aqiva's lemma, however, corresponds only to the preceding statement attributed to, "Those who make argument before sages." The two lemmas differ only on *denar* vs. a quarter of a *denar*.

18. T. M.S. 2:16

> Concerning Second-tithe produce which entered Jerusalem and contracted uncleanness:...
>
> Eliezer: If from Father, eaten outside; if from Offspring, then eaten inside.
>
> Aqiva: If contracted outside, then eaten outside; if contracted inside, then eaten inside...

The sayings of both masters respond to the superscription. *Father/Offspring* vs. *outside/inside* represent a complicated syzygy by reference to the particular law at issue in the pericope. As discussed in the comment on this pericope, Ushan masters, Meir and Judah, give different versions of Houses' disputes which further develop Aqiva's and Eliezer's positions. At T. M.S. 2:16 the Ushans' Houses' disputes are inserted between the superscription and Eliezer's and Aqiva's sayings.

19. M. Hal. 2:1/Sifré Num. 110/y. Hal. 2:1

> [Concerning liability of] exported produce [for dough-offering]:

Eliezer declares liable.
Aqiva declares exempt.

Both masters' lemmas respond to the superscription. The apodosis provides a fixed difference, *liable* vs. *exempt.*

20. T. Hal. 1:12

Concerning dough of a proselyte:
Before light crust formed, liable; after crust formed, exempt, words of Aqiva.
Yoḥanan b. Nuri: Before rolled out or kneaded, liable; after rolled out or kneaded, exempt.

Although the opinions of both masters respond to the superscription, their sayings are in fact independent of one another.

21. M. Hal. 4:4

Concerning dough-offering from one *qab* of dough:
Aqiva: Dough-offering.
Sages: Not dough-offering.

The opinions in the apodosis differ only in that the sages specify *not.*

22. M. Hal. 4:5

Concerning a piece of dough made by combining two one-*qab* pieces of dough from each of which dough-offering had previously been taken:
Aqiva declares exempt [from dough-offering].
Sages declare liable.

The apodosis provides a fixed difference, *exempt* vs. *liable.*

23. M. Hal. 4:9

Concerning [whether or not] vetches of Heave-offering [may be given to any priest]:
Aqiva permits.
Sages prohibit.

The apodosis of the dispute provides a fixed difference, *permits* vs. *prohibit.*

[24. M. Kil. 5:7

If wind blew seed before a person [into a vineyard:]:
Aqiva: If shoots sprout, should plow them under;
if reaches an early stage of ripening, shake it out;
if ripened, should be burned.

The form is defective. Aqiva's saying responds to the protasis but stands alone in the apodosis.]

Excluding M. Kil. 5:7, we have twenty-three (23) examples of the standard dispute-form. Of these twelve (12), about half of the total, contain apodoses which resemble disciplined patterns familiar from the Houses' traditions. [6] Five pericopae contain sayings with a fixed difference (nos. 13, 14, 19, 22: *exempt* vs. *liable*; no. 23: *permits* vs. *prohibit*). In four pericopae the sayings in the apodoses differ with regard to a number (no. 5: *one* vs. 2; no. 6: 10 vs. 8; no. 9: *both* vs. *first*; no. 17: *one* vs. 1/4). In two cases the difference is solely the presence and absence of the negative (no. 15: *not a fruit* vs. *fruit*; no. 21: *dough-offering* vs. *not dough-offering*). In one instance the difference between the two sayings in the apodosis entails the reversal of word-order and a minor change in wording (no. 1: *from every one* vs. *one from all*).

In three apodoses specific words which are not necessarily related to one another are set into opposition by reference to the legal problems at issue in the pericopae. "The poor" and "the landowner" are set off against one another in the discussions of gleanings in nos. 2 and 3. Similarly, *Father/Offspring* vs. *outside/inside* becomes a complex syzygy only by reference to the problem concerning uncleanness discussed in no. 18.

In six cases (nos. 4, 7, 8, 10, 11, 20) independent opinions of different masters are set into dispute-forms,—or at least in each case the pericope seems to have been formulated without regard for mnemonic considerations.

The form is interrupted twice by insertions separating the protasis from the opinions which would provide the apodosis. In no. 7 the interruption is merely, "Abba Saul says." In no. 18 the insertion includes two Ushan masters' different versions of a Houses' dispute. In one case, no. 16, Aqiva's opinion is not part of the proper dispute-form in the pericope and is in fact an independent saying added on at the end to balance the legal content of an expanded tradition. In only one case, no. 12, is there any doubt as to whether Aqiva's saying properly responds to the protasis given in the pericope.

Opinions are ascribed to anonymous sages nine times in a standard dispute-form. Seven times (nos. 1, 9, 13, 14, 15, 22, 23) the sages'

[6] *Phar.*, Vol. III, pp. 119-40.
[7] *Ibid.*, pp. 16-23.

sayings are balanced with Aqiva's in mnemonic patterns familiar from the Houses' traditions. Most of the named masters in the foregoing traditions are assigned independent opinions which are set in dispute-forms with sayings of Aqiva. Only three masters' names occur in more than a single tradition: Ishmael (nos. 2, 4, 5, 6, and 10); Eliezer (nos. 3, 10, 18, and 19), and Tarfon (nos. 10 and 11). Except for two of Ishmael's sayings (nos. 5 and 6), named masters' opinions are not given in dispute-forms in which apodoses exhibit mnemonic patterns.

B. A scriptural citation, and not a legal saying (as in A), may provide a protasis: *Scripture* + *X says,...Y says,...* This is in fact a close variation on the standard dispute-form.

1. Sifré Deut. 63

> ["You shall seek the place which the Lord your God will choose out... there you shall bring your offerings and your sacrifices, your tithes... (Deut. 12:5-6)]. "Your tithes."
>
> Aqiva says: Scripture refers to two tithes, one of grain and one of cattle.

The pericope gives only Aqiva's exegesis of the term, "your tithes."

2. Sifré Deut. 107

> "You shall bind up (*wṣrth*) the [Second-tithe] money [in your hand and go to the place...] (Deut. 14:25).
>
> ["Bind up" refers to] a thing which is bound up in the way that money usually is, words of Ishmael.
>
> Aqiva says: A thing upon which there is a figure (*ṣwrh*).

The masters' sayings balance in numbers of syllables; both focus on *wṣrth*. We find only two examples of this form. One is defective, and both occur in Sifré Deut.

C. *Anonymous law* + *X says* (*...Y says,...*). This form suggests a gloss on antecedent law. Frequently, however, the named masters' opinions reflect a difference from the preceding anonymous rule; such cases serve as variations on the dispute-form.

1. M. Pe. 4:5

> Three searches during the day: morning, midday, afternoon.
>
> Gamaliel: They said this only lest they decrease [the number].
>
> Aqiva: They said this only lest they increase [the number].

Aqiva's and Gamaliel's sayings balance perfectly. Both assume the first part of the law given in the protasis.

2. M. Pe. 5:8

> They do not give the poor less than half a *qab* of wheat or a *qab* of barley—
> Meir: Half a *qab*—
> a *qab* and a half of spelt or a *qab* of dried figs or a *maneh* of fig-cake—
> Aqiva: *Prs* [half a maneh]—
> half a *log* of wine—
> Aqiva: A quarter *log*—
> a quarter [*log*] of oil—
> Aqiva: An eighth of a *log*.

The masters, Aqiva three times and Meir once, dispute items on the anonymous list. In each case Aqiva or Meir gives a measurement one-half as great as that stated anonymously.

3. T. Pe. 2:21

> [Concerning] ears of corn in the straw and in the fields:
> These belong to the landowners.
> Said Aqiva: In this the landowners behaved generously.

Aqiva's saying assumes the anonymous rule about ownership of the corn.

4. M. Kil. 6:1

> How much for tillage of the vine? Six handbreadths in every direction.
> Aqiva says: Three.

Aqiva disputes the measure given in the anonymous rule.

5. T. Kil. 1:15

> One who sows, or weeds, or blows [Mixed-kinds of seeds] transgresses a negative rule.
> Aqiva says: Also one who allows [them] to grow transgresses a negative rule.

Aqiva adds an additional item to those listed in the anonymous statement. The repetition of "transgresses a negative rule" is out of phase with the form; if "also" is deleted, then Aqiva gives an independent saying.

6. M. Shev. 9:6

> One gathers (1) fresh vegetables until the moisture dries up, (2) dry [vegetables] until the second rainfall [after the 7th year], (3) leaves of reeds and leaves of vines until they fall off their stems, and (4) dry leaves until the second rainfall.
>
> Aqiva says: In all cases until the second rainfall.

Aqiva's saying disputes the first and third items listed in the anonymous rule.

7. M. Hal. 2:3

> One who cannot prepare his dough in cleanness should prepare *qab*-sized pieces and thus not prepare his dough in uncleanness.
>
> Aqiva says: He should prepare it in uncleanness and should not prepare *qab*-sized pieces

Aqiva's saying reverses the word-order of the anonymous rule, which it disputes.

8. M. Hal. 3:6

> Proselyte's dough: if prepared before conversion, exempt from dough-offering; if prepared after conversion, then liable for dough-offering.
>
> Aqiva says: Everything depends upon the forming of a light crust in the oven.

Aqiva's opinion disputes the anonymous rule. Aqiva's saying is formulated, however, in completely different language.

9. M. Or. 3:7

> Sages say: Only six things render [other produce] prohibited [when combined in a mixture with that produce].
>
> Aqiva says: Seven
>
> And these are they: (1) nuts of Perech, and (2) pomegranates of Badan, and (3) sealed jars [of wine], and (4) beet-root-tops, and (5) cabbage-stalks, and (6) Greek gourds.
>
> Aqiva says: Also loaves of householders.

The pericope contains two disputes, one between sages and Aqiva on *six* vs. *seven*, and the other between Aqiva and an anonymous rule regarding whether loaves of householders render other produce prohibited. As discussed in the comment on this pericope, I suspect that the latter dispute has generated the former.

10. y. Bik. 1:7

> Setting delays. Declaring does not delay.
> Aqiva says: Declaring delays.

Aqiva's saying disputes the last part of the anonymous rule. The difference is *not*.

All ten examples in the foregoing function as variations on the dispute-form. In four cases the anonymous rule and Aqiva's comment balance closely; they differ on numbers (no. 2: *one* vs. *one-half*, *half* vs. *quarter*, and *quarter* vs. *eighth*; no. 4: *six* vs. *three*), word-order (no. 7: *should prepare qabs and not in uncleanness* vs. *should prepare in uncleanness and not qabs*), and the use of *not* (no. 10: *declaring does not delay* vs. *declaring delays*). In two additional instances Aqiva's opinion implicitly differs from the anonymous rule with regard to the use of a negative, for Aqiva mentions an item which does not occur in the anonymous rule; that is, the differences in nos. 5 and 9 are whether allowing to grow *does* or *does not* transgress a negative rule and whether loaves of householders *do* or *do not* render other produce in a mixture prohibited. Twice general statements are attributed to Aqiva. In no. 6 the general statement uses vocabularly familiar from the foregoing anonymous rule ("until the second rainfall"); Aqiva specifically disputes only two out of four items listed in the anonymous rule. In no. 9, however, Aqiva's general statement does not take over the language of the anonymous rule (*prepared before/after conversion* vs. *depends on forming of a light crust*); Aqiva's position is completely independent of that which it disputes.

Aqiva obviously disagrees with the anonymous rule in no. 3 ("Fallen corn belongs to the householder"). His saying ("In this householders were generous"), however, comments on, rather than disputes, that rule. No. 1 also provides a case in which Aqiva's saying comments on the anonymous rule. No. 1 nonetheless gives a dispute: Aqiva and Gamaliel, both of whom assume the anonymous rule, disagree on the reason behind the law; the masters' sayings balance perfectly (*decrease* vs. *increase*).

D. Question-and-answer pattern: *Question* + *X says,...Y says,...*

1. M. Shev. 1:8

> Until when are they called seedlings?
> Eleazar b. ᶜAzariah: Until [their fruit] becomes common-produce.

Joshua: [C, K read, Until] 7 years old [K reads, 90 years].
Aqiva: A seedling is as its name [implies].

Each of the masters' sayings responds to the question. Each is, however, independent of the other answers.

2. M. Shev. 3:10

During the 7th year what should they do with dirt dug up while erecting a fence at the boundary of one's property?
He piles it up in the public domain and then straightens it out, words of Joshua.
Aqiva: As they do not clutter the public domain, so they do not straighten it out.

Aqiva's saying responds to Joshua's; Aqiva does not answer the question about what to do with the dirt. As discussed in the comment on this pericope, a prior formulation, without the question, stands behind this tradition.

3. M. Ma. 3:5

What type of courtyard [renders produce] liable for tithes?
Ishmael: A Tyrian style courtyard in which the vessels are watched.
Aqiva: Any that one opens and another closes is exempt.
Nehemiah: Any in which a man is not ashamed to eat is liable.
Yosé: Any which one may enter without someone asking, 'What are you seeking?,' is exempt.
Judah: [Concerning] 2 courtyards, one inside the other: the inner is liable, but the outer is exempt.

The masters' sayings assume a single principle: produce brought into a private courtyard becomes liable for tithes. Each saying gives, however, an independent formulation. It is striking that Yavneans and Ushans are grouped together.

In each of the three examples of the question-and-answer pattern, Aqiva's opinions are not intelligible without the question. Twice Aqiva's saying answers the question posed in the superscription but is formulated independently from the sayings of the other named masters (nos. 1, 3). In no. 2 Aqiva does not answer the question; instead he responds to the saying of the other master in the pericope. As noted above, a prior formulation, without the question, stands behind the tradition in no. 2.

E. Debate. Characteristic of a debate is the use of the past-tense, *said*, and *to him* (or *to them*).

1. T. Dem. 5:24

*m*ᶜ*śh š*- Our rabbis entered Samaritan villages and were served vegetables, which Aqiva tithed.
Said to him Gamaliel: How do you dare transgress the words of your colleagues; or, who gave you permission to tithe?
[Aqiva] said to him: Have I established a *halakhah?*
[Aqiva] said to him: I tithed only my own.
[Gamaliel] said to him: Know that you established a *halakhah.*

The attributive formularies of the debate carry forward the dialogue in the story. Gamaliel opens and closes the discussion. Aqiva's answer is naive. As noted in the comment on the pericope, the dialogue has been developed.

2. M. Ter. 9:2

[Concerning a field sown with seeds of Heave-offering:]
Tarfon: Only the poor priests should glean. Perhaps [poor Israelites] might forget and place [the gleanings] in their mouths.
Said Aqiva to him: If so, only the clean should glean.

Aqiva responds to the reason given for Tarfon's position. Aqiva puts forward a *reductio ad absurdum.* Tarfon does not reply.

In Houses' materials debates regularly develop out of dispute-forms. Neither of the foregoing examples corresponds to an extant Aqivan dispute-form. The sample obviously is statistically insignificant.

F. Juxtaposition of opinions of different masters; the saying of the second (and sometimes third or subsequent) master frequently depends upon the saying of the first. This form serves as a variation on the dispute-form.

1. M. Pe. 3:6

Eliezer: Land of the size of a quarter-*qab* is liable for *pe*ᵓ*ah.*
Joshua: That which produces 2 *se*ᵓ*ahs.*
Tarfon: 6 by 6 handbreadths.
Judah b. Bathyra: Enough to harvest and repeat. And the *halakhah* is according to his words.

Aqiva: Land of any size is liable for *pe^ɔah*, and for first-fruits, and to write a *prosbul* on its basis, and to be acquired along with movable property by money, or by document, or by presumption.

Joshua's and Tarfon's sayings assume the topic set in Eliezer's. The gloss about the *halakhah* separates the three masters' opinions from Aqiva's. Aqiva restates "is liable for *pe*ʾ*ah*" and adds several other obligations. Aqiva's saying disputes each of the foregoing opinions, although it most closely resembles the statement attributed to Eliezer. The difference between Aqiva and Eliezer is, *Land of the size of a quarter qab* vs. *Land of any size.*

2. T. Shev. 3:5

They clear away stones via the public domain, words of Joshua.
Aqiva: Just as one does not have the authority to make a clutter, so one does not have the authority to clear away stones.

In the context of T. Shev. 3:5 the masters refer to the problem of removing stones from private property during the Seventh-year. Aqiva's saying depends upon the reference to "public domain" in Joshua's statement. (M. Shev. 3:10 supplies a question, "What do they do with dirt?", to introduce the masters' opinions.) The two sayings in fact use different vocabulary. (*ršwt* in Joshua's statement refers to "public *domain*"; for Aqiva *ršwt* refers to the "authority" to clutter or to clear.)

3. M. Ter. 4:8

Joshua says: Black figs neutralize the white, and the white neutralize the black.
[Concerning] round cakes of pressed figs:
The large neutralize the small, and the small neutralize the large; the round neutralize the quadrangular, and the quadrangular neutralize the round.
Eliezer forbids.
Aqiva says: When what fell in can be distinguished, one does not neutralize the other; but when what fell in cannot be distinguished, one neutralizes the other.

The context is a series of disputes between Joshua and Eliezer concerning Heave-offering produce which becomes mixed with common produce. Aqiva responds neither to Joshua's saying nor to the preceding dispute-form (Eliezer's opinion on fig-cakes). Instead Aqiva speaks to the general question at issue. Although it is formulated independent of the foregoing, Aqiva's saying depends upon the context for intelligibility. As noted in the comment on this pericope, Aqiva's view conforms to the position consistently taken by Eliezer.

4. M. Ter. 6:6

> Eliezer says: They pay back from one kind for a different kind. Provided that he pays back from a better instead of from a worse kind.
>
> Aqiva says: They pay back only from one kind for its own kind.

The legal issue is whether substitutions can be made for Heave-offering. Aqiva's saying balances the first part of the statement attributed to Eliezer (*pay back from one kind for another* vs. *pay back only from one kind for its own kind*).

5. M. Ter. 10:11

> Yosé says: All [kinds of unconsecrated produce] that are boiled with beets are prohibited [to non-priests].
>
> Simeon says: A cabbage from irrigated soil with a cabbage from rain-watered-soil is prohibited, because the one absorbs [the juices from the other].
>
> Aqiva says: All which are cooked one with the other are permitted, except with the meat.

Aqiva's saying is formulated independent of the foregoing statements attributed to the Ushans. (K, P, and M read "Judah" in place of Aqiva.)

6. M. Ma. 4:6

> Eliezer says: The caperbush is tithed for stalks, and caperberries, and caper-flowers.
>
> Aqiva says: It is tithed only for caperberries, because they [alone] are fruit.

Aqiva's saying depends upon "the caperbush" in Eliezer's saying. Aqiva mentions only the item about which the masters agree—tithes are paid for caperberries. The gloss, "because they are fruit," makes the argument explicit. In a standard dispute-form, the topic-statement would be "stalks and flowers of the caperbush," and the masters would differ with regard to the use of the negative, e.g., *one tithes* vs. *one does not tithe*.

7. b. Yeb. 86a

Heave-offering to the priest and first-tithe to the Levite, words of Aqiva.

Eleazar b. [c]Azariah says: To the priest.

Eleazar's saying depends upon the last part of Aqiva's saying, "first-tithe to the Levite." This is a simple variation on the dispute-form, with the difference being, *Levite* vs. *priest.*

8. y. M.S. 14

Ishmael interpreted, 'And you shall give the money however much you want,' as a general statement; 'in cattle or in sheep or in wine or in liquor,' as a limitation; 'and in anything which you want' (Deut. 14:26), this too is another general statement. General statement—limitation—general statement: you reason in terms of the limitation. That is to say, just as the limitation is interpreted as something which is (a) produce or (b) the product of produce of the land, so too it can be only something which is (a) produce or (b) the product of produce of the land.

Aqiva interprets: Just as the limitation is interpreted as something which is (a) produce or (b) a product of produce or (c) is connected with acts preliminary to eating produce, so too I have only something which is (a) produce or (b) the product of produce or (c) something connected with acts preliminary to eating produce.

Aqiva's saying depends upon the citation of the verse and the exegetical principle in Ishmael's statement. The difference between the masters is that Aqiva adds (c), an extra item as part of the "limitation."

9. M. Bik. 3:9

Simeon b. Nanos says: They bedeck the first-fruits [with produce] other than the 7 species.

Aqiva says: They bedeck the first-fruits only [with produce] of the 7 species

This is a variation on the dispute-form. The masters' opinions balance. The difference is *they bedeck with other than* vs. *they bedeck only with.* In standard form the dispute would lend itself to a topic statement which focuses on the use of produce other than the 7 species (e.g., *they bedeck first-fruits with produce other than the 7 species*); and the masters would differ on *permitted* vs. *prohibited.*

The sample of items is small. Mnemonic devices are not noteworthy. In one pericope, no. 5, the masters give different opinions which are formulated completely independent of one another. In no. 3 Aqiva's position agrees with that attributed to another master, Eliezer, but Aqiva's saying is formulated completely independent of all of the other statements in the pericope. In four items (nos. 2, 6, 7, 8), the saying of one master depends upon that of another master. In one case (no. 2), however, the dependence relates solely to topic and not to language; and in the other three cases mnemonic considerations are not striking (no. 6: *stalks*, *berries, flowers* vs. *only berries*—which draws a gloss; no. 7: *Levite* vs. *priest*; and no. 8: Aqiva adds "something connected with acts preliminary to eating produce" to Ishmael's catalog).

Two items (nos. 4 and 9) exhibit opinions which balance. In both cases Aqiva uses an "only" (*ʾyn...ʾlʾ*) formulation. In no. 4 Aqiva alleges that one kind of produce cannot be substituted for Heave-offering of a different kind of produce; Eliezer allows substitutions. And in no. 9 Aqiva restricts to the 7 species the kinds of produce which can be used to bedeck first-fruits; Simeon b. Nanos allows other kinds of produce to be used.

One item (no. 1), as it stands, gives Aqiva's saying as independent of four preceding opinions. But the language of part of Aqiva's statement resembles that of one of the other masters, Eliezer, and a dispute between the two could readily be constructed (*Land the size of a quarter qab* vs. *Land of any size*). The difference is quarter *qab* vs. anything.

G. Witness-Form. The following items occur in a form which is not familiar from the traditions of Eliezer, Joshua, Gamaliel or Ishmael. This form is characterized by the past-tense, *said*, plus *before R. Aqiva*.

1-2. M. Shev. 8:9-10

> A hide anointed with oil of the 7th-year:
> Eliezer says: It is to be burned.
> But sages say: He should eat [produce of] equal value.
> They said before Aqiva: Eliezer used to say...
> He said to them: Silence. I shall not tell you what Eliezer says concerning it.
> And further they said before him: Eliezer used to say, 'He who eats the bread of Samaritans is like one who eats the flesh of a pig.'
> He said to them: Silence. I shall not tell you...

Anonymous individuals cite Eliezer's opinion on two different issues *before* R. Aqiva. In both instances the identical language is attributed to Aqiva, who refuses to reveal Eliezer's view. This implies that the anonymous parties seek to know Eliezer's true opinions, which clearly differ from those cited in the lemmas *said before R. Aqiva.*

3. T. Shev. 2:13

> Simeon Shizuri says: Egyptian beans which they planted from the outset for sheaves and also large beans and everything which is like them are tithed for the past [year] and are permitted in the 7th-year.
>
> But if [they are] not [one-third grown] they are forbidden in the 7th-year and are tithed for the following year.
>
> Said ben Azzai before R. Aqiva in the name of R. Joshua: Even after they have taken root.
>
> Aqiva reversed [his opinion] so as to teach according to the words of ben Azzai.

Simeon and Joshua differ with regard to the moment at which Egyptian beans become liable for tithes. Ben Azzai cites Joshua's opinion, "even after they have taken root," *before R. Aqiva.* The form is complex. First, there is a difference between Simeon and Joshua on *one-third-grown* vs. *taken root.* Second, there is ben Azzai's testimony concerning Joshua's opinion, to which Aqiva responds by reversing his own opinion so as to be in agreement with Joshua's rule.

4. T. Shev. 5:12

> Testified Judah b. Isaiah the spice-maker before Aqiva in the name of Tarfon that *qtp* [is subject to the laws of the] 7th-year.

The pericope gives *"testified,"* rather than *said.* It states, *before Aqiva,* however, and thus may be included as a witness-form. Judah simply states the view of another master, Tarfon, regarding the obligation of *qtp* for the laws of the 7th-year. Aqiva does not respond.

5. M. Ter. 4:13

> Said Yosé: A case came before Aqiva concerning 50 bundles of vegetables in the midst of which fell a similar [bundle of vegetables], half of which was Heave-offering. And I said before him, 'It should neutralize—not because the Heave-offering should neutralize in [a mixture of] 51 [parts], but

because there were there [among the bundles] 102 halves.'

Here Yosé reports an opinion which he himself previously delivered *before Aqiva* with regard to a specific legal problem. Aqiva does not respond.

It is striking that the *said-before-X*-form occurs five times in Aqiva's traditions on agriculture, which comprise approximately one-sixth of the entire tradition, and not at all in entire traditions of other major Yavneans. Nonetheless this is a very small sample of items. And the form is used in several different ways. In nos. 1 and 2 Aqiva is asked about the opinions of another master, Eliezer. These questions reflect an interest in the transmission of opinions of a specific master. By contrast, the items in nos. 3, 4, and 5 focus on the rules at issue. In no. 3 a named master, ben Azzai, cites an opinion and attributes it to another master, Joshua. Aqiva responds by reversing his previous view so as to teach in accord with Joshua's opinion. By contrast, in no. 4 Aqiva does not respond to Judah b. Isaiah, who cites an opinion and attributes it to Tarfon. In no. 5 Yosé, an Ushan, reports a rule he himself stated *before R. Aqiva* regarding a specific case. Again Aqiva does not respond.

H. First-person report: *Said X + I said/did...*

1. M. Ter. 4:13

See G5, above.

2. M. M.S. 2:7

House of Shammai say: A man should not change his selas [of Second-tithe money for] gold *denars*.

But House of Hillel permit.

Said Aqiva: I changed Gamaliel's and Joshua's silver for gold *denars*.

Aqiva's report supplies a story to show that the law is in accord with the view of the Hillelites.

I. *Added X + lemma.*

1. M. Kil. 1:3/T. Kil. 1:3

The turnip and the radish, and the cabbage and the cauliflower, the beets and the orach;

Added Aqiva: The garlic and the wild garlic, the onion and wild onion, and the lupine and the wild lupine,
Are not [considered] Mixed-kinds [when they grow] beside each other.

Aqiva adds a series of pairs to those listed in the foregoing.

J. *ʾmr X + lemma*

1. M. Shev. 6:2

[In the 7th-year] in Syria they work with [crop which is] detached but not with attached [crop]. They thresh and winnow and trample and bind into sheaves, but they do not reap grain or gather grapes or harvest olives.
Aqiva laid down a general rule (*kll ʾmr*): Everything which is similar to what is permitted in the land of Israel is permitted in Syria.

Aqiva states a principle. By contrast, the preceding anonymous statement focuses on details.

K. *X Taught + lemma*

1. M. M.S. 5:8

Said Judah: Formerly they used to send [the following instructions] to landowners in the provinces, 'Hurry and take care of your produce before the time for removal arrives; until Aqiva came and taught that all the produce which did not enter into the season of tithes is exempt from the removal.

The form is complex. Judah reports a tradition in which Aqiva's 'teaching' is set off against what was done 'formerly.' As noted in the comment on this pericope, "Formerly...until Aqiva came and taught" is formulaic; it distinguishes between different opinions and recurs elsewhere in the Aqivan tradition.

L. Narrative is not a form. Nonetheless stories provide a distinguishable sample of items. Most of the following are introduced by *mᶜśh b* or *š*-. The stories frequently provide illustrations of, or precedents for, law.

1. T. Dem. 4:13

Said Yosah: *mᶜśh š*- a shipment of beans arrived in Meron. And they came and asked Aqiva, and he permitted them [to buy all beans in] the market [without obligation for tithing].

[Later] they said to him, 'Master, the [supplies of imported beans] have diminished.' And the market returned to its previous condition.

m^{c}śh š- introduces the Ushan master's story. The incident illustrates a rule about obligation for tithing produce. Normally domestic produce is liable for tithes; in the face of competition from imported produce, however, liability may be temporarily waived. Aqiva seems to function in the story merely as an authoritative name.

2. T. Dem. 5:24

m^{c}śh š- Our rabbis entered Samaritan villages and were served vegetables, which Aqiva tithed.
Said to him Gamaliel: How do you dare transgress the words of your colleagues; or, who gave you permission to tithe?
[Aqiva] said to him: Have I established a *halakhah*?
[Aqiva] said to him: I tithed only my own.
[Gamaliel] said to him: Know that you established a *halakhah*.

m^{c}śh š- introduces the story. *Said to him* characterizes the debate-form, which is here considerably developed. In context the story precedes an account of how Gamaliel visited Samaritan territory and decreed that Samaritans' vegetables must be tithed, as Aqiva assumes. The narrative points up Aqiva's act as a precedent for law. Aqiva himself, however, is made to appear ingenuous.

3. M. Kil. 7:5

Said Yosé: *m^{c}śh b-* One who sowed his vineyard during the 7th-year, and the case came before Aqiva. And he said: 'A man cannot forfeit something which does not belong to him.'

m^{c}śh b- introduces the Ushan master's narrative. The case is a legal conundrum, and the decision attributed to Aqiva is a stock phrase. (In the preceding pericope, M. Kil. 7:4, it is attributed jointly to Yosé and to Simeon, another Ushan.) Aqiva functions as an authoritative name.

4. T. Shev. 4:21

m^{c}śh b- Aqiva picked an *etrog* on the first of *Shevat* and acted with it according to the words of the House of Shammai and according to the words of Liezer.
R. Yosah b. R. Judah [says]: According to the words of Rabban Gamaliel and according to the words of R. Liezer.

m^c^ŝh b- introduces the narrative. The story illustrates how Aqiva acted in a situation for which sages had provided different prescriptions. The Houses differ with regard to the time of the New Year for trees (M. R.H. 1:1); the story implies that Aqiva picked the *etrog* on the first of *Shevat* and then gave two different kind of tithes, one of which would be required on the Hillelite view and the other on the Shammaite view. Yosah b. Judah further alleges that Aqiva acted in accord with the views of both Gamaliel and Eliezer, who differ as to whether the *etrog* is tithed as a fruit or as a vegetable; this again implies that Aqiva gave two different tithes.

5. M. M.S. 5:9

> *m^c^ŝh b-* Gamaliel and the elders were travelling on a ship. Said Gamaliel: The tithe which I am going to measure is given to Joshua, and the land it grows on is rented to him. Another tithe which I am going to measure is given to Aqiva ben Joseph that he may possess it on behalf of the poor, and the land it grows on is rented to him.
>
> Said R. Joshua: The tithe which I am going to measure is given to Eleazar b. ^c^Azariah, and the land it grows on is rented to him.
>
> And they received rent from each other.

In context the narrative provides a precedent for the rule that at the time for removal a person who is at a distance from his field should designate tithes from his crop. Aqiva plays a subordinate role; no opinion is attributed to him.

6. T. M.S. 1:13

> [Concerning] cakes of saffron:
>
> Said Yosah:
>
> Yoḥanan b. Nuri approached Ḥalafta [and] said to him: What is the status of saffron-cakes? May they purchased with Second-tithe money?
>
> He said to him: They may not be purchased.
>
> He said to him: I am of the same opinion, but Aqiva said that they may be purchased.

The story reports a conversation between two Ushan masters concerning Aqiva's opinion about saffron-cakes. Yosah, an Ushan, is Ḥalafta's son.

7a. y. M.S. 5:5

> Ba used to tell the story: Leazar b. ^{c}Azariah used to take tithes from a garden which had 2 exits, one of which led to a cemetery. Aqiva ordered the other exit closed off, thus preventing Leazar, a priest, from returning to the garden. Num. 18-31 is cited to defend Aqiva's action. Leazar admitted defeat and returned all the tithes he had previously taken.

The narrative is much longer than the other stories. It includes passages in both Hebrew and Aramaic, a reference to Scripture, and an exegesis. The story illustrates the rule that one does not give first-tithes to priests.

7b. b. Yeb. 86b

> There was a garden from which Eleazar b. ^{c}Azariah used to take first-tithe. Aqiva moved the exit so that it faced a cemetery. Eleazar conceded to Aqiva.

Shorter than the narrative in no. 7a, this story illustrates the same law: priests do not receive first-tithe.

The sample of narratives is statistically insignificant. *m^{c}śh b-* or *š* introduces most of the narratives (nos. 1-5). Except for no. 7a, all of the stories are short. In two cases narratives provide illustrations for laws (no. 1: suspension of a *demaʾi*-regulation; no. 7: priests do not collect first-tithe). Two stories provide precedents for law (no. 2: Samaritans' vegetables must be tithed; no. 5: a person at a distance from his field designates tithes from his crop). Gamaliel figures prominently in both precedent-narratives; by contrast, Aqiva plays an ingenuous role in one (no. 2), and only a subordinate role in the other (no. 5). One case (no. 3) gives legal conundrum. And one story (no. 4) relates Aqiva's action to conflicting legal positions attributed to different masters.

M. Collection of Traditions. Beyond the single, simple pericope, larger units of tradition can be distinguished. In traditions about the Houses, about Yoḥanan b. Zakkai, and about Eliezer, Neusner distinguishes between "collections" and "composites." [8] The former consist of small units with separate legal opinions combined, each unit with its own

[8] *Eliezer*, Vol. II, pp. 53-60.

superscription, into a larger unit of tradition. Composites, by contrast, combine separate legal statements in a complex unit with a single superscription. In Aqiva's traditions on agriculture we find one example of a composite—and no collections.

1. M. Pe. 1:6

At any time one may give [part of his crop] for *pe'ah* and is exempt from tithes, until he finishes stacking.
And he may renounce ownership and is exempt from tithes, until he finishes stacking.
And he may feed to cattle, to a wild animal or to birds and is exempt from tithes, until he finishes stacking.
And he may take from the threshing-floor and sow and is exempt from tithes, until he finishes stacking, words of Aqiva.

Four separate rules are given. Each deals with exemption of crop from tithes; and in each case the process of stacking provides the principle which marks the expiration of the exemption.

iii. *Summary of Forms and Formulary Patterns*

The following table summarizes the forms and formulary patterns discussed above. (Some pericopae, it should be noted, yield more than one form: M. Ter. 4:13, for instance, includes both a first-person report and a witness-form.)

Table E

Summary of Forms and Formulary Patterns

Form or Pattern		*No. of times*
A.	Dispute-form	24
B.	Citation of Citation of Scripture + lemma	2
C.	Anonymous law + gloss	10
D.	Questions + answers	3
E.	Debate	2
F.	Juxtaposition of different masters' sayings	9
G.	Witness-form	5
H.	First-person reports	2
I.	*Added* X + lemma	1
J.	*Said* X + lemma	1
K.	X *taught* + lemma	1
L.	Narrative	7
M.	Large units of tradition	1
	Total	68

Slightly less than three-quarters of the identifiable forms and formulary patterns in Aqiva's traditions on agriculture are disputes (48 out of 68 items, or 71% of the total). Half of these are in standard form (A—24 items), and half are in variations (B, C, D, F—24 items). Although not statistically significant, the sample of examples of the witness-form (G—5 items) marks off Aqiva's tradition from the Houses' and the other Yavnean masters' traditions, for the latter contain few or no instances of the form.

The seven narratives are scattered in function. Two stories give illustrations of law. Two give precedents for law; both of these relate primarily to Gamaliel, however, and in one case Aqiva is mentioned only in passing. One story gives a legal conundrum, and it is not clear that Aqiva contributes anything more than a famous name. And one story explains an act performed by Aqiva by reference to conflicting opinions attributed to different sages.

Only one example of a large unit of tradition, a composite, occurs in the entire corpus. By contrast, complex units of tradition are relatively frequent in the Houses' materials and also occur in the traditions of Eliezer and Yoḥanan b. Zakkai.

No form can be identified with a particular circle of tradents. The number of examples of the witness-form is statistically insignificant. And the examples of the dispute, the predominant formulation in Aqiva's traditions on agriculture, match Aqiva with a variety of other masters. Among the disputes in standard form, only three masters' names occur in more than a single tradition; Ishmael occurs with Aqiva five times, Eliezer four times, and Tarfon two times. The incidence of intersections in examples of variations on the standard dispute-form shows a similar randomness. The identification of forms aids in the exegesis of Aqiva's traditions on agriculture but not in the determination of the history of those traditions.

CHAPTER FOUR

ATTESTATIONS

i. *Introduction*

An "attestation" provides a *terminus ante quem* for a tradition. Different sorts of attestations can be distinguished. First, the publication of works like Mishnah and Tosefta, which account for most of Aqiva's traditions on agriculture, provides a *terminus ante quem* for the traditions which the collections contain. Mishnah is generally taken to have been promulgated by Judah the patriarch at the end of the second century, and Tosefta probably was put together shortly afterwards. Since Aqiva died during the first half of the second century, more than sixty years separate his death from the compilation of his opinions in M.-T. This first sort of attestation, publication of M.-T., obviously provides no information about the nature and transmission of Aqiva's sayings during the master's lifetime or in the half-century after his death. It shows only that certain sayings were attributed to Aqiva by approximately A.D. 200.

A second sort of attestation derives from the content of legal sayings attributed to masters other than Aqiva. If another master makes a statement which assumes an opinion attributed to Aqiva, or if another master's statement develops Aqiva's view, or refines the legal theory upon which Aqiva's view is based, then it is evident that Aqiva's opinion predates the view attributed to the other master. If the other master is an Ushan, then the chronological sequence suggested by the attributions supports the logic internal to the development of the law.

This latter sort of attestation must be distinguished from mere reference to an Aqivan tradition by another master (e.g., *Said X, Aqiva used to say...*). Such references obviously reflect interest in the transmission of Aqivan sayings. They may even provide a "chain of tradition," an attributive formula which gives a series of specific masters' names: *Said X in the name of Y*. A chain is of interest with regard to the designation of circles of tradents. The reliability of such references depends, however, upon the reliability of attributions in general—and that in turn is measured best by reference to the logical development internal to discussions of discrete legal issues. [1]

The distinction between "attestation" and "mere reference" can be illustrated by the contrast between the traditions at T. M.S. 2:12 and 2:16. The same principle underlies the opinions attributed to Aqiva in the two pericopae. That principle is that the boundary of Jerusalem, understood as an imaginary line running parallel to the city-wall, is crucial to the disposition of problems relating to Second-tithe produce. The issue at 2:16 relates to Second-tithe produce which, once inside the city, is discovered to be unclean. Aqiva holds that the produce is redeemed and eaten inside the city if the uncleanness was contracted inside the city and outside if the uncleanness was contracted outside the city. Eliezer alleges that the source of uncleanness, and not the place at which uncleanness is contracted, is crucial; the produce should be eaten and redeemed outside if the source is a Father of uncleanness and inside if the source is an Offspring. In the same pericope Ushan masters, Meir and Judah, give Houses' disputes which develop the opinions attributed to the two Yavnean masters. Meir's and Judah's Houses attempt to correlate the different principles of Aqiva and Eliezer, e.g., Meir's Hillelites allege that the produce is redeemed and eaten inside the city, except if it contracts uncleanness from a Father outside. The logical development internal to the law, supported by the chronology of the attributions, provides an attestation to the Yavneans' opinions. Minimally we can say that Eliezer's and Aqiva's view must have preceded the opinions formulated by the Ushans. (The manufacture of Houses' disputes by Ushans is not uncommon. [2])

By contrast, in a discussion of olive presses attached to the wall of Jerusalem, Yosé merely alleges that a particular opinion is "the teaching" of Aqiva. That particular opinion is consistent with the view attributed to Aqiva at 2:16, and it may therefore be argued that the Ushan attestation at 2:16 also extends to the view attributed to Aqiva in 2:12. Yosé's reference to Aqiva's opinion, however, does not provide an attestation, although it does evidence Yosé's interest in the transmission of Aqivan traditions.

In this chapter I survey all references and attestations to Aqivan traditions on agriculture in M.-T. Yavnean references are taken up first

---

[1] Neusner's discussions of the development of the law in the first tractates in *Seder Tohorot* suggest the reliability, in general, of attributions in these tractates. See e.g., HMLP, Vol. III, Chapter 34, Attributions, pp. 237-72.

[2] J. Neusner, *Phar.*, Vol. III, p. 282, and HMLP, Vol. III, pp. 361-65.

(2 items), then Ushan (10 items), and then those attributed to masters of the generation of Rabbi (2 items). Finally I list those pericopae first attested by publication in M.-T. (37 items). The results of this chapter are mostly negative: attestation, like forms, prove to be of little help in distinguishing different strata among Aqiva's traditions on agriculture.

ii. *The Generations*

I. *Yavneh*

a. Abba Saul

1. T. Kil. 4:10

And [concerning] greens which stretch under the vine: Abba Saul says,
Aqiva says: One returns [the greens to their place].
Ben Azzai says: One trims [them].

Aqiva's and ben Azzai's opinions do not necessarily conflict (see comment on the pericope), which suggests that the dispute is artificial. The attribution to Abba Saul, a late Yavnean, provides a chain of tradition for the sayings of the earlier master(s): *Abba Saul says, Aqiva says,... ben Azzai says...* Normally, however, chains of tradition use the past tense, *said* (*Said X in the name of Y*, or *Said X said Y*).

b. Yoḥanan b. Nuri and Ḥalafta

1. T. M.S. 1:13

[Concerning] cakes of saffron:
Said Yosah:
R. Yoḥanan b. Nuri approached R. Ḥalafta [and] asked him:
What is the status of saffron-cakes? May they be purchased with Second-tithe money?
He said to him: They may not be purchased.
He said to him: I am of the same opinion, but Aqiva said that they may be purchased.

Yoḥanan reports Aqiva's opinion. Yoḥanan and Ḥalafta are Yavneans, and Yosah, Ḥalafta's son, is an Ushan. The pericope suggests an obvious line of transmission: Yoḥanan b. Nuri to Ḥalafta to Yosah.

Neither of the foregoing items supplies an attestation to an Aqivan opinion. In both cases Yavnean masters simply cite Aqiva's views.

II. Usha

a. Yosé/Yosah (b. Ḥalafta)

1. T. Dem. 4:21

Said Yosah:

mᶜśh š- A shipment of beans arrived in Meron. They asked Aqiva, and he permitted the purchase of all beans in the market without obligation for tithing; after the supply of imported beans was diminished, the market returned to its previous condition.

Yosah gives a story about Aqiva. Aqiva's view—that in certain circumstances the rules of *demaʾi*-produce may be suspended—is assumed in the story and not spelled out. The attribution to Yosah obviously provides evidence regarding the transmission of Aqivan traditions; it does not supply, however, an attestation to Aqiva's opinion.

2. M. Kil. 7:5

Said Yosé: *mᶜśh b-* One who sowed his vineyard during the Seventh-year, and the case came before Aqiva: he said, 'A man cannot forfeit something which does not belong to him.'

Yosé merely cites Aqiva's saying. Aqiva responds to a legal conundrum, the problem of Mixed-kinds of seed planted in a vineyard during the 7th-year. The saying attributed to Aqiva, 'a man cannot forfeit...,' occurs elsewhere. Indeed, it is attributed jointly to Yosé and to Simeon, another Ushan, in the preceding pericope, M. Kil. 7:4.

3. M. Ter. 4:13

Said Yosé: A case came before Aqiva concerning 50 bundles of vegetables in the midst of which fell a similar [bundle of vegetables], half of which was Heave-offering. And I said before him, 'It should not neutralize...'

Yosé merely cites the case which came before Aqiva. The tradition focuses on Yosé's opinion, not Aqiva's.

4. T. M.S. 1:13

See above, I.b.1.

5. T. M.S. 2:1

[Concerning vetches] of Heave-offering:

House of Shammai say: They soak in cleanness, and they grind and give as food in uncleanness.

But House of Hillel say: They soak in cleanness, and they grind and give as food in uncleanness.

But House of Hillel say: They soak and grind in cleanness, and they give as food in uncleanness, words of Judah.

Meir says:

House of Shammai say: They soak and grind in cleanness, and they give as food in uncleanness.

But House of Hillel say: Whatever concerns them in uncleanness.

Said Yosé: This is the teaching of Aqiva.

Therefore [Aqiva] says: They may be given to any priest.

But sages did not agree with him.

Yosé reports the 'teaching' of Aqiva: Heave-offering vetches may be handled in uncleanness. Meir attributes that opinion to the House of Hillel. M. M.S. 2:14, like Yosé, attributes that specific opinion to Aqiva. Yosé obviously does not attest Aqiva's view.

6. T. M.S. 2:12

[Concerning] olive presses in or attached to the wall of Jerusalem:

House of Shammai say: They do not redeem Second-tithe produce in such places, nor do they eat lesser sanctified things in them.

But House of Hillel say: The area from the wall and inwards is considered inside the city, and from the wall outwards is considered outside the city.

Said Yosah: This is the teaching of Aqiva.

The prior teaching was,

> House of Shammai say: They do not redeem Second-tithe produce in such places nor do they eat lesser sanctified things there.
>
> But House of Hillel say: Lo, they are like the chambers of the Temple—whatever the exit of which is to the inside is inside and whatever the exit of which is to the outside is outside.

Yosah reports the 'teaching' of Aqiva: an imaginary line, parallel to the boundary of the city, divides the room. Yosah obviously does not provide an attestation for Aqiva's opinion. But cp. Judah's and Meir's opinions at T. M.S. 2:16.

b. Judah (b. Ilai)

1. M. Kil. 3:3

One seeks to sow a row of vegetables in the midst of a field planted with another kind of vegetable:
Ishmael says [He may not do so] unless there is an open furrow extending from one end of the field to the other.
Aqiva says: An area in length six handbreadths and fully as wide.
Judah says: In width a *prsh*.

At issue is the demarcation of the area in which a row of vegetables can be planted within a field previously planted with a different kind of vegetable. Judah's saying depends upon Aqiva's. Judah in fact disputes the measure which Aqiva gives for the width of the area. A *prsh* is smaller than six handbreadths. Although in context Judah's opinion assumes Aqiva's, it cannot be shown that Judah's view represents a development upon that of the earlier masters.

2. M. M.S. 5:8

Said Judah: Formerly they used to send to landowners in the provinces, 'Hurry and take care of your produce before the time for removal arrives.' Until Aqiva came and taught that all the produce which did not enter into the season of tithes is exempt from the removal.

Judah simply cites Aqiva's legal innovation.

3. T. M.S. 2:16

Concerning 2nd-tithe produce which entered Jerusalem and contracted uncleanness:
House of Shammai: Redeemed and eaten inside.
House of Hillel: Redeemed and eaten inside, except that which contracted uncleanness by a Father outside—words of Meir.
Judah says:
House of Shammai: Redeemed and eaten inside, except that which contracted uncleanness by a Father outside.
House of Hillel: Redeemed and eaten outside, except that which contracted uncleanness by an Offspring inside.
Leazar: If by a Father—outside; by an Offspring—inside.

Aqiva: If contracted outside—then outside; inside—then inside.
Said Simeon b. Leazar: Houses disputed only with regard to that which contracted uncleanness by a Father inside *or* by an Offspring outside—
House of Shammai say: Eaten and redeemed in the place in which it contracted uncleanness.
House of Hillel say: Redeemed in same place and eaten in any place.

Aqiva and Eliezer differ on a major principle: What criterion pertains to the disposition of unclean 2nd-tithe produce in Jerusalem? Aqiva holds that the place in which uncleanness is contracted (whether inside or outside the city) is crucial; Eliezer alleges that the source of uncleanness is decisive. The Houses' opinions, as formulated by the Ushans, reflect the effort to correlate the views attributed to the two Yavnean masters. Meir's and Judah's Houses assume that both categories, the place of contraction and the source of uncleanness, are relevant to the problem. The chronology of the attributions supports the logic of the development of the legal positions; the Ushans thus supply an attestation to the Yavneans' views. Simeon's reformulation represents still a further refinement. The manufacture of Houses' disputes by Ushans is not uncommon. [3]

4. Sifré Num. 110

Judah says:
[Concerning] imported produce:
Eliezer declares it exempt...
And Aqiva declares it liable [for dough-offering]...
[Concerning] exported produce:
Eliezer declares it liable...
Aqiva exempts it...

Judah simply reports the Eliezer-Aqiva disputes. He does not provide an attestation to the Yavnean masters' opinions.

c. Simeon (b. Yoḥai)

1. T. Kil. 1:2

Added R. Aqiva: The garlic and the wild garlic, and the onion and the wild onion, and the lupine and the wild lupine.

---

[3] Ibid.

> Said Simeon: Aqiva taught only with regard to the first two pairs; but the lupine and the wild lupine are not considered Mixed-kinds when they grow beside each other.

Simeon refers to a teaching of Aqiva regarding pairs of items which are considered Mixed-kinds when they grow beside each other. The Ushan master presumably assumes the list of pairs which Aqiva "added." Simeon alleges, however, that the list is in error: Aqiva did not teach that each of the pairs listed is considered Mixed-kinds. In any case, Simeon focuses on the accurate transmission of Aqivan opinions on the problem.

The foregoing includes only eleven (11) items with attributions to merely four Ushan masters (Yosé—6 times; Judah—4 times; Meir and Simeon—once each). Among these traditions I can identify only one attestation (Meir + Judah; T. M.S. 2:16). No chain of tradition occurs.

Reference to Aqiva's "teaching" occurs three times, twice with attributions to Yosé (T. M.S. 2:1 and 2:12) and once with an attribution to Simeon (T. Kil. 1:2). In one case Judah seems to gloss an Aqivan dispute (M. Kil. 3:3). In two other cases Judah reports Aqiva's opinion, once as part of a dispute-form (Sifré Num. 110) and once in a setting which suggests that Aqiva's opinion represents a legal innovation (M. M.S. 5:8). Yosé gives three *m*[c]*śh*-stories which refer to Aqiva; but the sayings attributed to Aqiva in two of the stories are dubious (T. Dem. 4:21; M. Kil. 7:5), and the third story reports Yosé's, and not Aqiva's, opinion (M. Ter. 4:17). Yosé also reports a fourth story which includes a reference to Aqiva by a Yavnean master, Yoḥanan b. Nuri (T. M.S. 1:13).

III. Bet Shearim

a. Simeon b. Eleazar

1. T. Ma. 2:20

> Simeon b. Eleazar says in the name of Aqiva: [Produce brought into] any courtyard which one opens and [another] one closes is exempt from liability for tithes [= Aqiva's statement at M. Ma. 3:5].

Simeon b. Eleazar may be a late Ushan. I include him in the category of "Bet Shearim" in order to distinguish between him and other masters, Yosé, Judah, Simeon, Meir, who clearly belong to the generation of Usha.

The pericope provides a chain of tradition for the saying attributed to Aqiva at M. Ma. 3:5.

b. Yosah b. Judah

1. T. Shev. 4:21

m^{c}śh b- Aqiva picked an *etrog* on the 1st day of *Shevat* and acted with it according to the words of both Houses.

Yosah b. Judah: According to the words of Gamaliel and Liezer.

Yosah's lemma depends upon the story about Aqiva's picking an *etrog*. The Houses differ with regard to the date of the beginning of the new year for trees (M. R.H. 1:1); Gamaliel and Eliezer differ on whether the *etrog* is tithed as a fruit or as a vegetable (M. Bik. 2:6). Presumably Aqiva gave two tithes, and, in the first instance, his action is explained by reference to the different opinions of the two Houses. Yosah b. Judah further explains Aqiva's unusual action by reference to the opinions of the two other Yavnean masters. Yosah attests the story about Aqiva giving two tithes.

Of the two traditions which I have designated as attributed to masters of the generation of Bet Shearim, the first gives a chain of tradition (Simeon b. Eleazar; T. Ma. 2:20). The second tradition provides a late attestation to an enigmatic action by Aqiva (Yosah b. Judah; T. Shev. 4:21). Neither pericope contains an attestation to an Aqivan legal position.

IV. M.-T.

Aqivan traditions on agriculture in the following pericopae are neither attested nor referred to prior to their occurrence in M.-T.

1. M. Pe. 1:6
2. M. Pe. 3:2
3. M. Pe. 3:6
4. M. Pe. 4:5
5. M. Pe. 4:10
6. M. Pe. 7:7
7. M. Pe. 8:5
8. T. Pe. 2:21
9. T. Dem. 5:24

10. M. Kil. 3:6
11. M. Kil. 5:7/T. Kil. 1:15
12. M. Kil. 6:1
13. M. Shev. 1:8
14. M. Shev. 3:10/T. Kil. 3:5
15. M. Shev. 4:6
16. M. Shev. 6:2/T. Shev. 4:12
17-18. M. Shev. 8:9-10
19. M. Shev. 9:6
20. T. Shev. 2:13
21. T. Shev. 5:12
22. M. Ter. 3:3
23. M. Ter. 4:5
24. M. Ter. 4:8
25. M. Ter. 6:6/T. Ter. 7:9/T. Ter. 7:10
26. M. Ter. 9:2-3
27. M. Ter. 10:11/T. Ter. 9:4
28. M. Ma. 3:9
29. M. Ma. 4:6
30. T. Ma. 3:14
31. M. M.S. 2:7
32. M. M.S. 5:9
33. T. M.S. 2:16
34. M. Hal. 2:3/T. Hal. 1:9
35. M. Hal. 3:6/T. Hal. 1:12
36. M. Hal. 4:9
37. M. Or. 3:7
38. M. Bik. 3:9

iii. *Summary*

The foregoing has been an effort to determine whether it is possible to identify different strata, by generation, within the corpus of Aqivan traditions on agriculture. The results are almost entirely negative. Of the fifty-two (52) pericopae surveyed, almost three-quarters (38, or 73% of the total) contain traditions which are neither attested nor referred to prior to their occurrence in M.-T. No Yavnean attestations occur. Only one Ushan attestation can be identified. And in one instance a master of the generation of Bet Shearim provides a late attestation to a story about an unusual action of Aqiva—but not to a legal opinion attributed to the Yavnean master.

In the whole corpus only two chains of tradition occur. In one case a Yavnean master, Abba Saul, reports Aqiva's opinion; in the other Simeon b. Eleazar, a late Ushan, reports Aqiva's opinion.

The Ushan masters, Yosé, Judah, and Simeon account for nine references to Aqivan traditions on agriculture. They provide no chains of tradition. Judah refers to one of Aqiva's innovative legal positions, and Simeon and Yosé show an interest in accurately specifying Aqiva's "teaching." Yosé also reports several stories which refer to Aqiva—but Aqiva's legal opinions are not central to the stories. Strictly speaking, of course, the nine pericopae which contain Ushan references to Aqivan traditions on agriculture are themselves attested only by occurrence in M.-T. Nonetheless it is striking that relatively so few traditions are referred to Yavneans (2 instances out of 52, or 4% of the total) and by Ushans (no more than 12 instances out of 52, or 23% of the total).

CHAPTER FIVE

AQIVA AND THE LAW. CONCLUSIONS

i. *Introduction*

This chapter focuses on how Aqiva's traditions relate to the spectrum of legal issues in the individual tractates in M.-T. *Zera^cim*. Law in the tractates frequently reflects development through at least two stages, at Yavneh and at Usha, before ultimate redaction during the generation of Judah the patriarch at the end of the second century. The development of mishnaic law cannot be measured, however, into neat stages. Neusner, in his *History of the Mishnaic Laws of Purity*, has observed that metaphorical language drawn from geology, the search for "strata" in the law, and the like, does not accurately portray the issues involved in the study of the development of law in M.-T. Neusner prefers to speak of the "weaving" of the law. [1] The image derives from traditional language, for the Hebrew word for tractate, *masseket*, also means a web on a loom. A *masseket* in M.-T. represents the weaving together of different opinions and traditions on related legal problems. With a length of cloth a thread of a certain color may begin in one corner and continue without interruption through the length of the material. Or a thread of a primary color may at some point become intertwined with a thread of a different color to produce still a third hue. So with a tractate a single legal principle might be espoused without interruption from one generation to the next, or at some point it might be correlated with a different principle and be brought to bear on a problem undreamt of in a previous generation. In this chapter I ask about Aqiva's role as a weaver of the law in the different tractates in M.-T. *Zera^cim*.

Three considerations render Aqiva's corpus in M.-T. *Zera^cim* of significant interest. First, the size of Aqiva's tradition is, in absolute numbers, far larger than that of any other Yavnean master. Only a few Ushans have comparable traditions. How, we want to know, do the issues of Aqiva's tradition relate to the legal agenda in the ultimate redaction of the individual tractates? Are Aqiva's issues central to the development of the tractates, or are they not? The second consideration,

---

[1] HMLP, Vol. III, pp. 273-76.

the remarkable distribution-pattern of Aqiva's traditions, raises similar questions. As discussed in Chapter Two, the distribution of Aqivan pericopae in absolute numbers closely approximates the sizes of the different tractates as measured by reference to the numbers of chapters into which each tractate is divided. Can some correspondence be discerned between the distribution of Aqivan traditions and the specific legal problems taken up and formally worked out by the ultimate, and most careful, redactors of the material? It is possible to imagine that an editor could have introduced Aqivan pericopae into a tractate at any stage in the redaction process. Indeed, the evidence discussed in this chapter suggests exactly that conclusion. On the basis of the content of his traditions and their relation (or lack thereof) one to another, it is difficult to discern a proto-tractate in Aqiva's corpus in *Zeraᶜim*. Our question in this chapter is how in fact do Aqiva's positions relate to the content, and logical development, of the legal issues woven together in the different tractates. At issue obviously is the nature of Aqiva's influence on the legal agenda of masters in subsequent generations.

The third consideration is a negative one. *Prima facie* it would be preferable to begin this study with the identification of a core of Aqivan traditions, "Yavnean pericopae" in the sense that they give a Yavnean master's views on Yavnean issues. Development and application of Aqiva's principles could then be traced through the work of subsequent generations. As noted in Chapters Three and Four, however, indications external to the content of the law do not provide a formidable Yavnean "core" for Aqiva's corpus. The study of the forms of Aqiva's sayings yields information interesting for the exegesis of the master's opinions, but nothing concerning the development of his tradition. Only one, or at most two, firm Ushan attestations occur in the entire corpus. If the attributions supplied in M.-T. could be relied upon, the situation would be considerably less complicated. To date Neusner has shown that in the first tractates in *Seder Tohorot* attributions generally are reliable; Yavnean masters, for instance, do not discuss developments that proceed from fundamental principles introduced by Ushan masters. In the traditions I have surveyed in Part One I have discovered little or no evidence to suggest that attributions in *Seder Zeraᶜim* are any less reliable. The necessary work on the individual tractates, however, lies in front of us. For the present a more tentative approach is called for.

Measured against the issue at stake, the efforts in this chapter are necessarily modest. I survey the tractates in M.-T. *Zera^cim* in the order in which they occur. If a tractate contains more than one or two Aqivan pericopae, I briefly sketch the legal problems with which that tractate deals. Then I review Aqiva's traditions in the tractate and relate those traditions to the areas of concern in the tractate as a whole. Minimally we can distinguish between tractates in which Aqivan traditions relate to major areas of concern and tractates in which they do not. Obviously we measure "major" issues by criteria supplied by the redactors of the material. The proportion of space devoted to an issue is one important consideration. Another is the logical centrality of an issue to the law in a tractate. Certain tractates, such as *Terumot* and, to a lesser extent, *Kila*ʾ*im*, draw special attention, because Aqivan traditions relate to legal principles fundamental to their agenda.

ii. *The Tractates*

a. *Pe*ʾ*ah*

In tractate *Pe*ʾ*ah* attributions to Aqiva occur more frequently than to any other Yavnean master (8 times). Among the Ushans only Judah's name occurs as many times.

The tractate focuses on the following issues:

I. Regulations relating to produce liable for *pe*ʾ*ah:* quantities, place to be left in a field, time-limits (M. 1:1-6).

II. Definition of a field: divisions of areas within fields; minimum size of a plot (M. 2:1-3:8).

III. Methods of taking *pe*ʾ*ah* (M. 4:1-9).

IV. Gleanings: cases of doubtful gleanings; eligibility of persons to take gleanings (M. 4:10-5:6).

V. Forgotten things: sheaf in a field; contents of a vineyard (M. 5:7-7:6).

VI. Poor people: time-limit on exclusive right to *pe*ʾ*ah* and other gifts; credibility regarding tithing (M. 7:7-8:9).

VII. Poorman's tithe: amounts; eligibility; penalty for misappropriation.

An Aqivan tradition occurs at M. 1:6. *Pe*ʾ*ah* is exempt from tithes, and Aqiva's saying designates the time-limit of the exemption. *Pe*ʾ*ah* may be given after the finish of the harvesting process, the limit proposed by Aqiva; but crop designated as *pe*ʾ*ah* subsequent to that moment continues to be liable for tithes. *Pe^ᵓah* is in fact an issue secondary to Aqiva's tradition, which focuses on liability for tithing. Several items besides *pe*ᵓ*ah* (ownerless property, cattle-fodder, seed of produce taken from a threshing-floor), all of which are exempt from tithes, are also mentioned in the pericope. The primary issue suggests that the tradition would be more appropriate in the context of a discussion of tithing. In any case, the pericope contains the only reference to a Yavnean in the first unit of materials in the tractate. It is the last item in that unit and does not relate to the pericope which precedes it.

Two of Aqiva's traditions (M. 3:2, 3:6) focus on the definition of a field for the purposes of giving *pe*ᵓ*ah*. At M. 3:2 Aqiva holds that in a partially harvested field *pe*ᵓ*ah* should be collected for each individual section. In effect each section constitutes a separate field. The Houses (M. 3:1) and an Ushan (Yosé at M. 3:4) deal with the same issue. Aqiva's position is consistent with that attributed to the House of Shammai and to Yosé. (An anonymous statement at T. Pe. 1:9 also is consistent with Aqiva's view.) The lack of development in the formulation of the issue, as attributed to masters of different generations, is striking.

Aqiva also focuses on an issue related to the definition of a field at M. 3:6. Aqiva holds that crop on land of any size is liable for *pe*ᵓ*ah*. Other Yavneans—Eliezer, Joshua, Tarfon, Judah b. Bethyra—suggest larger areas. In context Aqiva lists *pe*ᵓ*ah* as only one of several items. "Land of any size" also obligates for first-fruits and provides substance enough for the purpose of writing a *prosbul* or acquiring movable property. As at M. 1:6, Aqiva's saying goes beyond the immediate issue relating to *pe*ᵓ*ah*. And again as at 1:6, Aqiva's saying occurs at the end of a larger unit of materials. (M. 3:7-8 do not relate to *pe*ᵓ*ah* at all; they follow from Aqiva's statement at 3:6.) The question of the minimum size of an area, in the context of *pe*ᵓ*ah*, is not taken up in sayings attributed to masters after Yavneh.

Aqiva occurs once in a tradition relating to technical matters of taking *pe*ᵓ*ah*. He disputes with Gamaliel concerning the reason for specifying three searches—no more, no fewer—during a single day (M. 4:5). It is implied that the designation, "three searches," precedes the dispute of the Yavnean masters. The issue does not recur in M.-T.

The unit of materials dealing with gleanings at the outset gives a dispute between Aqiva and Ishmael regarding a case of doubt—harvested crop which falls over the top of the hand of the harvester or over the top of his sickle (M. 4:10). Aqiva alleges that such produce belongs to the landowner and not to the poor. I discern no principle underlying Aqiva's view or tying his position to that expressed in subsequent pericopae which deal with other cases of doubtful gleanings. Another Yavnean, Eliezer (M. 5:2), and Ushans, Meir and Simeon b. Gamaliel, also deal with cases of doubtful gleanings. A pericope at T. 2:21 gives a case in which Aqiva assumes that produce (corn that falls among straw) which might be considered as doubtful gleanings in fact belongs to the landowner. Again I discern no principle tying Aqiva's specific view to another tradition.

Aqiva occurs in one tradition relating to clusters of grapes left in a vineyard. Aqiva and Eliezer dispute regarding the status of grapes in a vineyard which consists solely of defective clusters (M. 7:7). Aqiva holds that the contents of the vineyard belong to the poor. A glossator supplies a scriptural warrant for Aqiva's view: "And from your vineyard you shall not take defective clusters" (Lev. 19:10). The definition of "defective clusters" is discussed by Ushans, Judah and sages, at M. 7:5.

At M. 8:5 Aqiva allegedly glosses, and disputes, specific items on a list of minimum quantities of produce, including fig-cake, wine and oil, consigned to the poor. The tradition obviously assumes a complex of rules relating to Poorman's tithe. Curiously Meir glosses, and disputes, one of the items in the anonymous list in the same way that Aqiva does. Another Yavnean, Abba Saul, responds to the same issue in a saying formulated in a general statement, a sentence, that is, a formulation completely different from that in which Aqiva's and Meir's sayings occur. The question of minimum quantities for Poorman's tithe is not further expanded in the tractate.

Aqiva does not seem to have contributed significantly to the development of the major issues in the tractate. One of Aqiva's traditions relates primarily to tithing and only secondarily to *pe᾽ah* (M. 1:6). Two traditions deal with the definition of a field, an issue to which the tractate devotes considerable attention. The first tradition (M. 3:2) gives Aqiva's opinion on the separation of sections in a single field; curiously the formulation of Aqiva's view is identical with that of the Houses' views and the view of an Ushan in other pericopae on the same problem. The second case (M. 3:6) relates to the minimum size of a field, a question to which only Yavnean masters respond. In one case Aqiva seems to gloss prior law (M. 4:5). In several pericopae Aqivan sayings on discrete cases relate to issues dealt with by masters of later generations (doubtful gleanings, M. 4:10, T. 2:21; defective clusters in a vineyard, M. 7:7; minimum quantities of Poorman's tithe, 8:5). With one possible exception (the definition of defective clusters, not an issue for Aqiva and Eliezer, is disputed by Ushans), no development can be discerned from one generation to the next. Clearly Aqiva's traditions, however developed and refined, would not have yielded a tractate like the one we find in M.-T. *Pe³ah.*

b. *Dema³i*

T. provides two *m*ᶜ*śh*-stories. At T. 4:13 Yosé's story alleges that Aqiva would suspend *dema³i*-regulations in a market-place in order to protect domestic produce against cheap imported produce. T. 5:24 describes a controversy between Aqiva and Gamaliel concerning the status of Samaritans' vegetables. Aqiva assumes that the vegetables must be considered wholly untithed. M. Dem. contains no Aqivan traditions. An anonymous pericope at M. 7:4 assumes, as does Aqiva in the story in T., that Samaritans' vegetables are considered wholly untithed.

c. *Kila³im*

Eight Aqivan traditions occur in M.-T. Kil. The tractate focuses on the following areas:

I. Flora and fauna which together are not Mixed-kinds (M. 1:1-9).
II. Mixed-kinds of seeds in fields (M. 2:1-3:9).
III. Mixed-kinds of seeds in a vineyard (M. 4:1-7:8).
IV. Mixed-kinds of animals (M. 8:1-6).
V. Mixed-kinds of cloth (M. 9:1-10).

Aqiva's traditions deal only with problems in the first three areas, which constitute the main body of the tractate.

Three Aqivan traditions relate important principles to problems of Mixed-kinds of seed in a field. In one case Aqiva sets an absolute ban on allowing Mixed-kinds of seeds to grow (T. 1:15). Aqiva alleges that a person may not ignore a case of Mixed-kinds once he becomes aware of the situation. Aqiva is the only master to whom this principle is ascribed. M. gives the principle without attribution in a summary catalog at 8:1, and anonymous statements in M. and T. assume Aqiva's principle in discussions of specific problems. M. 2:3-4, for instance, elaborately describe procedures which must be followed before seed of one kind can be planted in a field previously planted with seed of a different kind; the pericopae assume that at no time may Mixed-kinds be allowed to grow.

Two other Aqivan traditions on Mixed-kinds of seeds assume another important principle, namely, the appearance of Mixed-kinds must be avoided. In one case (M. 3:3) Aqiva holds that the area alloted to one kind of vegetable planted in a field previously planted with a different kind of vegetable must be separated from the area of the old crop by a space six handbreadths in length and "fully as wide." In a second pericope (M. 3:6) Aqiva focuses on the specific problem of rows of gourds planted in a field previously planted with rows of onions; gourds, which are leafy and spread quickly, may become entangled with the onions. Aqiva holds that no out-of-the-ordinary precautions must be taken to protect against the appearance of Mixed-kinds. Ishmael, another Yavnean, disputes Aqiva's opinion in both pericopae. In one of the traditions (M. 3:3) an Ushan, Judah, glosses, and disputes, Aqiva's opinion. The underlying principle, which is fundamental to the tractate, is given explicitly in an anonymous statement at M. 3:5: "all that the sages prohibited was decreed only for the sake of appearance." The Houses assume the principle in a pericope at M. 2:6. It obviously is not Aqiva's contribution to the law on Mixed-kinds.

The same major principles occur in Aqiva's traditions on Mixed-kinds in a vineyard. Aqiva holds that Mixed-kinds in a vineyard must be removed as soon as they are noticed (M. 5:7). The specific problem relates to seeds blown by the wind into a vineyard. The products of such seeds must be uprooted at whatever stage they are first observed; since the seeds were planted inadvertantly, the owner of the vineyard does not forfeit his vines. Aqiva alleges, however, that delay results in the forfeiture of the vines.

In another tradition Aqiva, as reported by Abba Saul, speaks to the problem of the appearance of Mixed-kinds in a vineyard. Aqiva prescribes what to do if greens become entangled with a vine. The opinion of another Yavnean, ben Azzai, is cited along with Aqiva's. The pericope supplies further evidence that the ban on the apperance of Mixed-kinds was assumed at Yavneh.

Aqiva's opinion on the tillage of a vine, that is, the area needed for the growth of a plant, is out of phase with the view generally given in the tractate. Aqiva alleges that the tillage of a vine has a radius of three handbreadths (M. 6:1). The figure usually given is six handbreadths.

Yosé reports a story in which Aqiva allegedly gave a ruling in the case of a man who planted Mixed-kinds in a vineyard during the Seventh-year. The story is suspect, first because it gives a perfect legal conundrum, and second because Yosé ascribes to Aqiva a stock-phrase, "A man cannot forfeit what does not belong to him." That statement recurs elsewhere without attributeion to Aqiva. In the preceding pericope it is attributed jointly to two Ushans, Simeon and Yosé; Yosé's story about Aqiva provides a precedent for the Ushan's statement.

In summary: two major principles recur in Aqiva's traditions on Mixed-kinds. The ban on allowing Mixed-kinds to grow seems to be his contribution to the law; at least it is explicitly ascribed to no one other than Aqiva. Anonymous statements in M. and T. develop Aqiva's principle in situations which focus on issues related to intention. By contrast to the first principle, the ban on the appearance of Mixed-kinds evidently is accepted by other masters at Yavneh. Aqiva and one other Yavnean, and the Houses as well, dispute details in the application of the principle. Aqiva is the only Yavnean credited with listing pairs of items which are not Mixed-kinds when they are planted in the same field; but the significance of this fact is not clear. In his definition of the tillage of the vine Aqiva stands alone; his view on the radius of the area is one-half the usual figure given. Clearly Aqiva's contribution to the law in the tractate is significant. The ban on allowing Mixed-kinds to grow is taken up and applied in many different situations. Nonetheless the framework of the tractate obviously goes beyond Aqiva's agenda on Mixed-kinds. As with Aqiva's traditions in M.-T. Pe., we are left to ponder the question of the prior shape of Aqiva's tradition. Disciple-circles probably transmitted the master's principles and views on specific situations; but there is no evidence to suggest that the collection of Aqiva's sayings generated the redactional activity reflected in M.-T. Kil.

d. *Shevi^{c}it*

Eight Aqivan traditions, in ten separate pericopae, occur in M.-T. Shev. The tractate focuses on the following areas:

I. Tending crops during the period immediately prior to the Seventh-year: orchards; fields of vegetables and of other produce (M. 1:1-2:10).

II. Work performed during Seventh-year to prepare field for eighth year, e.g., fertilizing, building fences, pruning, cutting (M. 3:1-4:10).

III. Use of produce grown in Seventh-year: specific items; commerce; time-limits (M. 5:1-9, 7:1-9:9).

IV. Geographical areas to which regulations of Seventh-year pertain (M. 6:1-6).

V. Release of debts (M. 10:1-9).

Aqivan sayings relate to each of the areas except for the last.

In one pericope (M. 1:8) Aqiva speaks to a problem of tending crops during the period immediately prior to the Seventh-year. Seedlings may be tended during that period, and the question is, What is a seedling? Aqiva is one of three Yavneans who suggest definitions. Aqiva holds that a seedling "is what its name implies"; presumablv that limits a seedling to a plant one year old or less. By contrast, Eleazar b. ᶜAzariah and Joshua suggest far longer periods of time (4 or 5 years and 5, 6, or 7 years, respectively).

Two Aqivan traditions relate to the issue of preparatory work performed during the Seventh-year. Aqiva holds that, during the Seventh-year, reeds may be cut in the usual way (M. 4:6). Against Aqiva, Yosé the Galilean alleges that reeds can be cut down to no closer than one handbreadth from the ground. In a second tradition (M. 3:10; T. 3:5) an Aqivan saying is related to the problem of dirt removed from a field by way of a public thoroughfare during the Seventh-year. Aqiva opposes piling the dirt temporarily in the public domain. But the problem concerning the Seventh-year is secondary to Aqiva's statement. The saying relates in a primary sense to the issue of effecting a change in the public domain; Aqiva states that just as one may not clutter the public domain, so too one may not clear it of an obstacle.

Three of Aqiva's traditions concern the use made of produce which grows during the Seventh-year. Only one of the three (M. 9:6), however, states Aqiva's own opinion on a problem. The issue is the time after the Seventh-year beyond which produce of the Seventh-year can no longer be eaten. Aqiva holds that for all purposes the second rainfall of the eighth year serves as the terminal point. After that rainfall produce of the Seventh-year must be destroyed. Aqiva's saying glosses, and disputes, an anonymous statement which gives different time-limits for different categories of produce. Ushans discuss the time of removal of produce of the Seventh-year (T. 7:17-18); Aqiva is the only Yavnean master to speak to the issue.

In a second tradition on the uses made of produce which grows in the Seventh-year, Aqiva responds to a saying ascribed to ben Azzai concerning the status of an anomalous sort of vegetable, Egyptian beans. Ben Azzai, citing Joshua's opinion, alleges that Egyptian beans become liable for tithes from the moment that they take root; whether that happens before or after the start of the Seventh-year determines liability for tithes. The pericope notes that Aqiva "reversed" his opinion and accepted ben Azzai's opinion. Aqiva's previous position is not stated, although a contrary opinion (Egyptian beans become liable when one-third fully grown) is ascribed to Simeon Shizuri at the outset of the same pericope.

A third tradition on the uses made of produce of the Seventh-year (M. 8:9) is of interest for reasons unconnected with Aqiva's opinion on the problem at issue. Disciples ask Aqiva about Eliezer's opinion concerning a hide anointed with oil of the Seventh-year. Aqiva refuses to divulge Eliezer's true opinion. Presumably Eliezer's view was more liberal than the opinion ascribed to him (the hide should be burned) in the pericope in M. Aqiva's own opinion on the matter is not explicated. A second tradition (M. 8:10), unrelated to issues of produce of the Seventh-year (it concerns Samaritans' bread) but set in the same form ('They asked Aqiva...He refused to divulge...') follows the pericope about the hide anointed with Seventh-year oil. These pericopae are intriguing as examples of the transmission, and explicit manipulation, of one master's traditions by another master. The examples, however, are unique in M.-T. and contribute little to the composition of tractate *Shevi*ᶜ*it.*

One Aqivan tradition (M. 6:2; T. 4:12) relates to the status of produce grown in Syria. Aqiva alleges that what is permitted in Israel during the Seventh-year is also permitted in Syria. What is of interest is whether the status of land in Syria is in all cases considered comparable to that of land in Israel, thus rendering what is prohibited in Israel also prohibited in Syria. In context that seems to be Aqiva's position; but the matter, clearly a controversy at Yavneh, is not certain. At M. Hal. 4:7 Eliezer and Gamaliel, older contemporaries of Aqiva, dispute regarding the status of land in Syria. Eliezer holds that it is liable to the regulations of the Seventh-year. Gamaliel relinquishes all claims on Syrian land, including liability for the Seventh-year. An anonymous statement at M. Hal. 4:7 claims that the law first followed the view of Eliezer but subsequently was revised in favor of Gamaliel's opinion. Ushans also discuss the problem (T. Hal. 2:5; also M. Ma. 5:5).[2]

---

[2] S. Kanter, *Gamaliel*, pp. 54-60.

In summary: Aqiva's sayings do not relate to the central issues of the tractate. Of eight traditions, only two deal with significant principles. Aqiva alleges that Seventh-year produce may be used until the second rainfall during the eighth year (M. 9:6). Aqiva's position concerning the second principle, however, is in fact unclear; he states that what is permitted in the land of Israel is also permitted in Syria but does not mention explicitly whether things prohibited in the land are also prohibited in Syria (M. 6:2; T. 4:12). In two cases Aqivan sayings relate to matters of detail: seedlings are "what their name implies" (M. 1:8); and reeds may be cut in the usual way during the Seventh-year (M. 4:6). Twice Aqiva's own position on a particular problem is not given, or is not stated explicitly: Aqiva "reversed" to follow ben Azzai's, and Joshua's, view concerning the moment that Egyptian beans, an anomalous variety of plant, become liable for tithes (T. 2:13); and Aqiva refuses to divulge Eliezer's true opinion concerning a hide anointed with oil of the Seventh-year (M. 8:9). The legal issue in a second tradition concerning a suppressed tradition of Eliezer is totally irrelevant to the subject of the Seventh-year (M. 9:10); it occurs in the tractate purely for formal reasons. And one tradition, concerning effecting a change in the public domain, relates to the Seventh-year only by virtue of editorial manipulation (M. 3:10, T. 3:5).

e. *Terumot*

Seven Aqivan traditions occur in eleven (11) separate pericopae in M.-T. None of the pericopae is referred to prior to its occurrence in M.-T.

We can identify the following areas of concern in the tractate:

I. Persons who may not separate Heave-offering (M. 1:1).

II. Gifts that are valid despite improper procedures (M. 1:2-2:6).

III. Mechanics of giving Heave-offering: agency; order; amount (M. 3:1-4:6).

IV. Mixtures of Heave-offering with other produce: neutralization of Heave-offering; effects on common produce (M. 4:7-5:9).

V. Misappropriated Heave-offering, including penalties for misuse, product of Heave-offering sown in a field, and eligibility of priests to receive gifts (M. 6:1-9:7).

VI. Uses of Heave-offering produce (M. 11:1-10).

Two issues recur throughout the tractate. First is the role of intention in the separation of Heave-offering. And second is the question of whether one category of produce can be substituted for Heave-offering of a different category of produce.

One Aqivan tradition focuses on the problem of intention as part of a valid gift of Heave-offering (M. 3:3). Aqiva alleges that separate gifts by partners are both valid offerings; although the individuals may be unaware of each other's gift, each gives produce with the proper intention and thus makes a valid gift. In the only other reference to this problem an Ushan, Yosé, introduces the question of the amounts of the respective gifts: if the first partner gave "in measure," then his gift alone is valid; if not, then the second partner's gift alone is valid. The sages with whom Aqiva disputes, like Aqiva, know nothing about the proper "measure" of a gift of Heave-offering. The sages allege that only the first gift is valid; the second gift, regardless of the intention of the second partner, is unnecessary. Aqiva stands against both the sages and Yosé, who hold that only one of the gifts can be valid. Yosé's criterion of "in measure" develops the sages' position.

Aqiva opposes the notion that substitutions can be made from one category of produce for Heave-offering of a different category of produce. That notion is consistently ascribed to Eliezer (M. 2:1, 6:6). Numerous statements, with two exceptions all anonymous, give the contrary view: they prohibit giving unclean produce for clean (M. 2:1; T. 3:18-19), one kind of produce for a different kind (M. 2:4, T. 2:4), raw products for processed foodstuffs (M. 1:4, 9-10), worse for better products (M. 2:6). The two exceptions, one a statement against paying back for misappropriated Heave-offering (M. 6:6, T. 7:9) and one against the substitution of produce less than one-third fully grown for mature Heave-offering produce (T. 7:10), ascribe the ban on substitutions to Aqiva. Each attribution to Aqiva occurs in the context of an Eliezer-Aqiva dispute-form. Most likely Eliezer's view is an innovation in previous Pharisaic law. [3] The tractate, however, is evidently built up out of Aqiva's principle, against substitutions, and that principle may be no less an innovation than Eliezer's. In the absence of evidence regarding prior Pharisaic law the question cannot be answered.

Aqiva follows Eliezer's view on the neutralization of Heave-offering that gets mixed with common produce (M. 4:8; T. 5:10). What can

---

[3] J. Neusner, *Eliezer*, Vol. II, pp. 326-30.

be distinguished within the mixture should be removed. Heave-offering in such a mixture, regardless of its proportion to the common produce, is not neutralized. The Heave-offering is neutralized only if it cannot be distinguished by size, shape, color, or whatever, so long as the requisite quantity of common produce is present in the mixture. In a series of disputes with Eliezer, Joshua argues that distinctions such as color are irrelevant; on Joshua's view, what matters is solely whether the Heave-offering and the common produce are present in the mixture in the requisite proportions. Ushans pursue more complicated problems. Yosé, for instance, reports on the case of a bundle of vegetables, half of which were Heave-offering, that fell in among fifty bundles of vegetables (M. 4:13). The case allegedly "came before" Aqiva; but the tradition gives only Yosé's opinion on the problem.

Aqiva is one of four Yavneans who dispute concerning the maximum amount of a crop which can be designated as Heave-offering (M. 4:5). Aqiva and Tarfon place no limit on the amount—with the proviso that some little bit be kept back. By contrast, Ishmael limits the maximum offering to half of the crop and Eliezer to merely ten per cent (10%). Yavneans do not discuss the standard measure for Heave-offering. An anonymous statement (M. 1:7) notes that no standard measure is given for Heave-offering; Houses' opinions for good, medium, and poor gifts are reported at T. 5:3.

With regard to the product of Heave-offering seeds sown in a field, Aqiva dismisses as farfetched the notion (Tarfon's) that only poor priests may glean the crop (M. 9:2). The crop should be sold to priests at the price of Heave-offering, but, according to Aqiva, special precautions need not be taken during gleaning against rendering the produce unclean.

An Aqivan tradition deals with mixtures of common produce with prohibited meat (M. 10:11; T. 9:4). Meat obviously is not prohibited by virtue of being Heave-offering, however, and the proper context of the tradition is not clear.

In summary: the tractate seems to be built up out of principles ascribed to Aqiva. Aqivan traditions relate to two major areas of the tractate, the role of intention in a gift of Heave-offering and the possibility of substitutions of one category of produce for Heave-offering of a different category. Aqiva holds that proper intention renders valid separate gifts from partners. Aqiva does not take into consideration the amounts of the separate gifts; that issue, the standard measure for Heave-offering, is raised by an Ushan statement on the problem of partners' Heave-offering. Aqiva opposes the substitution of one category of produce for Heave-offering of a different category of produce (M. 6:6; T. 7:9, 10). Eliezer alleges the opposite. The tractate is built up out of the principle attributed to Aqiva. Aqiva takes over Eliezer's view on the neutralization of Heave-offering in a mixture with common produce: the latter neutralizes the former only if the Heave-offering cannot be distinguished by virtue of size, shape, color, or the like, and if the proportion of common produce in the mixture is large enough (M. 4:8, T. 5:10). Aqiva sets no limit on the maximum amount of a crop which can be designated as Heave-offering (M. 4:5); the issue is considered only by Yavneans, who in turn do not consider the standard measure for a gift of Heave-offering.

f. *Ma^c^aserot*

Aqivan traditions occur in five pericopae in M.-T. Ma. The tractate deals with the following areas:

I. Definition of liability for tithes: general principles (M. 1:1).

II. Designation of moments at which specific items become edible, and thus subject to tithes, although the items may be eaten as snacks (M. 1:2-3).

III. Designation of moments at which the processing of specific items is considered completed, and thus the items are obligated for tithes and cannot be eaten as snacks (M. 1:5-8).

IV. Activities which render produce liable, including commerce, bringing produce into a house or a courtyard, actions by laborers in a field (M. 2:1-3:10).

V. Anomalous cases, including the tithing of preserved fruits, Sabbath-regulations relating to tithes, snacks taken from a vat of olives or from a winepress, the eating of produce not usually eaten by people (M. 4:1-6).

VI. Liability for re-planted produce (M. 5:1-2).

VII. Sale of produce to untrustworthy persons (M. 5:3-4).

VIII. Additional anomalous cases, including Syrian produce (M. 5:5, 7-8).

Aqivan sayings relate only to IV, V, and VIII.

The issue of intention underlies two Aqivan traditions on the status of produce in a courtyard. Bringing foodstuffs into a courtyard signals the intention to eat the produce, which is consequently rendered liable for tithes. Aqiva defines a courtyard which does not obligate produce for tithes as one to which one person opens the gate and another person closes the gate (M. 3:5). Aqiva's saying, which is referred to by a late Ushan, Simeon b. Eleazar, assumes the same principle as do statements ascribed to Ishmael, a Yavnean, and to Nehemiah, Yosé, and Judah, Ushan masters: only a courtyard which is closed, or guarded, and thus is comparable to a private house, renders produce brought therein liable for tithes. In a second tradition on produce in a courtyard, Aqiva specifies the procedure by which grapes, pomegranates, and melons which happen to grow inside a courtyard are to be harvested (M. 3:9). Aqiva disputes with Tarfon on the problem. Both Yavnean masters assume that special precautions must be taken in harvesting such produce; they differ only concerning the nature of the specific precautions.

In one tradition Aqiva deals with the liability of a crop purchased from a gentile (T. 3:14). If the crop is purchased after it has become edible, then it is not liable for tithes; if before, then it becomes liable at the moment that it does become edible. The principle which Aqiva applies to this one case recurs throughout the tractate.

Aqiva holds that the caperbush, an anomalous plant, is tithed only for its berries (M. 4:6), presumably because people do not usually eat the other parts of the plants. Against Aqiva, Eliezer holds that the caperbush is also tithed for its flowers and stalk.

In summary: a principle which is fundamental to the tractate, produce becomes liable for tithes from the moment that it becomes edible, is ascribed to Aqiva in one tradition (T. 3:14). Two Aqivan traditions relate to the issue of intention as it pertains to the liability of produce in a courtyard; Aqiva addresses one main issue, the status of produce which grows inside a courtyard (M. 3:9). Aqiva also states that the caperbush, an anomalous plant, is tithed only for its berries (M. 4:6). Aqivan sayings do not relate to major areas of the tractate and thus, although one important principle is ascribed to Aqiva, it is difficult to imagine that Aqivan interests have significantly influenced the agenda of the tractate.

g. *Maᶜaser Sheni*

Nine pericopae in M.-T. M.S. mention Aqiva. Ushans attest to at least one of Aqiva's opinions. And a Yavnean refers to one Aqivan position. The tractate focuses on the following issues:

I. Uses to which Second-tithe produce and money cannot be put (M. 1:1-2:4).

II. Coins of Second-tithe money (M. 2:5-10).

III. Second-tithe produce and money in Jerusalem (M. 3:1-8).

IV. Second-tithe produce and problems related to uncleanness (M. 3:9-13).

V. Rate at which Second-tithe produce is exchanged (M. 4:1-3).

VI. Designation of Second-tithe money (M. 4:4-8).

VII. Presumption concerning articles found, e.g., beside a road, regarding Second-tithe (M. 4:9-12).

VIII. Fourth-year produce in a vineyard (M. 5:1-5).

IX. Removal of tithes in fourth and seventh years (M. 5:6-15).

Aqiva allegedly holds that Second-tithe money may be used to buy inedible items which contribute to the process of preparing foodstuffs. Such items include saffron-cakes used as food-coloring (T. M.S. 1:13). Yoḥanan b. Nuri, a Yavnean, refers to Aqiva's opinion.

Most of Aqiva's sayings relate more directly to issues of the holiness attached to Second-tithe produce and money. With regard to the protection of the holiness attached to Second-tithe money, a Houses' dispute on exchanging Second-tithe money of silver for gold draws a gloss by Aqiva, who explains that he followed the view of the House of Hillel in an action performed on behalf of Joshua and Gamaliel (M. 2:7). In another tradition on the exchange of species of Second-tithe money, Aqiva specifies instructions for the exchange of silver coins for copper in Jerusalem (M. 2:9). Both traditions on the exchange of Second-tithe money obviously assume a larger corpus of regulations.

Two traditions focus still more directly on issues of holiness. Both traditions relate the sanctity of the city of Jerusalem to Second-tithe produce. In one case Aqiva alleges that Second-tithe produce may be redeemed and eaten at any time that it enters within the area circumscribed by an invisible boundary-line which runs parallel to the city wall (T. 2:12). Thus Second-tithe produce may be redeemed in a room set into the wall even though the only access to that room may be from outside the city. The point is that the sanctity of the city operates without reference to physical obstructions. The second case occurs in the only tradition for which there is a solid Ushan attestation. Aqiva holds that the disposition of Second-tithe produce which, once inside Jerusalem, is discovered to have contracted uncleanness depends upon the location in which the uncleanness was contracted (T. 2:16). As in the previous tradition, Aqiva relates a problem concerning the holiness of Second-tithe produce to the sanctity of the city. If the uncleanness was contracted outside the city, then the produce must be taken outside and be redeemed and eaten there; if inside, then it should not be taken outside. By contrast, Eliezer holds that the source of uncleanness, not the location at which the uncleanness is contracted, is crucial. The sanctity of the city is not relevant on Eliezer's view. In T. Ushans develop Aqiva's view and try to correlate it with Eliezer's position regarding the sources of uncleanness. Discussion in both M. and T. logically passes on from the nature of the sanctity of Jerusalem to excurses on the nature of the sanctity attached to the Temple. The question is whether the holiness attached to the Temple is demarcated by an imaginary boundary, as Aqiva in T. alleges concerning the sanctity of Jerusalem, or whether it can be contained by a physical obstruction, such as a wall.

One Aqivan tradition implies an innovation in the procedures of the removal of tithes and of produce from which tithes have not been separated during the fourth and seventh years of the seven-year cycle (M. M.S. 5:8). Judah alleges that Aqiva introduced the principle that unripe produce, which was not yet liable for tithes, should be exempt from removal. The issue does not recur elsewhere.

In a *m*ᶜ*śh*-story Gamaliel names Aqiva as recipient of tithes from a crop on behalf of the poor (M. 5:9). The underlying issue in the pericope concerns to whom tithes should be paid, specifically whether priests may collect first-tithe. The tradition does not give Aqiva's opinion on the question. (Stories at y. M.S. 5:5 and b. Yev. 86a-b report that Aqiva restricts the collection of first-tithe to Levites.)

In summary: one Aqivan tradition deals with the issue of uses to which Second-tithe money cannot be put, an issue which draws a good deal of discussion in the tractate. Several Aqivan traditions focus on the nature of the holiness attached to Second-tithe produce and money. Aqiva deals with the transference of sanctity from one species of coin to a different kind of species. Of most interest are two traditions in which Aqiva correlates the sanctity of Jerusalem with that attached to Second-tithe produce. The holiness of the city, according to Aqiva, operates within a boundary marked by an imaginary line running parallel to the city wall; it is not affected by physical obstructions. Aqiva holds that Second-tithe produce brought inside the boundary of the city, even into a room within the city wall which has no access to the city itself, may be redeemed and eaten. Aqiva further alleges that the sanctity of the location determines the disposition of Second-tithe produce which contracts uncleanness.

Aqivan traditions do not relate to issues to which a proportionately large amount of space is devoted in the tractate. Such issues include the disposition of Second-tithe produce which gets mixed with common produce, the mechanics of the redemption of Second-tithe produce, presumption concerning produce and coins found in a public place, misappropriated tithe, and questions related to the produce of vine-yards in the fourth year. One Aqivan tradition deals with the removal of tithes in the fourth and seventh year; allegedly Aqiva contributes an important innovation, the exemption from removal of produce less than one-third fully grown. M.-T. contain no hint of Aqiva's view on the problem of whether or not a priest should collect first-tithe. On the face of it Aqivan interests are not responsible for the development of the tractate.

h. *Ḥallah*

Aqiva occurs in five traditions in eight separate pericopae in M.-T. Hal. The tractate focuses on the following areas:

I. Products liable for dough-offering and/or tithes (M. 1:1-9).
II. Liability of imported produce (M. 2:1-2).
III. Dough-offering and problems relating to uncleanness (M. 2:3, 8).
IV. Measure of dough liable for dough-offering (M. 2:4-7).
V. Moment liability incurred (M. 3:1-6).
VI. Liability of combinations of foodstuffs (M. 3:7-4:6).
VII. Liability of produce from Syria and from different districts in the land of Israel (M. 4:7-11).

One Aqivan tradition deals with the liability of imported produce (M. 2:1). Against Eliezer, Aqiva holds that the location of the produce at the moment at which it is made into dough determines its liability; obligation for dough-offering is incurred only inside the land; the location at which the produce was grown is irrelevant. Eliezer holds that domestic produce is always liable and foreign produce always exempt, even if the former should happen to be exported or the latter imported prior to being made into dough. As with the problem of unclean Second-tithe in Jerusalem (T. M.S. 2:16), Aqiva focuses on the boundaries within which an act takes place, and Eliezer focuses on the source by which holiness is transmitted or affected. The issue of imported produce is discussed by at least one Ushan master, Judah (M. 2:2; y. Hal. 2:1, 58b).

Three of Aqiva's sayings relate to the mechanics of giving dough-offering. Aqiva holds that dough-offering should be given in measure even in a situation in which a person cannot roll dough in a state of cleanness (M. Hal. 2:3). The alternative, proposed by unnamed sages, is to prepare small clumps of dough the size of a *qab*, thereby avoiding liability altogether. Aqiva alleges that liability should not be avoided. Aqiva's view on the minimum quantity liable for dough-offering is not given. Presumably Aqiva holds that it is larger than a *qab*. The Houses dispute this question in a tradition reported at M. Ed. 1:2; a post-Houses compromise position, cited at M. Ed. 1:2, is given at M. Hal. 2:6. The Houses' opinions do not occur in tractate *Ḥallah*. The issue of a minimum specification occurs in an Aqivan tradition at M. 4:4-5. Aqiva holds that a gift from a single *qab* of dough is a valid offering. Unnamed sages reject that view. The pericope assumes that one *qab* is less than the minimum measure. Aqiva's view is that a non-obligatory gift can be valid as dough-offering. Ushans, Eliezer b. Jacob and sages, discuss the same issue (T. Hal. 2:5). The third Aqivan tradition relates to the moment at which obligation for dough-offering is incurred. Aqiva holds that liability can be incurred until the dough forms a light crust in the oven (M. 3:6; T. Hal. 1:12). Other Yavneans, Yoḥanan b. Nuri and Judah b. Bethyra, propose specific moments at which the obligation is incurred; for instance, Yoḥanan holds that flour made from wheat becomes liable at the moment at which the dough is rolled out. (M. reports a series of pericopae, immediately prior to citing Aqiva's saying, which assume Yoḥanan's view.)

One Aqivan tradition relates not to dough-offering but rather to Heave-offering. Aqiva alleges that vetches designated as Heave-offering may be given to any priest (M. 4:9). Vetches are not usually obligated for Heave-offering, on Aqiva's view, for people usually do not eat them; and therefore it is not necessary to take precautions against their falling into the hands of untrustworthy priests if by chance they should be designated as Heave-offering.

In summary: Aqivan traditions focus on issues of the mechanics of giving dough-offering—the minimum quantity of dough which incurs liability; at what stage in the baking-process the obligation is incurred;

protection against contracting uncleanness. One Aqivan tradition deals with the status of imported produce and relates to the sanctity attached to the land of Israel. One tradition relates to Heave-offering and not to dough-offering. No Aqivan traditions deal with liability for dough-offering in different geographical districts, with combinations of food-stuffs, or with the explicit comparison of dough-offering with Heave-offering and tithes. Aqivan interests are obviously not central to the range of the law in the tractate.

i. *ᶜOrlah*

Only one Aqivan tradition occurs in M.-T. Or. (M. 3:7). The pericope focuses on items which, when mixed with other produce, will render the other produce prohibited. Aqiva adds the "loaves of a householder" to an anonymous list of such items. Aqiva may refer to loaves made from dough of Heave-offering produce; but the matter is not clear.

j. *Bikkurim*

Only one Aqivan saying, in a dispute with Simeon b. Nanos, occurs in M.-T. Bik. (at M. 3:9). The issue concerns the decoration of the baskets in which first-fruits are carried to Jerusalem. Aqiva restricts the decoration to fruits of the seven-species.

iii. *Conclusions*

In conclusion I take up two questions. The first relates to the literary framework of Aqiva's corpus on agricultural laws; and the second concerns the man behind the tradition. First I deal with the relation between Aqiva's sayings and the legal agenda of the individual tractates. In this regard I distinguish between three groups of tractates: those to which Aqiva contributes central principles; those in which Aqiva deals with significant issues but does not himself contribute basic principles; and those in which Aqivan sayings do not play a significant role at all. The second question relates to the unity of conception in Aqiva's traditions on agriculture. Here I specify the recurring principles which Aqiva applies in different legal settings. These principles reflect the philosophical issues which underlie the Aqivan tradition. In this regard I refer to Aqivan positions regarding areas of law other than those discussed in M.-T. *Zeraᶜim*; we see that Aqivan principles on topics in *Seder Tohorot* are consistent with Aqivan principles now familiar to us from *Seder Zeraᶜim.*

As we have seen in the review of Aqiva's sayings in the individual tractates, in no case does Aqiva set the agenda of a tractate. We can distinguish, however, two tractates, *Terumot* and *Kilaʾim*, to which Aqiva contributes central principles. By "central" I mean principles which are taken up and developed in the dominant dialectic of the tractate. In M.-T. Ter. several anonymous pericopae apply Aqiva's ban on substitutions to situations which Aqiva himself does not discuss. The ban on substitutions is ascribed only to Aqiva; the opposite principle, in favor of substitutions, is attributed to Eliezer and occurs only in statements attributed to him. In M.-T. Kil. the ban on allowing Mixed-kinds to grow is ascribed solely to Aqiva. Anonymous pericopae spell out implications of the ban, e.g., in discussions of actions which may properly intervene between observing Mixed-kinds and uprooting the offending variety of plant. Both tractates also include Aqivan sayings which respond to issues or assume principles that are not solely Aqivan. In M.-T. Ter. the issue of intention, for instance, draws discussion by Eliezer and Joshua as well as by Aqiva. And with regard to mixtures of Heave-offering with other produce, Aqiva reproduces Eliezer's opinion; Eliezer's and Joshua's opinions are in fact spelled out in formulations far more elaborate than is Aqiva's. Similarly in M.-T. Kil. Aqiva assumes a central principle which seems to have been accepted by other Yavneans, namely, the very appearance of Mixed-kinds must be avoided. In two disputes between Aqiva and Ishmael, for instance, both masters assume that some sort of separation must intervene between different vegetables planted in a single field; the differences between the two masters relate to the dimensions of the intervening areas required for the separate cases.

In several tractates Aqivan sayings relate to significant issues but do not themselves contribute central principles. In M.-T. Pe., for instance, Aqiva speaks to a fundamental issue, the definition of a field; but Aqiva's position, which relates the definition of a field to the landowner's intention as signified by reference to the times at which he harvests his crop in separate patches in a single field, does not seem to be further developed in the tractate. Similarly Aqiva supplies a time-limit for the exemption of *peʾah*-produce from tithes; but the issue is not central to the tractate. In M.-T. Shev. Aqiva alleges that the second rainfall during the eighth year constitutes the time for removal of all kinds of produce of the Seventh-year; the issue is not crucial to the tractate. Of greater interest is the problem of the liability of crop which grows on land in Syria. Aqiva speaks to the issue, but his view is not clear. In M.-T. Ma. Aqiva's sayings, like those attributed to other Yavneans, assume that produce brought into a courtyard becomes liable for tithes; Aqiva, along with Ishmael and Tarfon, explores problems that represent developments out of that principle.

It is more difficult to judge the role of Aqiva's sayings in M.-T. M.S. and M.-T. Hal. In each tractate Aqiva contributes significant principles which do not generate further refinements. These principles seem to be tangential to the main interests reflected in the redaction of the tractates. In M.-T. M.S. Judah alleges that Aqiva supplies the rule exempting produce not yet liable for tithes from removal; that rule represents a significant legal innovation, but the problem of the removal of tithes does not figure prominently in the tractate. Aqiva also contributes an important principle concerning the sanctity of the city of Jerusalem; Ushans expand Aqiva's position, which focuses on the designation of the boundaries of the city, by reference to the intention of a pilgrim as he enters Jerusalem with his Second-tithe produce. These discussions are given in T.; it is not clear to me how M. develops Aqiva's views, if it does at all. In M.-T. Hal. Aqiva alleges that liability for dough-offering is incurred only by dough prepared inside the land of Israel; the location of the field in which the produce used for the dough grew, whether it is inside the land or outside, is not relevant. Other Yavneans, Eliezer and Gamaliel, assume that crop which grows outside the land does in some cases incur liability for dough-offering without regard to whether or not it is brought into the land. It is again not clear to me whether Aqiva's view is further developed in the tractate; it obviously does not occupy the pivotal position of Aqiva's contributions to law in M.-T. Ter. and M.-T. Kil.

In a third group of tractates Aqiva's sayings contribute little or nothing of central importance. M.-T. Or. and M.-T. Bik. each contain a single Aqivan statement; neither saying relates to the central principles of the tractates. T. Dem. yields two stories about Aqiva. In one of the stories Aqiva acts on the assumption that Samaritans' produce should be considered wholly untithed; that view is reflected in an anonymous statement in M. but does not seem to be of central importance in the tractate.

The redaction of materials in M.-T. obviously goes beyond the legal interests expressed in the Aqivan corpus. Even M.-T. Ter., which more than any other tractate depends upon and further develops an Aqivan principle, includes discussions of legal issues in which Aqiva does not participate. It has been suggested that Aqiva organized a corpus of traditions, a "mishnah," as distinguished from "The Mishnah" edited by Judah the patriarch at the end of the second century; indeed, it has been alleged that Aqiva stands behind a collection of traditions which was transmitted and augmented by masters at Usha and which was eventually authorized by Rabbi. [4] With regard to traditions on agricultural laws I see no evidence to support either suggestion. There is nothing to indicate that Aqiva is responsible for a proto-tractate dealing with any topic that occurs in *Seder Zeraᶜim.* The results here are in accord with the results of the survey of forms in Chapter Three: the redaction of the tractates sets the parameters of our study; our rudimentary methods cannot reconstruct the shape of Aqiva's corpus prior to that redaction.

The results are quite different, however, when we turn to the conceptual framework suggested by Aqiva's traditions, for we can identify recurring principles in the Aqivan corpus as it is reported in *Seder Zeraᶜim.* Time and again Aqiva raises two major issues in connection with legal problems in different tractates. The first issue is the definition of domains, in time and in space, the fixing of boundaries; and the second is the role of intention. The two issues are in fact related, for Aqiva frequently proposes to set boundaries or define domains by reference to the intentions expressed by the actions of individual men. We see this occur in the following ways. In M.-T. Pe. Aqiva defines a field by reference to the time at which a man harvests his crop; if a landowner harvests sections of his crop in a single field at different times, then each section, according to Aqiva, constitutes a separate field and is liable for *peʾah* on its own. Thus a landowner's intention, signaled by his harvesting sections of crop in a single field at different times, defines separate areas, in effect separate fields, for the purposes of *peʾah.* Aqiva's ban on allowing Mixed-kinds of things to grow represents an extreme application of the notion that different crops, and the areas in which the crops grow, must be kept quite separate. Aqiva's view is developed by reference to questions about what sorts of actions may intervene between the observation of Mixed-kinds and their removal; the issue obviously concerns the sorts of actions which signal the intention to remove the Mixed-kinds and those which signal the opposite. In M.-T. Ter. Aqiva alleges that proper intention renders valid separate gifts of Heave-offering from partners; the gifts are apportioned according to the

[4] Epstein asserts, for example, that Aqiva is the "father of the mishnah, that is, 'of our Mishnah,'" *Tannaim*, p. 71.

respective shares of crop owned by the two partners. In M.-T. Ma. Aqiva deals with the liability of produce brought into a courtyard; Yavneans commonly assume that bringing foodstuffs into a closed courtyard, which is comparable to a private house, signals the intention to eat the food as a formal meal and thus renders it liable for tithes. In M.-T. M.S. Aqiva relates the sanctity attached to Second-tithe produce to the holiness which operates within the boundary of the city of Jerusalem; the issue of the intention of the pilgrim, as signified by his bringing Second-tithe into the city, underlies Aqiva's view, which is further refined by Ushan masters. And in M.-T. Hal. Aqiva permits the gift of dough-offering from a piece of dough less than the minimum size obligated for the offering; the intention of the donor, on Aqiva's view, renders the gift valid.

We recognize Aqiva's concern with the issue of intention in areas of law outside of *Seder Zera^cim*. Neusner has shown that in M.-T. Kel. Aqiva focuses on the role of intention in the determination of the status of a utensil. Aqiva argues that "[i]t is the intention of the user, not the traits intrinsic to the utensil, which governs the status of the object," [5] that is, whether or not an object is considered susceptible to uncleanness (= useful) depends upon the intention of the person who uses the utensil. It follows from Aqiva's principle that secondary uses of an object must be taken into consideration in the determination of its susceptibility for uncleanness. Nonetheless in the determination of the usefulness of vessels Aqiva's sayings represent an effort to find a balance between the needs of a particular man, a private conception of usefulness, and the function of a utensil quite independent of the intention of any specific individual. [6]. The search for a balance between the intention of a particular person and the traits intrinsic to a physical object is familiar from Aqiva's traditions in *Seder Zera^cim.* The recurring problem is to define the actions by which the intention of a private person affects the status of objects in the public realm.

The search for a metaphysic underlying Aqiva's legal traditions goes considerably beyond the scope of this study. For the present we note that the nature of the human will, the issue which, in Aqiva's traditions, is formulated in terms of the role of intention in abstract legal situations, recurs as a major issue in Jewish literature from Palestine during the first century. The prophet of the Ezra Apocalypse, for

---

[5] HMLP, Vol. III, p. 333.
[6] *Ibid.*, pp. 334-35.

instance, explains the disastrous war against Rome by fixing on man's sinful nature:

> in truth there is none of the earth-born who has not dealt wickedly, and among those that exists who has not sinned (IV Ezra 8:35).

The prophet assigns an ironic role to the exercise of the intellect:

> O thou Earth, what have you brought forth, if the mind is sprung from the dust as every other thing! It had been better if the dust itself had even been unborn, that the mind might not have come into being with it. But as it is, the mind grows with us, and on this account we are tormented, because we perish and know it (IV Ezra 7:62-74).

On the prophet's view, men inevitably sin. The mind merely makes men conscious of transgressions. Given the inevitability of sin, men would be better off without consciousness. In a different context, a series of statements on temptation, the Synoptic Gospels present a similarly stark view of the nature of sin:

> If your hand or your foot causes you to sin, cut it off and throw it away; it is better for you to enter life maimed or lame than with two hands or two feet to be thrown into the eternal fire. And if your eye causes you to sin, pluck it out and throw it away; it is better for you to enter life with one eye than with two eyes to be thrown into the hell of fire (Matt. 18:8-9 // Mark 9:43-47).

Here an active response is vividly related to consciousness of sin. The means by which man proceeds to sin are to be removed or closed off. In still a different context, a consideration of the relation of will to the prescriptions of law, Paul focuses on the gap between intention and action. "I do not understand my own actions .For I do not do what I want, but I do the very thing I hate" (Rom. 7:15). Carnal man, on Paul's view, is separated off from the spiritual, the ideal realm of "the law." Paul claims ironically that knowledge of the law leads to knowledge of sin:

> If it had not been for the law, I should not have known sin. I should not have known what it is to covet if the law had not said, "You shall not covet" (Rom. 7:7).

Aqiva's traditions surveyed above clearly enough differ from each of these other sources. By contrast to the prophet of the Ezra Apocalypse, Aqiva assumes an important role for the mind. A legal system, such as the one for which Aqivan statements provide building-blocks, depends upon the exercise of the intellect. By contrast to the vivid statements in the Synoptic Gospels, Aqivan traditions deal with subtle legal problems. Aqiva's approach to those problems assumes the application of views on fundamental issues upon which the Synoptic Gospels focus more directly. The contrast with Paul's work makes this clear. Paul discusses the nature of "the law," a consideration external to the legal process. Aqiva's traditions in *Seder Zera^{c}im* quite obviously are internal to the process. Yet it would be difficult to recognize in the details of law in Aqiva's traditions an explicit concern for the sorts of sin to which Paul devotes a great deal of attention. Paul's agenda is formulated in terms which include discussions of almost all of the commonplace items given in the catalogue of evils at Rom. 1:29-31: envy, murder, strife, deceit, malignity, gossip, slander, hatred of God, insolence, haughtiness, boastfulness, invention of evil, disobedience to parents, foolishness, faithlessness, heartlessness, and ruthlessness. By contrast, Aqiva's legal traditions in *Seder Zera^{c}im* deal with issues of tithing and the protection of the holiness attached to various sorts of crops. We have seen little or no evidence in the traditions themselves to suggest that these issues related to the everyday activities of large numbers of Jews in Palestine in the first part of the second century. Indeed, we note that legal traditions in M.-T., by contrast to the writings collected in IV Ezra, the Synoptic Gospels, and the Pauline corpus, simply do not spell out the purpose(s) for which they have been compiled so elaborately. Thus although Aqiva's legal traditions relate to a familiar question, the nature of the human will, the context of the Tannaitic investigations, and not the philosophical and religious questions implicitly at issue, becomes primary. By that I mean the legal process, which includes tight reasoning and careful literary formulation of discrete problems, becomes all-absorbing. Immersion in the process obviates the need on the part of traditional participants to specify goals and precedures in terms external to the process. The study of Aqiva's traditions in *Seder Zera^{c}im* suggests, however, the rich possibilities attendant on the effort to explain the process, that is, to explain the complexity and inner logic of earliest rabbinic Judaism.

BIBLIOGRAPHY

Note: The bibliography lists two sorts of items: first, materials which have been regularly consulted for exegetical purposes in Part One; and second, works cited in the text and in footnotes. Previous monographs on Aqiva have not been systematically surveyed. I have discovered that such works without exception focus on issues, e.g., biography, religious philosophy, to which this study can be considered only a preliminary effort. For instance, in *Akiba, Scholar, Saint and Martyr,* L. Finkelstein does not explicitly refer to any of the pericopae which I discuss in my study.

I. CLASSICAL RABBINIC TEXTS, MSS., TRANSLATIONS

a. Mishnah

Mishnah Codex Parma 138, Jerusalem, 1970.

Mishnah Codex Paris: Paris 328-329, Jerusalem, 1973.

Mischnacodex Kaufmann A 50, Jerusalem, 1968.

The Mishnah on which the Palestinian Talmud Rests, ed., W. H. Lowe, Cambridge, 1883; repr. Jerusalem, 1967.

Mishnah Naples, p.e., 1492, repr. Jerusalem, 1970.

Shishah Sidre Mishnah, ed., Chanoch Albeck, 6 vols., Jerusalem, 1954-59.

The Mishnah, trans., Herbert Danby, Oxford, 1933.

b. Tosefta

The Tosefta, ed. with a brief commentary by Saul Lieberman, vol. I, *Zera^c^im*, New York, 1955.

Tosefta, ed., M.S. Zuckermandel, repr. Jerusalem, 1963.

c. Palestinian Talmud

Palestinian Talmud, Venice, p.e., 1522-23. Repr. n.p., n.d.

——, *Leiden ms. Cod. Scal 3*, Jerusalem, 1971.

——, *Codex Vatican 133*, Jerusalem, 1971.

——, New York, 1959.

d. Babylonian Talmud

Babylonian Talmud, Vilna, 1895, repr. Jerusalem, 1968.

——, *Codex Munich 95*, 3 vols., Jerusalem, 1971.

e. Other

Finkelstein, Louis, ed., *Sifra or Torat Kohanim According to Codex Assemani LXVI*, New York, 1956.

——, ed., *Sifré on Deuteronomy*, New York, 1956.

Hoffmann, David, ed., *Midrash Tannaim*, Berlin, n.d.

Horowitz, H. S., ed., *Sifré d'Be Rab*, repr. Jerusalem, 1966.

——, ed., *Sifré Zuṭṭa zum IV Buch Moses*, repr. Jerusalem, 1966.

II. SECONDARY LITERATURE

Aleksandrov, G. S., "The Role of Aqiba in the Bar Kochba Rebellion," in J. Neusner *Eliezer,* Vol. II, pp. 422-36.

Alon, G., "The Sociological Approach for the Investigation of the Halakhah" (Heb.), *Studies in Jewish History in the Times of the Mishna and the Talmud*, Tel Aviv, 1970², Vol. II, pp. 181-227.

Bacher, Wilhelm, *Tradition und Tradenten in den Schulen Palästinas und Babyloniens. Studien und Materialien zur Entstehungsgeschichte des Talmuds*, Leipzig, 1914; repr., Berlin, 1966.

Bokser, Baruch M., *Samuel's Commentary on the Mishnah. Its Nature, Forms and Content*, Part 1. Mishnayot in the Order of *Zeraᶜim*, Leiden, 1975.

Epstein, Jacob N., *Introduction to the Literature of the Amoraim* (Heb.), Jerusalem, 1962.

——, *Introduction to the Literature of the Tannaim* (Heb.), Jerusalem, 1957.

——, *Introduction to the Text of the Mishnah* (Heb.), Two Volumes, Jerusalem, 1964².

Feldman, Uriah, *Flora of the Mishnah* (Heb.), Tel Aviv, n.d.

Feliks, Judah, *Agriculture in Palestine in the Period of the Mishnah and Talmud* (Heb.), Jerusalem, 1963.

Finkelstein, Louis, *Akiba. Scholar, Saint and Martyr*, Philadelphia, 1936.

——, *The Pharisees. The Sociological Background of Their Faith*, Philadelphia, 1962³.

Freedman, Harry, "Aqiva," *Encyclopedia Judaica*, (Jerusalem, 1972), Volume I, pp. 487-91.

Gereboff, Joel, *Tarfon*, unpublished Ph.D. dissertation, Brown University, Providence, 1977.

Gilat, Isaac, "As to the Applicability of the Laws of Plowing and Seeding for the Seventh-year," (Heb.), *Sinai* 70, 1970, pp. 200-10.

Ginzberg, Louis, "Akiba," *Jewish Encyclopedia*, (New York, 1912), Volume I, pp. 304-10.

——, "The Significance of the *Halachah* for Jewish History," *On Jewish Law and Lore*, Philadelphia, 1955, pp. 77-124.

Green, William S., *The Traditions of Joshua ben Hananiah. A Form-Critical Study*, unpublished Ph.D. dissertation, Brown University, Providence, 1974.

Heschel, Abraham Joshua, *The Theology of Ancient Judaism* (Heb.), (New York, 1962-65).

Hoffmann, David, *Die erste Mischna und die Controversen der Tannaim*, Berlin, 1882.

——, *Zur Einleitung in die halachischen Midraschim*, Berlin, 1886-87.

Hyman, Aaron, *Histories of the Tannaim and Amoraim* (Heb.), Three Volumes, Jerusalem, 1964.

Jastrow, Marcus, *A Dictionary of the Targumim, the Talmud Babli and Yerushalmi, and the Midrashic Literature*, repr., New York, 1967.

Kanter, Shammai, *Gamaliel of Yavneh*, unpublished Ph.D. dissertation, Brown University, Providence, 1974.

Kohut, Alexander, *Aruch Completum*, Eight Volumes, Vienna, 1926².

Konovitz, Israel, *Rabbi Akiba. Collected Sayings, in Halakah and Aggadah in the Talmudic and Midrashic Literature*, Jerusalem, 1965.

Kosovsky, Chayim J., *Thesaurus Mishnae*, Four Volumes, Jerusalem, 1960.

——, *Thesaurus Tosephtae*, Six Volumes, Jerusalem, 1932-61.

Krauss, Samuel, et al., *Supplement Volume* to Kohut, *Aruch Completum*, New York, 1965.

Levi, J., *Wörterbuch über die Talmudim und Midraschim*, Four Volumes, Leipzig, 1876-89; Berlin, 1924.

Levine, Baruch, *In the Presence of the Lord. A Study of Cult and some Cultic Terms in Ancient Israel*, Leiden, 1974.

Lieberman, Saul, *Greek in Jewish Palestine*, New York, 1965[2].
——, *Hellenism in Jewish Palestine*, New York, 1950.
——, *Sifré Zuṭṭa*, New York, 1968.
——, *Tosefta Ki-fshutah. A comprehensive commentary on the Tosefta*, New York, 1955- .
——, *Tosefeth Rishonim*, Jerusalem, 1938-39.
Lightstone, Jack, *The Rabbinic traditions concerning R. Ṣadoq the Yavnean,* unpublished M. A. dissertation, Brown University, Providence, 1974.
Löw, Immanuel, *Die Flora der Juden*, Four Volumes, Vienna, 1924-34.
Neusner, Jacob, *Development of a Legend*, Leiden, 1970.
——, *Eliezer ben Hyrcanus*, Two Volumes, Leiden, 1973.
——, *History of the Mishnaic Law of Purities*, Leiden, 1974-77.
——, *The Idea of Purity in Ancient Judaism*, Leiden, 1973.
——, *The Rabbinic Traditions about the Pharisees before 70*, Leiden, 1971.
——, ed., *The Modern Study of the Mishnah*, Leiden, 1973.
Porton, Gary G., "According to R. Ishmael. A Palestinian Amoraic Form," in *Approaches to Ancient Judaism: Theory and Practice* (ed., W. Green; Missoula, forthcoming.)
——, *The Traditions of R. Ishmael. Part One, The Non-exegetical Materials*, (Leiden, 1976).
Scholem, Gershom G., *Jewish Gnosticism, Merkabah Mysticism and Talmudic Tradition*, New York, 1965[2].
——, *Major Trends in Jewish Mysticism*, New York, 1961[3].
Sperber, Daniel, "Palestinian Currency Systems during the Second Commonwealth," *Jewish Quarterly Review* 56, 1966, pp. 273-301.
——, *Roman Palestine, 200-400. Money and Prices*, Ramat Gan, 1974.
Urbach, Ephraim E., "The Traditions about *Merkabah* Mysticism in the Tannaitic Period" (Heb.), in *Studies in Mysticism and Religion Presented to Gershom G. Scholem*, Jerusalem, 1967, pp. 1-28 (Hebrew section).
Yalon, Hanoch, *Introduction to the Vocalization of the Mishna*, Jerusalem, 1964.
Zahavy, Tzvee, *Eleazar ben ᶜAzariah*, unpublished Ph.D. dissertation, Brown University, Providence, 1976.
Zuri, J. S., *Rabbi Aqiva* (Heb.), Jerusalem, 1925.

INDEX TO BIBLICAL AND TALMUDIC REFERENCES

BIBLE

PSEUDEPIGRAPHA

MISHNAH

TOSEFTA

SIFRA AND OTHER MIDRASHIM

PALESTINIAN TALMUD

BABYLONIAN TALMUD

MAIMONIDES, *CODE*

GENERAL INDEX